Art
of the
Osage

Dear Jim
we had a wonderful book
Time putting this
and exhibition together.
I learned so much

cheers

John Nunley
May 20. 2019

Art
of the
Osage

GARRICK BAILEY
DANIEL C. SWAN

With contributions by
JOHN W. NUNLEY
E. SEAN STANDINGBEAR

SAINT LOUIS ART MUSEUM

in association with

UNIVERSITY OF WASHINGTON PRESS
Seattle and London

Published in conjunction with
the exhibition *Art of the Osage,*
Saint Louis Art Museum,
March 13–August 8, 2004

Saint Louis Art Museum
1 Fine Arts Drive
St. Louis, MO 63110
www.slam.org

University of Washington Press
P.O. Box 50096
Seattle, WA 98145
www.washington.edu/uwpress

Library of Congress Control Number: 2003105591
ISBN 0-295-98387-6 (cloth)
ISBN 0-89178-085-8 (paperback)

The paper used in this publication meets the minimum requirements of American National Standard
for Information Sciences—Permanence of Paper
for Printed Library Materials, ANSI Z39.48-1984.

Front cover: Roach and Spreader with Hair
Ornament (cat. 9)
Back cover: Shield (cat. 46)
Page 2: Blanket (detail, cat. 1)
Page 26: Mirror Board (detail, cat. 23)
Page 48: Child's Blanket (detail, cat. 59)
Page 108: Peyote Fan (detail, cat. 69)
Page 136: Feather Bonnet (detail, cat. 80)
Page 156: Garters (detail, cat. 95)
Page 194: Blanket (detail, cat. 108)

Project manager: Mary Ann Steiner
Designed by Susan E. Kelly and Jeff Wincapaw
Typeset by Marie Weiler
Edited by Kris Fulsaas
Proofread by Laura Iwasaki
Color separations by iocolor, Seattle
Produced by Marquand Books, Inc., Seattle,
    for the University of Washington Press
Printed and bound by CS Graphics Pte., Ltd.,
    Singapore

Contents

) Foreword (

It is a privilege and honor for the Saint Louis Art Museum to present *Art of the Osage* in this year that celebrates the bicentennial of the formal transfer of the upper Louisiana Territory from France to the United States and Lewis and Clark's departure on their famous expedition to the West. The Osage people had a noteworthy history in the Midwest long before the Louisiana Territory was so named, and their artistic and social traditions both preceded and survived the 1764 establishment of St. Louis at the junction of our two great rivers. The works of art presented in this book and the exhibition it accompanies give testimony to the dynamic aesthetic of Osage art and life.

We have been very fortunate to have had the wholehearted support of the Osage Tribal Council in developing the exhibition. Former Chief Charles Tillman Jr. responded to our early ambitions for the exhibition with enthusiasm and cooperation. His successor, Chief Jim Gray, has been equally supportive and helpful. With their endorsements, we have been able to identify the finest examples of Osage art in private collections and public institutions around the country and abroad. We have been introduced to active Osage artists and Osage historians, as well as to the staff of the Osage Tribal Museum, which has provided us with information on the history and use of these singular works of art. It is our pleasure to have had them as our partners in this endeavor.

The more than one hundred works of art selected for *Art of the Osage* have been lent by people and institutions whose generosity has accommodated our intention to present the greatest range and highest quality of

Osage artistry. To those individuals who have separated themselves from particularly dear examples of their heritage and to those institutions that have temporarily diminished their Osage holdings, we express particular appreciation.

We thank Garrick Bailey, professor of anthropology at the University of Tulsa, and Daniel C. Swan, former curator at the Gilcrease Museum and now director of the Chucalissa Museum, University of Memphis, for serving as authors of the book that accompanies the exhibition and as unofficial consultants to the exhibition. Their lifelong work with the Osage has benefited this project in the information and insight they provided. Sean Standing-Bear and John Nunley are commended for their vision and leadership of the project. We are grateful to Leonard Maker for his informed review of the manuscript, and it has been our good fortune to work once again with the University of Washington Press.

Generous support for the exhibition and publication of *Art of the Osage* has been provided by The Henry Luce Foundation, The Edward L. Bakewell Jr. Fund, and The Aileen and Lyle Woodcock Fund for the Study of American Art. Our thanks extend as well to Nancy Pillsbury Shirley and Crosby Brown, whose support and belief in this project have been constant.

Brent R. Benjamin
Director
Saint Louis Art Museum

) Acknowledgments (

This publication of *Art of the Osage* and the exhibition it accompanies are the culmination of years of planning and creative ideas from many interesting and dedicated individuals. It is my privilege to express our thanks to those we name below and to those artists whose names have been lost to us, to caretakers who have protected and handed down these precious objects, and to the many people who have preserved and upheld the rich continuity of Osage culture.

The Saint Louis Art Museum takes this opportunity to acknowledge the early encouragement of St. Louis collectors Ray Cooperman, Joe Kinker, and Ben Thompson; their passion for the history and art of the Osage has been constant since our first meetings in the 1980s. Jackie Lewis-Harris, a former assistant curator at the Museum, added new enthusiasm in the early 1990s when she and Kathryn Red Corn discussed the possibility of an exhibition of Osage textiles. Although those early ideas did not come to fruition, good seeds were sown—among the Osage, within the St. Louis community, and at the Museum—and the project was revived with new energy when a meeting in Pawhuska, Oklahoma, the seat of the Osage Tribal Council, brought together Chief Charles Tillman Jr., Garrick Bailey, Sean StandingBear, Charles Banks Wilson, and Leonard Maker. Nancy Pillsbury Shirley, whose friendship with the Osage is one of destiny, organized that meeting in Pawhuska. As an adopted Osage herself, she has supported the Tribe and this project both spiritually and financially. We soon invited Dan Swan, then Head Curator at the Gilcrease Museum in Tulsa who had worked with the Osage for twenty years, to contribute his expertise, and our working team was in place. I cannot imagine a better mix of knowledge, experience, and deep love of Osage material. In forums that ranged from traditional meetings to visits with Osage elders and artists to our being welcomed at the annual E-Lon-schka dances in Pawhuska, together we worked out the details, found the exceptional objects, and ferreted out the histories of this amazing selection of Osage art.

We are indebted to Chief Tillman for his early support and for getting the word out about us in the Osage community. The Osage Tribal elections of June 2002 brought in a new administration headed by Chief James Gray, who was immediately supportive of this endeavor. Chief Gray is responsible for bringing in Kathryn Red Corn of our earlier acquaintance and now Director of the Osage Tribal Museum, which has provided key loans to this exhibition while kindly offering our staff a large space to photograph objects there. We are so grateful for the wisdom and great humor of the late Preston Morrell, whose spirit still seems to guide this project. Preston was the Road Man for the Black Dog Church in Hominy, Oklahoma. His position was passed on to Leonard Maker, another man whose generosity about the Osage experience is matched by a watchful eye for accurate information about his people and their culture. We appreciate his careful reading of the manuscript and his sure, but gentle, revisions when needed.

Many other members of the Osage community have shared their knowledge and hospitality with us. We are grateful to Christine No Ear, Mr. and Mrs. Raymond Red Corn, Harry Red Eagle Jr., Everett and George Waller, Romain Shackleford, Geoffrey Standing Bear, Charles Red Corn, and Andrew "Buddy" Red Corn. The Osage Tribal Council and the Osage Tribal Museum have been supportive and helpful throughout.

———————

Both the book and the exhibition have benefited from the cooperation and generosity of the following lenders and lending institutions and their staffs. We thank Arnold L. Lehman, Susan Kennedy Zeller, and William Siegman from the Brooklyn Museum of Art; Nancy J. Blomberg and Lewis Sharp from the Denver Art Museum; Graham W. J. Beal and Michelle S. Peplin at the Detroit Institute of Arts; Mr. and Mrs. Timothy L. Drone; Jonathan Haas, Dorren Martin-Ross, and John W. McCarter at the Field Museum of Natural History; Gordon Julich, Laura King, and John Peterson at Fort Osage, Jackson County Parks & Recreation; Hillary Kitz and Daniel Swan of the Gilcrease Museum in Tulsa; Denise Daenzer and Tina Wodiunig at the Nordamerika Native Museum in Switzerland; Tomas Michel and Sonja Schierle at the Staatliches Museum für Völkerkunde (Linden Museum) in Stuttgart; William Green and Nicolette B. Meister at the Logan Museum of Anthropology at Beloit College; Alex W. Barker and Dawn Scher Thomae at the Milwaukee Public Museum; Robert Archibald and Diane Mallow at the Missouri Historical Society; Bruce Bernstein, Joe Don Brave, Sarah Demb, Patricia L. Nietfeld, Erik Satrum, and Richard West at the National Museum of the American Indian, Smithsonian Institution; Susan Crawford, Candace Green, Douglass H. Erwin, Felicia Pickering, and Deborah Hull-Walski from the National Museum of Natural History, Smithsonian Institution; Kathryn Red Corn at the Osage Tribal Museum; Christy Abraham, Marcia Y. Manhart, Shelby Tisdale at the Philbrook Museum of Art; Nancy Pillsbury Shirley; Douglas J. Brewer and Jennifer White at The Spurlock Museum, University of Illinois at Urbana-Champaign; Margaret Jennings, Barbara Standingbear Hoge, Patrick Standing-Bear, and Sean StandingBear; Paula Stabler; Alan Waldt, and William Wierzbowski at the University of Pennsylvania Museum of Archaeology and Anthropology; and William McKale at the U.S. Cavalry Museum.

It is a pleasure to credit colleagues who have aided our progress on *Art of the Osage*. Bill Mercer, Curator of Native American Art at the Portland Art Museum, and Candice Green, Curator at the National Museum of Natural History, Smithsonian Institution, were helpful as the exhibition developed. Professor Simon Ottenberg encouraged our association with the University of Washington Press. We can't forgo this opportunity to credit the late Donald Ellegood, former director of the press, for bringing so many books on Native American art and culture to print, and we thank J. Patrick Soden, the Press's current director, for continuing to seek out American Indian subject matter. Special thanks to the staff of the Press and Marquand Books for bringing this book to its timely publication.

I thank Brent Benjamin, Director of the Saint Louis Art Museum, for his full support of this project. His rigorous review of the various phases of its development upheld the aesthetic level of our selection. We are grateful to Linda Thomas, Assistant Director for Collections and Exhibitions, and Connie Homburg, former Assistant Director for Curatorial Affairs, for their supportive direction in the many aspects of a developing exhibition. Mary Ann Steiner, Head of Publications for the Museum, provided the expertise and experience that guided this book

to its completion. The coordinating efforts of our Photography Manager Patricia Woods and fine photographic skill of David Ulmer resulted in the wonderful images you see in the following pages. Jeanette Fausz, Registrar, brought her expertise to the movement, safety, and care of Osage objects. Thanks also to: Jon Cournoyer, Senior Graphic Designer, and Jeff Wamhoff, Exhibition Designer, for the exhibition graphics and installation design; Susan Patterson, Manager of Information Technologies, for the Web presentation; Barbara Decker and Ann Burroughs, Educators, for their thoughtful editorial assistance; Brian Benben, Registration Assistant, for his help preparing the art objects for photography; Zoe Perkins, Conservator, for her careful review and conditioning; Steve Schenkenberg, Grant Writer, for his resourceful search for funding; Cathryn Goodwin, Network Administrator, and Ella Rothgangel, Collections Database Administrator, for their diligent care of the digital images and data.

Special thanks to to the research assistants who have contributed to the progress of *Art of the Osage*. Michelle Arens began early files for Osage art in known collections; Chris Jeannot tracked down the majority of the Osage collections from which we have drawn our final list; and R. Michael Barnett helped throughout the final phase by pursuing details, hunting down documents, and solving difficulties that cropped up along the way. Tammy O'Connor contributed her expertise in assembling the comparative illustrations.

Among the many individuals who have offered insights and encouragement are Indian art historian Ralph T. Coe; Christian Feest, professor of anthropology at the University of Frankfurt; Peter Bolz at the Ethnologisches Museum in Berlin; Jean Paul Rouselout at the Staatliches Museum für Völkerkunde; J. Frederick Fausz and Patty Wright at the University of Missouri, St. Louis; John W. Behrer at the Missouri Botanical Garden; Chester Cowen at the Oklahoma Historical Society Photo Archive; Margaret Hardin at the Los Angeles Museum of Natural History; and Julia Lookout. Special thanks to Dorothy Nunley and Manon Herzog.

John W. Nunley
Morton D. May Curator of the Arts of Africa, Oceania, and the Americas
Saint Louis Art Museum

The Osage people have one of the most distinctive and significant Native artistic traditions in the United States. Unlike the arts of most other Native American communities, Osage art has never been commercialized. Osage artisans have made and continue to make items only for members of their families or for other members of the Osage community. Although contemporary Osage art shows direct continuity in decorative motifs and basic forms with Osage art from earlier periods, it is still a dynamic and evolving artistic tradition. Uninfluenced by external market forces, it represents one of a declining number of truly indigenous living Native artistic traditions in the United States.

Early historic Osage art did not exist as separate and distinct from other aspects of culture. Unlike artists in Western/European societies, Osage artists did not produce art for art's sake. Instead, art was integrated with and inseparable from their material culture as well as an expression of their religious beliefs and practices.

To the Osage, the universe and everything within it was the purposeful creation of *Wakonta*, an all-controlling invisible force. The universe was a perfect, logically integrated structure, in which all naturally occurring things had been endowed by *Wakonta* with unique physical and behavioral qualities. Through observation of the world in which they lived, the Osage were able to create a model of the universe based on the varying characteristics of the different natural phenomena of which they were aware. Within this cosmic model, every different form of animal, bird, plant, cloud, and other natural phenomena was given a special set of symbolic meanings and purposes based on its known physical and behavioral qualities.

Osage material culture, and thus its art, is best understood by looking at individual objects from within the context of this cosmic model. Not all human needs could be directly satisfied in the universe as it had been created by *Wakonta*. As a result, humans were provided by *Wakonta* with the ability to rearrange the differing elements present in the universe to create new things

that would have new meanings to serve uniquely human needs and purposes.

To the Osage, the making of a material object involved rearranging the natural elements created by *Wakonta* into something new. Each newly made material object would have its own individual meaning and purpose. This process involved first defining those elements in the universe that represented the range of qualities needed to bring about the intended objective of the material object. These elements might consist of particular woods, hides, feathers, colors, textures, etc. For example, the wood of a cedar or willow tree was symbolic of everlasting life; the feather of a hawk was associated with courage, while that of a crow was a symbol of destruction; and the color white symbolized life, the color black, death, the color red, the sun or the source of life. Designs, symbolically representing parts of the cosmos, might be used to further enhance the intended purpose of the object. These elements were then crafted into a form suitable for its intended purpose. Once made, the object itself and its form became endowed with their own symbolic significance, which was a composite of those qualities present in all of the elements used in its construction.

Whether the material object was elaborately decorated or left plain depended not on individual choice but on its intended symbolic meaning and purpose. To attempt to divide Osage material culture into art objects (items that are aesthetically pleasing) and nonart (purely functional) objects is to impose an artificial Western concept. This does not mean that the Osage did not have an aesthetic sense. Rather, Osage craftspeople attempted to make objects, all objects, as beautiful as possible. Traditional Osage material culture and art were synonymous, and they are treated as such in this text.

Osage people did, however, distinguish different categories of material/art objects. Some objects had only a domestic or utilitarian function, other objects were used only in rituals, while most objects potentially could be used for either domestic or ritual purposes. Regardless of their use, all objects were made from materials that were gifts from *Wakonta* to humans, and even the most mundane domestic objects made by the Osage were, in a sense, "sacred." *Wakonta* had provided deer for the use of humans; therefore items of everyday clothing made out of deerskin were sacred and had to be treated with respect. Other objects had strictly ritual or ceremonial functions, and in those the Osage also recognized a higher level of sacredness. Certain objects used in their rituals were *wa-xó-be*, a term that means "to be made sacred," or consecrated for ritual use. These objects were made only for use in ceremonies. The most important *wa-xó-be* were the sacred bundles, which are discussed in Chapter 2, Osage Cosmology. It should be noted, however, that most objects ritually used in ceremonies were not *wa-xó-be*. Pipes, for example, were an important ritual object that were not considered *wa-xó-be*.

The symbolism used in Osage art is complex and sophisticated. The material arts were a means by which the people recorded and transmitted important cultural knowledge while simultaneously showing their reverence for *Wakonta's* creations and praying for *Wakonta's* continued blessing. The making of any object was a religious act, and implicit in this act was a prayer.

———

While most people can readily appreciate the aesthetic qualities of Osage material objects and the technical skills used in their creation, they can only appreciate the full meaning and significance of such objects within the context of Osage culture and history. To understand the development of Osage art, it has to be placed within the context of Osage cultural history. Since French contact in the last decades of the seventeenth century, virtually every aspect of Osage lifestyle has changed. From self-sufficient farmers and hunters, they have become part of a cash economy, supporting themselves primarily by working for wages or salaries. The traditional Osage Tribal Religion is gone. Today Osages are Christians, usually Catholics, Quakers, and Baptists, or Peyotists. In their everyday lives, whether they live in one of the small towns in Osage County or the larger cities of Tulsa or Oklahoma City, there is little that readily distinguishes them from their non-Osage neighbors. They wear the same styles of clothing, drive the same kinds of automobiles and trucks, live in the same types of houses, shop at the same stores and malls, watch the same tele-

vision programs and movies, and usually eat the same foods as their neighbors. Yet the casual observer might attach too much significance to such overt or visible similarities. The Osages are neither fully assimilated nor acculturated into the generic "American world." In fact, today's Osages live in two worlds. They are fully integrated into the regional economies of the areas in which they live. At the same time, they also live in their socially distinct Osage world, with their own communities and their own cultural events and activities.

To understand why Osage artistic tradition is still viable and vibrant, we need first to understand the continuity in Osage culture. What truly distinguishes the Osage people and has allowed for such a strong degree of cultural continuity is their very different history of contact with Europeans. Two critical factors set their history apart from the histories of most other tribes. First, there was never a major war between the Osages and European or American peoples. As a result, they never suffered the humiliation of military defeat. Second, except for a few brief periods, over the past three hundred years the Osages have been a relatively wealthy people. They have always possessed something that the French, the Spanish, or the Americans wanted and were willing to pay for. In the eighteenth and most of the nineteenth century it was furs, hides, and robes. In the late nineteenth and twentieth centuries it was money, land, and mineral rights. In their relationships with traders, government officials, merchants, oilmen, ranchers, and all their white neighbors, the Osages have always acted and usually been treated as equals. As a result, Osage people today are as confident of their history and their culture as their ancestors were three hundred years ago. This pride and confidence in themselves are the major factors in the continuity of Osage culture and art.

———

The development of and change in Osage art can be divided into two broad historical periods: the period from 1673 to 1900 and the twentieth century. Osage art and cultural history are presented in this book in seven chapters. The first three chapters, Early Osage Art and History, Osage Cosmology, and Osage Daily Life: Living Life as a Prayer, cover the period from the 1670s to 1900.

Chapter 1 discusses two main topics. The first is Osage economic and political history from French contact in 1673 to Osage removal to Indian Territory (Oklahoma) in 1872. Although these two centuries were a time of tremendous change, the Osage were able to maintain their cultural autonomy and economic self-sufficiency. Trade with the French, Spanish, and Americans made the Osage wealthy and introduced them to a wide range of new materials and technologies. The second part of this chapter focuses on Osage material culture during the early and midnineteenth century and the effects of metal tools, blankets, trade cloth, silk ribbons, and glass beads on Osage art and material culture.

Chapter 2, Osage Cosmology, focuses on traditional Osage Tribal Religion. The religious beliefs and practices discussed in this chapter predated French contact and persisted throughout the entire period. In this chapter, the religious ideas and concepts that underlie the making of Osage material objects and art are explained in detail. From their observations of the universe, ancient Osage people defined a cosmic model in which everything had symbolic meaning and significance. Everything the Osage did, from the performance of a ritual to the making of material objects, was based on this model. In its basic conceptual structure, the organization and performance of a religious ceremony is the same as the making of a material object. The ritual is just far more complex in its use of symbolism and its purpose more abstract.

Chapter 3 looks at Osage daily life during the early and midnineteenth century. It shows how the same cosmic model structured the daily social and political life of the Osage and discusses the range and use of domestic material objects. This chapter concludes with a brief but important discussion of the collapse of the traditional religious and cultural institutions of the Osage that occurred in the waning decades of the nineteenth century.

The next three chapters of the book are concerned with Osage life during the twentieth century. Following the collapse of their traditional religious structure, the Osage adopted the Peyote Religion. Chapter 4, The Osage Peyote Religion, discusses the new Peyote Religion that dominated Osage life at the turn of the twentieth century.

The Peyotists almost totally rejected and extinguished the teachings, the symbolism, and the rituals of the earlier traditional religion. A whole new set of religious symbols and ritual items was created by the Peyotists, and their church houses and meetings became the focal point of not just Osage religious life, but their social and cultural life as well. As the Peyote Church was becoming increasingly dominant during the first two decades of the twentieth century, income in the form of royalty payments from oil and natural gas were bringing the Osage vast wealth.

Focusing mainly on the period of the late teens and 1920s, Chapter 5, The Richest People in the World, discusses the Osages' growing wealth and its effects on their lifestyle. Wealthy beyond belief, many Osages spurned the domestic material culture of their ancestors and adopted a generic American lifestyle. This same period saw the reemergence of the E-Lon-schka dance societies and the creation of War Mothers dance societies, the subject of Chapter 6, Osage Dancing Societies and Organizations. During the 1920s, these dance societies were subordinate to the Peyote Religion as the focal point of Osage life. However, as the Peyote Church began to wane in membership and relative importance, particularly in the years following World War II, these societies took on increasing social and cultural importance. Today dance societies, especially the E-Lon-schka, are the focal point of Osage community life and cultural activities. While the Peyote Church is still important in the maintenance of Osage culture and the production of Osage art, only a small minority of Osage still actively participate in the religion. Today the Osage artistic tradition is maintained primarily by the participants in E-Lon-schka and War Mothers societies.

This volume concludes with Osage Aesthetics—A Curatorial View, an essay by John W. Nunley and E. Sean StandingBear, who look at Osage art and material objects in terms of their aesthetic themes and qualities.

Garrick Bailey
Professor of Anthropology
University of Tulsa

This tribe [the Osage], though living, as they long have, near the borders of the civilized community, have studiously rejected everything of civilized customs . . . strictly maintaining their primitive looks and manners, without the slightest appearance of innovations. —George Catlin, 1844

In 1673 Father Jacques Marquette and Louis Joliet, traveling from Quebec via Lake Michigan, became the first French explorers to reach the Mississippi River and note the presence of the Osage. At that time the Osage villages were located along the Osage River, in the southwestern portion of present-day Missouri. How long the Osages had lived in this region is not known, but it is generally agreed that they had not been long in this location. Oral traditions of the Osage and the closely related Kansa, Omaha, Ponca, and Quapaw speak of a time when they were all one people living to the east on the banks of a great lake. Later they began moving westward along the Ohio River. Only after crossing the Mississippi River did they begin to separate and disperse. The people who were to become the Quapaw moved south to eventually settle near the mouth of the Arkansas River. The groups who were to become the Omaha and Ponca migrated north and west, eventually settling along the middle portion of the Missouri River. The last separation was that of the Kansa and the Osage. The Kansa moved farther west to the Kaw River, while the Osage moved south of the Missouri River and up the Osage River. The timing of these migrations and separations is not clear, but since all five tribes speak mutually intelligible Siouan languages, it could not have long predated French contact.[1]

The religious symbolism of the Osage and the four other related tribes leaves little doubt that they were the historical descendants of the earlier Mississippian peoples who flourished during the period between A.D. 1000 and 1500 and constructed the great temple mound complexes of the central and southern Mississippi Valley. The only question unanswered is which one or ones of these highly developed prehistoric chiefdoms were the Osage associated with. Some scholars have suggested an association with the so-called Fort Ancient peoples, who occupied portions of the upper Ohio Valley. Others have noted cultural similarities with Cahokia, the greatest of all the Mississippian cities, located just east of St. Louis. Given the generalized nature of their migration stories, the answer could be either or both.

Independent French fur and hide traders quickly followed Marquette and Joliet. In the early 1680s, it was reported that two French traders were already trading with some of the tribes on the Missouri, and in 1693 it was noted that two traders were attempting to open trade with the Osage and the Missouri tribes. By 1699 a thin arc of French forts, missions, and settlements stretched from the St. Lawrence west through the Great Lakes and south down the Mississippi River to the Gulf of Mexico. From these bases French traders worked, expanding their trade network to tribes both to the east and to the west. By 1704 there were more than a hundred traders operating along the Missouri and Mississippi Rivers. Of particular importance to the Osage were the French settlements and missions among the Illini tribes. Not only did they serve as convenient bases for the traders visiting the

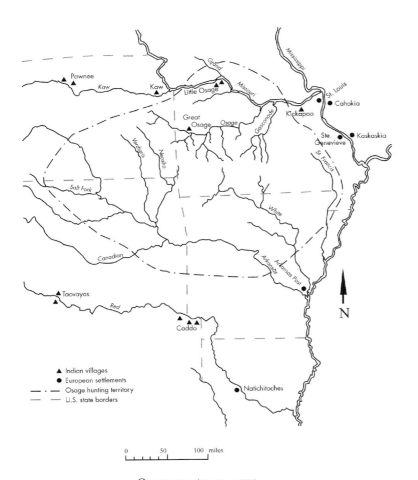

FIGURE 1.1 Osage country, ca. 1775.

sites, items of European manufacture—metal tools, ornaments, and glass beads—greatly outnumber native products. The stone, shell, and clay objects of native manufacture found on these village sites give few indications about Osage art.[2] Trade, together with the fact that most items made and used by the Osage were of perishable materials such as wood, leather, plant fibers, horn, bone, and quill, means that we know little concerning Osage art and material culture before contact with the French. While it is possible that some of the sacred items found in clan and tribal sacred bundles may date from the late seventeenth century or may even predate European contact, this cannot be ascertained. Except for some archaeological materials, the earliest known Osage art objects, as well as the earliest known drawings and paintings of Osage people, date no earlier that the first decades of the nineteenth century. The most that can be said about precontact Osage art is that it most likely made use of the same basic forms and decorative techniques as those of neighboring Prairie peoples.

The Fur and Hide Trade

French trade goods quickly became a necessity for survival. The earliest trade goods and those of greatest initial importance were guns and metal weapons such as knives, tomahawks, axes, and spearheads. These items served to increase the Osages' efficiency in hunting and gave them a military advantage over neighboring tribes who either lacked them or had fewer of them. Once they acquired European weapons, however, the Osage and other tribes became dependent on traders for a steady supply of powder, flints, and lead balls and as a means to replace weapons as they broke, wore out, or were lost.

Trade and the dependence on trade disrupted the prevailing balance of power among the tribes of the region and increased the level of intertribal warfare. In many cases, increased warfare was the result of preexisting hostilities between tribes, and those with regular supplies of guns and other metal weapons undoubtedly used the advantage of new and better weapons to settle old grudges with their enemies who lacked them. However, most of the increased warfare was directly related to the nature of the trade itself.

French traders exchanged their goods for a wide range of animal products. Deer hides and bearskins were the

Osages, they were sufficiently close that the Osages themselves could travel to trade at the settlements.

At almost the same time that the first French traders arrived, the Osage acquired their first horses, from the Plains tribes to the west. Horses soon proved to be as significant to the Osage as were the French and their trade goods. In the century that followed, the combined effects of trade and horses dramatically changed the lifestyle of the Osage and significantly affected their relationships with neighboring tribes.

Little is known about the material culture and the associated artistic traditions of the Osage at the time of French contact. French traders made available to the Osage a wide array of new metal tools—axes, saws, scissors, needles, and awls—as well as new materials such as cloth, ribbons, glass beads, and yarn that could be used to make or decorate goods. So quick were the Osage to adopt European trade items that even on the earliest known Osage village most important, but there was also a market for fox, beaver, marten, otter, wildcat, weasel, muskrat, and wolf skins and pelts. There was even a limited trade in bear grease and buffalo wool. With the development of trade, native hunters began killing far more of these animals than when they had been hunting only for their own needs. Overhunting soon diminished the numbers of game animals in the traditional hunting territories of the tribes most actively involved in the trade.

Indian captives, or slaves, were also a valuable trade item. With few French settlers in Louisiana, the market was at first limited. However, this changed in 1717 when John Law and his Company of the Indies were granted a commercial monopoly on Louisiana. Interested in the economic development of Louisiana, the French government recruited and sent settlers to the colony to establish farms and plantations. Within a few years, more than eight hundred French colonists had settled in the Illinois country, in sites at St. Charles, St. Genevieve, St. Philippe, and Prairie du Rocher. At the same time, plantations for growing rice, tobacco, and indigo were established by other colonists in the lower Mississippi Valley. The local market for Indian slaves increased, particularly in the lower valley, where they were used as plantation labor along with African slaves.

In the development of trade and the intertribal wars that followed, geography was on the side of the Osage. The earliest French trade routes were established along the Missouri and Mississippi Rivers, with the French settlements in the Illinois country serving as one of the main centers for this trade. Located along one of the main tributaries of the lower Missouri, the Osage villages were readily accessible to independent traders. Osage trading parties also visited the settlements in the Illinois country, so from the very earliest period the Osage were actively involved in the trade, a fact evidenced by the wealth of trade goods found on their early village sites.

The same was not true for all of their neighbors, particularly the Caddoan-speaking peoples of the middle Arkansas River Valley to the west and south. The French trade network was slow to expand westward up the Arkansas Valley, so the Caddoan peoples living in the valley had relatively few guns or other metal weapons. Poorly armed, the Caddoan peoples became the main target for raiding parties of Osage, Quapaw, and other

Siouan tribes seeking captives to sell to the French.[3] By 1740 the wars had taken a toll and many of the Caddoan tribes started to abandon their villages on the Arkansas and Canadian Rivers to move south of the Red River.[4] The war between the Osage and the Caddoans came to a temporary halt with the outbreak of the French and Indian War in 1756. The French troops in Louisiana and Canada needed all of the guns, flints, shot, and powder available to fight the British, and traders had little to supply the warring tribes.

With the defeat of France in 1763, Louisiana was divided between Britain and Spain. The English occupied the portion east of the river, and Spain took control of the land west of the Mississippi. Although numbering only about six thousand, the Osage were by this time well armed and militarily the most powerful tribe in the newly created Spanish Louisiana. Furs and hides were the main exports of the colony, and the Osage became the wealthiest tribe in the colony by supplying more hides and furs to traders than did any other tribe.

The change in the political status of Louisiana proved highly beneficial to the Osage. In 1764 Pierre Laclède moved his trading post to the west bank of the Mississippi, to a site called St. Louis. French settlers on the east bank of the river, finding themselves in what had become British territory, soon followed Laclède. The following year, Fort de Chartres and its garrison also moved across the river to St. Louis. The establishment of St. Louis on the west side of the river provided the Osage with even greater accessibility to trade.

In 1769 the first Spanish governor arrived in Louisiana and made several important changes in the Indian policy of the colony. There would be no independent free traders; all traders would have to be licensed and supervised by the government. The gun trade would be regulated, with munitions to the tribes limited so as to be sufficient only for hunting. Finally, Indian slavery was abolished in Spanish Louisiana.

Unlike the Caddoan tribes to the west, the Osage were now located close to the new British traders on the east bank of the Mississippi. That the Osage were the major source of furs and hides in Louisiana was a factor not lost on either the British traders or Spanish officials. Fearing encroachment by British traders, the Spanish government chose not to enforce its quotas of guns and other munitions on the Osage and other tribes along the Missouri River.

Once rearmed, the Osage made quick work of the remaining Caddoan villages on the Arkansas and Canadian Rivers. By the early 1770s, the remaining villages had been abandoned, the survivors having fled either south of the Red River or north to the Platte River. The Osage now laid claim to a vast, rich hunting territory that stretched from the Missouri River south to the Red River and from the Great Plains eastward almost to the Mississippi. Now in relative security, the Osage dramatically changed their economic activities and adopted a new seasonal pattern. After planting crops near their permanent village, all the villagers would travel west to hunt the vast herds of buffalo on the Great Plains. When the hunt was over, they would return home to harvest their crops. After the harvest, the villagers would again travel to the plains for the fall buffalo hunt; then when it was over, they would again return to their permanent village. During the winter, small parties of hunters would disperse throughout the Ozarks and the middle Arkansas Valley to hunt and trap, returning home in the spring for planting. Because of the increased distances involved in these seasonal movements, horses became critical to the Osage. The new hunting cycle proved extremely successful. In the 1750s and 1760s, it was estimated that the Osage and Missouri together marketed about eighty packs of furs and hides annually. By 1800 the Osage alone annually traded about nine hundred and fifty packs of furs and hides.

In 1803 the United States purchased Louisiana. One of the purposes for the purchase was to acquire land on which the eastern tribes, which were being displaced by white settlers, could be relocated. Negotiations for removal of the eastern tribes began almost at once.[5] The region best suited and selected for relocating the eastern tribes included the Arkansas Valley, the Ozark Plateau, and the south side of the Missouri Valley. There was only one problem: that area included the eastern portion of the Osage hunting range and their primary winter hunting and trapping region. American officials found what Spanish officials had discovered almost two generations earlier: the Osage were the wealthiest and best-armed tribe west of the Mississippi.

It proved fortuitous for American officials that just prior to the start of treaty negotiations, the Osage had abandoned their old village sites on the Osage River and relocated their villages farther west. Most of their villages were moved to sites along the Verdigris and Neosho Rivers, tributaries of the Arkansas. There appear to have been several reasons for these moves. René Auguste Chouteau, a French trader, had been given a monopoly on the Osage trade in 1794. In 1802 the Spanish trader Manuel Lisa was given the license to this valuable trade. Still having trading privileges and a trading post on the Arkansas, Chouteau was able to persuade most of the Osages of the Upland Forest village to abandon the Osage River and move their village southwest to Three Forks, where the Arkansas, Verdigris, and Grand Rivers come together. This Osage village became popularly known as Claremore's Village. A second reason for the moves was the increasing numbers of Indians from the eastern part of the United States now settling west of the Mississippi. The villages on the Osage River were increasingly vulnerable to attack by raiding parties from these tribes, especially when most of the villagers were absent on the summer and fall buffalo hunts. A third reason would have been that by moving their villages west, the Osages would be closer to the plains and the buffalo herds, making their seasonal hunting trips to the plains shorter and less arduous.

In 1808 the Osage signed a treaty with the United States, ceding most of their land in Missouri and Arkansas. In return, the Osage received annuities, a federal factory or trading post at Fort Osage on the Missouri River, and the right to hunt on the ceded tract until it was settled. The Osage thought that the new immigrants would be white settlers. Little did they realize that most of the immigrants would be eastern Indians who would be dependent on hunting the same game animals that the Osage counted on for trade.

As eastern tribes began to be resettled on the ceded lands, they came into ever-increasing conflicts with Osage hunting parties. Particularly aggressive were the Cherokee. In 1817 and 1821 Cherokee war parties attacked Claremore's Village at the lower Verdigris River. Hoping to separate the Osage and the Cherokee, the U.S. government negotiated a second treaty in

FIGURE 1.2 Clermont, son of Claremore the Town Maker, primary chief of Osage Indians in 1834. From George Catlin, LNAI, plate 150; courtesy Missouri Historical Society, St. Louis.

1818 in which the Osage ceded their portion of the Arkansas Valley as far west as Three Forks. A third treaty was negotiated in 1825 in which the Osage ceded most of their remaining territory, except for a narrow strip of land fifty miles wide and running from just west of the present Kansas-Missouri border west to the boundary of Mexico. In return, the Osage were to receive $7,000 a year in cash or merchandise. Despite the treaty, Claremore's Village and about fifteen hundred Osages remained outside the boundaries of the new reservation.

The Treaty of 1825 was negotiated in anticipation of the removal of the remaining eastern tribes. The western boundaries of Missouri and Arkansas were now seen by American government officials as the "permanent Indian frontier." The lands just west of that line would be the new home of the displaced eastern tribes, a place where they could live unmolested and undisturbed by white settlers. In 1830 Congress passed the Indian Removal Act. Under its provisions, treaties would be negotiated with the remaining tribes in the east, exchanging their lands for new reservations west of the line. Between 1830 and 1839, voluntarily or by force, almost seventy-five thousand eastern Indians were relocated to new reservations west of the line. The majority of these immigrants were resettled on lands once claimed by the Osage and abutting their reservation. Overwhelmed by the sheer numbers of immigrant Indians, Claremore's Village was abandoned in 1839 as its residents moved north and joined the other Osage on their reservation.

The resettlement of eastern tribes had devastating effects on the Osage economy. The eastern tribes, too, counted on hunting for much of their subsistence. The massive relocation resulted in overhunting, and the supply of deer, elk, and other game resources was rapidly depleted in the Ozark Plateau and middle Arkansas Valley. As a result, the Osage had to rely more heavily upon buffalo hunting. At the same time, the tribes of the southern plains—the Kiowa, Comanche, Cheyenne, and Arapahoe—were reacting with greater hostility to Osage hunting parties, which by the mid-1830s could not venture west of the Arkansas River for fear of attack. Caught between the displaced eastern tribes and the Plains tribes, the once wealthy Osage were growing hungry and impoverished.

Following the Texas Revolution of 1835–36, the Texas Rangers turned their attention to the Kiowa and Comanche. At the same time, hostilities broke out between these tribes and the Cheyenne to the north. Finding themselves cut off from their sources of guns and other munitions, the Kiowa and Comanche made peace with the Osage. With peace between them, the Osage became the major source of trade goods for the Kiowa and Comanche and gained for themselves greater access to the buffalo herds west of the Arkansas.

Osage annuity goods, guns, powder, lead, blankets, cloth, brass buckets, and other items received from the U.S. government were traded to the Kiowa and Comanche for buffalo robes, horses, and mules, which had a ready market in the trading posts and white stores on and off the Osage reservation. The profits of this trade proved enormous for the Osage. For a gun costing $20, they could receive one or two mules, which they could resell for $40 to $60. Throughout the 1840s, the volume of this trade increased. In 1847 alone, the Osage sold to white traders more than $60,000 worth of horses and mules that they had acquired from the Kiowa and Comanche. The Osage were once again not only self-sufficient but also prosperous.

Starting in the 1850s, the permanent Indian frontier was breached by white settlers. In what is now eastern Kansas, new removal treaties were negotiated with the tribes who would be moved south into the newly defined Indian Territory in present-day Oklahoma.

Early Trade and Osage Material Culture

We have little information on Osage material items at the time of French contact. In-depth knowledge of Osage art and material culture dates only to the first decades of the nineteenth century, when the earliest paintings and drawings of the Osage were made, the first descriptions of their domestic life were written, and the first known material items were collected.[6] What is now thought of as "traditional" Osage art and material culture actually date from a period almost one hundred fifty years after the people had started trading with the French. Not surprisingly, Osage material culture of this period strongly reflects influences from the trade. Catlin was mistaken in his appraisal of the Osage, cited at the beginning of this chapter. In fact, the Osage had so thoroughly integrated European trade items into their material culture that he could not recognize them.

While guns and metal weapons had been the earliest items of significance traded to the Osage, as the number of traders and the volume of trade increased during the eighteenth century, the inventory of goods grew increasingly diverse. By the beginning of the nineteenth century, traders were not only supplying the Osage with guns, metal weapons, and tools, they were also providing a wide-ranging array of domestic and luxury goods that quickly became necessities: brass buckets, iron kettles, awls, scissors, needles, files, saws, hawk bells, pin brooches, earrings, brass crucifixes, blankets, beads, cloth, wool yarn, and silk ribbon among them.[7] These goods had a profound effect not only on the general lifestyle of the Osage but on their artistic traditions as well.

Many pre-European art forms either disappeared altogether or became diminished in importance. At the time of contact, the Osage made and used a variety of utilitarian jar-shaped pottery vessels decorated with incised designs. By 1750 brass buckets and iron kettles had completely replaced those vessels, and pottery was no longer being made.[8] Woollen trade blankets were softer and easier to wear than robes made of buffalo hides or bearskins, so that while painted buffalo robes and bearskins continued to be used for bedding and seating, blankets increasingly replaced them as wearing apparel. The only problem the Osage found with the early trade blankets was that they were solid colors of white, dark indigo, scarlet, or green.[9] To enhance the aesthetic appeal of the blankets, the Osage eventually began to decorate them.

Trade cloth, some woollen and some of other fibers, began to replace leather for clothing. Wool broadcloth, usually black or dark blue and red, became the cloth of choice for making men's breechcloths and leggings and women's skirts and leggings. More brightly colored cloth, made of cotton or other light fabrics, sometimes printed with designs, was used for shirts and blouses.[10] Whether the use of more easily tailored cloth actually changed the styling of Osage clothing or merely replaced leather is unclear.

The Osages had traditionally carved a variety of useful items. Bowls, ladles, and spoons were carved out of maple, ash, or other woods, as were pipe stems, war clubs, and cradleboards. Buffalo horns were made into spoons.[11] Antlers, particularly those of elk, were carved into handles for tools of all kinds and for "spreaders" that were affixed to the deer-tail "roaches," or headdresses, that Osages wore on their heads.[12] Red catlinite stone traded from Minnesota as well as black stone quarried in eastern Kansas were carved into pipes and pipe bowls. French traders introduced a range of metal knives, files, and saws that could be used as tools to make these items. However, the effects of the new, more efficient, more effective tools on traditional Osage items are difficult to determine. Precontact wooden and antler objects have not survived. We don't know for certain how or whether the metal tools affected the forms or the decorative motifs cut or carved on these items. The only clues are in the stone pipes. We know that the stone pipes made by Osages during the historic period were more finely made and had far more elaborate decorative carving on them than those from the late prehistoric period.

French traders also introduced to the Osage a range of silver jewelry items: round brooches of various sizes, ear ornaments, bracelets, and armbands, all decorated with cutout or stamped designs. Originally, French silversmiths made these silver trade items, but by at least the early nineteenth century, Indian craftsmen from some of the Great Lakes tribes had their own tools and were buying sheet silver to make their own jewelry.[13] There is no mention of the first silversmiths among the Osage, but by the later nineteenth century, some Osage were fashioning ornaments out of German silver (a nonsilver alloy), which had replaced silver as the metal of choice for jewelry made by Prairie and Plains tribes in the mid-nineteenth century.

Most trade items could be placed within the Osage cosmic model. Metal objects were symbolically equated with copper, which the Osage and their ancestors had long used in limited quantities. The forms and functions of items could also be integrated into their symbolic model. Thus, a knife was symbolically a knife whether it was stone or metal. The same was true for ax heads, tomahawks, spear points, and most other items of trade. However, this was not true for all materials that traders introduced. The availability of new items provided the Osage with new means for making and decorating material goods: colored glass beads, silk ribbon, and wool yarn totally revolutionized the use of design elements on material objects. Glass, silk, and wool had no place in their cosmic model and no symbolic meaning or significance. In Chapter 2, Osage Cosmology, the full importance of this factor becomes more evident. The only thing of symbolic importance about these items was their color. As long as the colors and the design motifs created by the colors were compatible with the intended symbolic meaning and purpose of the object, they could be used on virtually any object. The Osage began using beads, yarn, and ribbon to add symbolically significant design elements to virtually any object to which they could be attached. The ribbon, beads, and yarn could be substituted for one another or even combined. There can be little doubt that the availability of these materials profoundly affected the amount and complexity of decorative designs found on Osage objects during the late eighteenth and nineteenth centuries.

Glass beads were one of the earliest and most popular trade items introduced to the Osage. There were two basic types of beads: large ones that could be worn on or as necklaces, and small ones that could be sewn on leather or cloth. Of the wide variety of necklace beads traded to the Osage, some were polychromes made with different colors of glass to create designs, others were monochromes, and some were translucent. The beads varied in size and shape. Some were spherical, others were ovoid or tubular, and they could be either faceted or smooth. In many cases, the beads were simply strung together and worn as a necklace. In other cases, they were strung on necklaces together with bear claws or eagle talons and wrapped with fur.[14]

Smaller beads for embroidery also varied in size, color, and shape. They were available in white, red, blue, green, black, pink, orange, and various shades of those colors. All were monochromes, either solid in color or translucent, and either smooth or faceted.[15] Beadworkers could vary the colors to create an almost infinite range of geometric and curvilinear designs. In fact, a skilled beadworker could reproduce almost any design in beads. The Osage, like all tribes, had their own range of generally distinctive designs and color preferences, which changed over time. For the most part, Osage beadwork designs were geometric and symmetrical, with the design split into two balanced, mirror-image halves, but there were other designs that featured hands, horse heads, and other motifs.

Beadwork appears to have replaced quillwork and painting as the most popular way to decorate many objects. Beads were used to decorate virtually anything to which they could be attached, and a wide range of different beading methods developed. Simple stitching was used to apply beads to tanned leather and cloth.

To apply beads to leather, the beadworker would string five to seven beads together and sew them down with sinew in the so-called lazy stitch.[16] On cloth, each bead would usually be sewn down with cotton thread. Osage beadworkers typically decorated clothing and moccasins with narrow strips of beads and, unlike some of their neighbors, they rarely beaded an item entirely.[17]

The Osage used looms for beading belts and garters. Although still narrow relative to their length, loomed pieces were often much wider than the beaded strips done directly on leather or cloth. Most loomed pieces were produced using commercial thread; however, wool yarn, usually red, was frequently used instead.

For decorating the wooden handles of feather fans and rattles, beadworkers would use a netted stitch. Since the beads could not be directly attached to the wood, they were held in a thread netting that formed a beaded tube, which could be fitted over the handle as a tight cover.

Before contact with Europeans, the Osage, like most Prairie tribes, produced a range of loom- and finger-woven items using either native plant fibers or buffalo hair. Large storage bags known as "feast bags" were loom-woven using plant fibers. Other large bags made to hold sacred objects were loom-woven of buffalo hair. Belts, garters, and small bags were also made of buffalo hair, but they were done in a finger-weaving technique. At least as early as the eighteenth century, women had begun to unravel worn-out trade blankets and reuse the yarn in their own weaving. At first the yarn was used only to add color to bags, belts, and other items woven of plant fibers or buffalo hair. It was probably not until yarn became more readily available during the nineteenth century that the Osage began to weave these items entirely out of yarn.[18]

Ribbon appliqué work consisted of making long decorative strips, using various colors of silk. Designs were created by cutting and/or folding the strips of ribbon and sewing them together. The completed strip was then sewn onto an item of clothing or blanket for decoration. The type of appliqué work produced by the Osage during the nineteenth century does not have any known native North American or European prototypes. The designs produced in Osage ribbon work are all traditional American Indian designs. With few exceptions, ribbon work was applied to trade cloth and trade blankets. These factors

seem to indicate that the particular type of ribbon work made by the Osage was an indigenous innovation that was developed in the eighteenth century by the tribes of the Great Lakes or the Mississippi Valley.[19]

Beadwork, ribbon work, and yarn work made up the three alternatives for decorating an item of clothing. Blankets could be decorated with beadwork, ribbon work, or yarn work, or even a combination of the three. Most frequently, blankets included three panels of ribbon work, one across the bottom and two going partway up each side to form a U-shape. Sometimes isolated design elements made from single pieces of silk cut in the shape of either hands or horses would be sewn along the bottom part of the U and outlined with beads. In other cases, three large finger-woven yarn belts or panels would be sewn crossways on a blanket. Still other blankets were decorated with a single panel of beadwork that had been applied to either leather or cloth—a so-called "blanket strip"—which was sewn across the blanket at its midpoint. Finally, some blankets were decorated with complex isolated designs of spot beading. Both the yarn- and bead-decorated blankets were sometimes further embellished with ribbon-work panels.

Men's and women's cloth leggings, as well as breechcloths and skirts, could be decorated with either beadwork or ribbon work. While ribbon work was the most common decoration on breechcloths and skirts, some clothing also included isolated beaded designs. Leggings, in contrast, were decorated with either a long beaded panel design or a panel of ribbon work. An interesting aspect of legging decoration is that the same designs could be used on a beadwork panel and a ribbon-work panel.

Although the materials and some of the tools used in making these items would change, the basic forms, techniques of decoration, and design elements that had evolved by the early nineteenth century are the very same ones used by the Osage today. There is, however, one major difference. The rich symbolic meanings of most of the forms and designs were lost or eroded following the collapse of traditional religious institutions and practices at the turn of the twentieth century. And the adoption of the Peyote Religion has resulted in the use of new symbolic forms and designs.

CAT. 1

BLANKET

early 20th century
wool and silk
59 × 72 × 7¾ inches
Denver Art Museum Collection, Native Arts Acquisition funds, 1953.131

Osage women wear blankets like this one during formal events. The horse motif indicates prosperity and, at times, the literal surnames of particular families. The horses are enclosed on three sides by double-sided lightning bolts that create an additional set of bolts as they interact with the surrounding color fields. The gold and white bilateral patterns, which are bisected by the line where the blue and red bands meet, depict converging arrows. Frequently, such blankets were placed on horses to be given away in gestures of gratitude and good faith.

GOURD RATTLE

glass beads, copper, brass, bronze, gourd, protein
combination, and horsehair
25 × 3 × 3 inches
Department of Anthropology, Smithsonian Institution

The patriotic attitude suggested by the
flag on the handle of this rattle conveys
the fact that the Osage have never been at
war with the United States. This was the
personal gourd rattle of Chief Bacon Rind
(Wah-she-hah). The bells attached to the
rattle's fringe may be a carryover from the
days when weapons were adorned with
hawk bells. The lightning motif around the
base of the handle is meant to imbue the
user with power. The Christian medal on
the handle refers to Christ, whose head
crowned with thorns is symbolically represented on the gourd by the zigzag line that
encircles it.

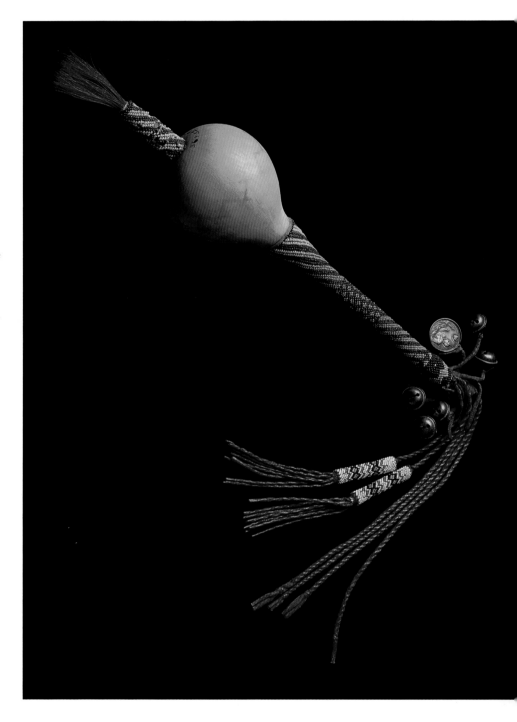

CAT. 3

SPLIT-HORN HEADDRESS

hair, feathers, horn, hide, glass beads, fur, silk, wool,
cotton, and sinew
49 × 9 inches
Brooklyn Museum of Art, Museum Expedition 1911,
Museum Collection Fund

Shunkahmolah, a leader of the Black Bear clan priesthood, presented this headdress to ethnologist and Indian scholar Francis La Flesche, who worked with the Osage in the early part of the twentieth century. The headdress was used in connection with ritual preparations for the hunt. The body of the kingfisher bird attached to the back symbolically unites the Osage Sky people and the Osage Earth people in the hunt. The kingfisher comes from the sky and hunts in the water, so it travels in the realms of both sky and earth. The northern-harrier and red-tailed hawk feathers attached to the lower half of the headdress give the hunter the power to move quickly and effectively, which would help ensure a successful hunt.

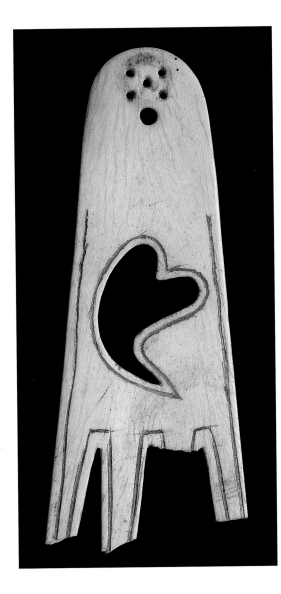

CAT. 4

ROACH SPREADER

bone
6⁵⁄₁₆ × 2³⁄₈ × ³⁄₈ inches
National Museum of the American Indian,
Smithsonian Institution

Made of elk antler, this roach spreader
helped secure the headdress, or roach, to
the head. It also functioned to hold a tail
feather from an adult eagle. The flat platform supported three other components:
a cylinder made from the upper wing bone
of a mature eagle; a wooden stick that fit
inside the cylinder to support the feather;
and a metal stopper to prevent the stick
from falling out. A braid of hair was pushed
through the large hole and held in place
with another small stick. The projections
at one end symbolize the *hó-e-ga*, the snare
of life. This spreader features a bleeding
heart design in which the artist has pushed
the asymmetrical lines to their limits while
retaining its full sensuality.

CAT. 5

MAN'S SHIRT

wool with embroidery and brass
30½ × 62³⁄₁₆ × ¹³⁄₁₆ inches
National Museum of the American Indian,
Smithsonian Institution

The dramatic representation of the
severed hands on the front of this red
shirt is an image that only a man of great
stature was allowed to wear. To secure
such a right, the man would have earned
many war honors. The elongated yellow
forms outlined by white lines suggest ear
stretchers. The bottom lozenge design
represents an ear perforator and terminates in a stylized fleur-de-lis. The single
blue hand on the back of the shirt is
framed by a V configuration consisting
of connected diamond shapes that end
in another fleur-de-lis.

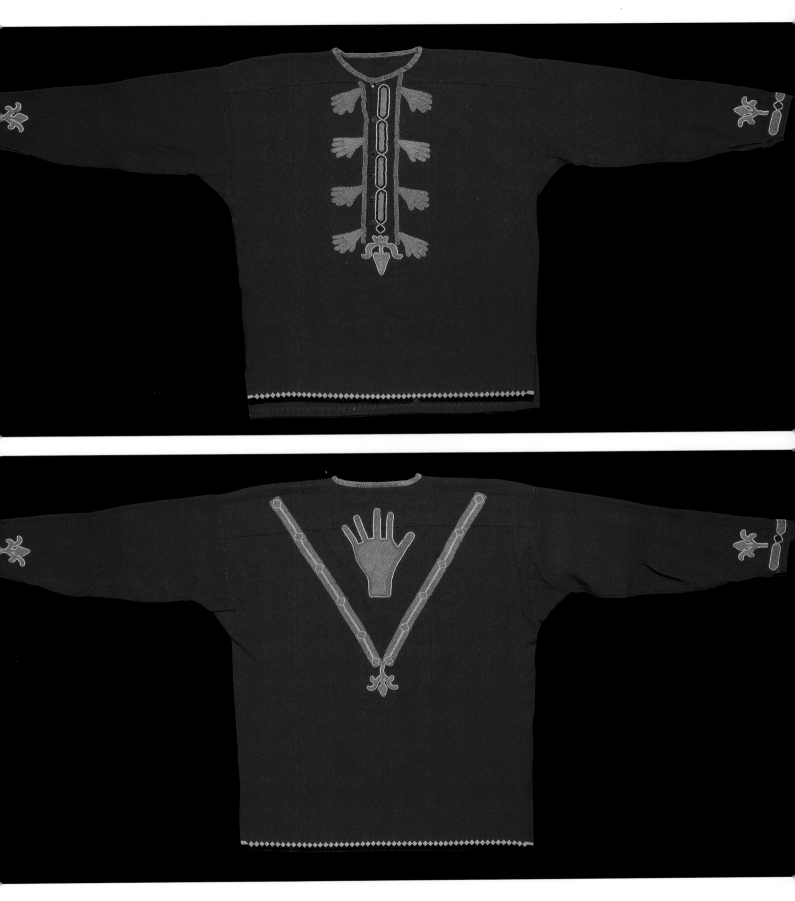

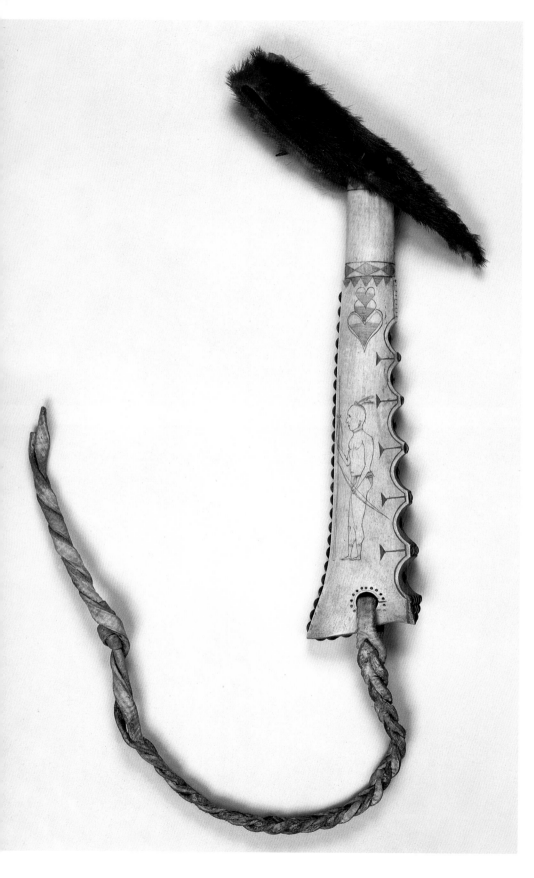

CAT. 6

QUIRT

ca. 1833
antler, brass, fur, and hide
length: 38³⁄₁₆ inches
Linden-Museum Stuttgart

This highly detailed quirt, or riding whip, may illustrate the personal narrative of the man who made it. On one side, the hunter-warrior with a lance and bow in his hands stands beneath three stacked hearts that appear to be half filled with blood. On the reverse side, the hunting dog companion is running beneath a warrior who holds a scalp. Above the warrior are three stacked hearts drained of blood. Perhaps this is a narrative about three enemies who were subdued by the warrior. The scalloped edge of the object refers to the *hó-e-ga*, the snare that both gives and takes life.

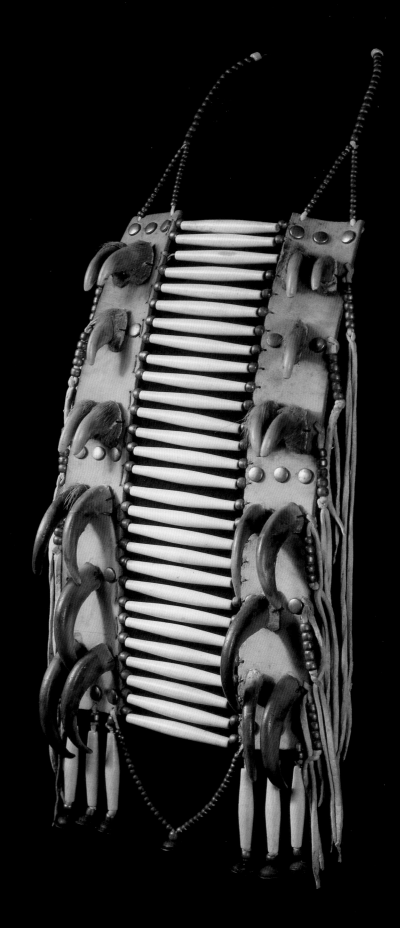

CAT. 7

BEAR CLAW BREASTPLATE

porcelain, bear claws, hide, and metal
18 × 10 inches
Osage Tribal Museum

The ingenious artist who made this chest
armor used a complete set of claws from
a single bear to establish the flowing composition of the piece. The claws on the
breastplate are arranged from small at the
top to large at the bottom, giving it a strong
sense of weight, balance, and significance.
The power and deadly force conveyed by
the open claws would have given pause to
an enemy and advantage to the wearer. The
bones placed in the center of the breastplate could deflect a blow from a battle-ax,
and the hawk bells suspended from the
bottom would announce the presence of
a formidable warrior.

PIPE

wood, stone, hide, and pigment
stem: 9/16 × 9/16 × 10 5/8 inches
bowl: 4 15/16 × 3 1/8 × 1 inches
National Museum of the American Indian,
Smithsonian Institution

The simplicity with which the two does and the buck are rendered recalls the great cave paintings created at Lascaux some 17,000 years ago. The artist who carved this pipe utilized organic lines to breathe life into the still images. This was a personal pipe used primarily for pleasure. The T shape of the catlinite bowl is common among Osage pipes.

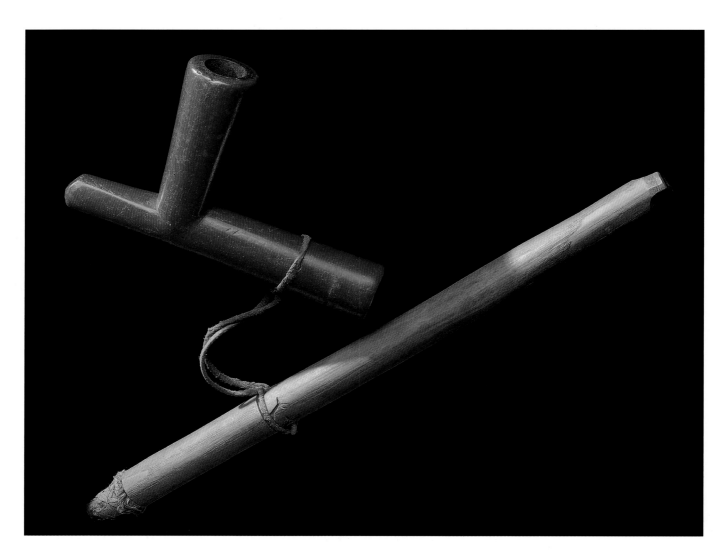

CAT. 9

ROACH AND SPREADER WITH HAIR ORNAMENT

deer hair, feathers, beads, and pigment
43 × 9 inches
Private collection

This roach, or headdress, is still worn in the
E-Lon-schka dances. Made of the long black
hairs from the chest of a mature male wild
turkey and dyed red hair from the underside
of the white-tailed deer's tail, these elements
symbolize the fire, ashes, and destruction
of a prairie fire. Placement on the head is
determined by holding one's palm on the
bridge of the nose and extending the middle
finger toward the top of the head. At that
spot, a piece of hide is braided with the hair,
and both are pushed together through the
large hole on the platform of the elk-antler
spreader. A small piece of wood or bone
is pushed through the braid to secure the
headdress. The incised geometric design
on the platform represents a stylized war
hawk of the Black Bear clan.

CAT. 10

WAMPUM BEAD NECKLACE

ca. 1840
shell, glass beads, brass, and ribbon
24 × 2 inches
Private collection

The term *wampum* originated on the East
Coast, where the polished shell beads used
as money were later produced for commercial use. The word itself most likely derives
from a Native American language. These
irregularly shaped shell beads are cut from
the central core of the hairpipe shell found
in saltwater bodies. In ancient times, the
hair-thin hollow core of the shell was used
as a pipe stem. Removing the outer layers
of shell is difficult and time-consuming.
These kinds of beads came to be valued
above all other kinds of beads by the Osage.
The nineteenth-century glass beads on this
necklace were added in the midtwentieth
century.

HEAD EFFIGY WAR PIPE

stone, wood, sinew, leather, hair, fiber cord, pigment,
glass beads, and copper alloy
25 × 2 × 2 inches
Department of Anthropology, Smithsonian Institution

This sacred pipe once belonged to the
people of the Wind clan. It was smoked
to consecrate the decision to declare war.
The white beads are made of shell, and the
narrow tubes between the beads are made
of hammered copper. Pieces of scalp and
hair fragments are attached near the mouthpiece. The pipe's shaft represents the body,
or torso, of "the symbolic man." The underside of the bowl depicts a face whose eyes
are consecrated with red paint. The gaze
of the symbolic man is remarkably subtle,
yet very powerful as it looks upon future
death and destruction. Prayers to *Wakonta*
for a successful war party would be carried
in the pipe's sacred smoke.

CAT. 12

MIRROR BOARD

wood, metal, and glass
13 × 6 × 1 inches
Osage Tribal Museum

The bottom of this hand mirror is shaped
in the form of a *hó-e-ga*, the symbolic snare
that holds all life. In the ancient religion,
two ceremonial arrows were used to signify
life and death. Representations of these
arrows are incised and painted on the board.
The commercially made enamel paint and
the pronged studs that adorn the surface
would have been purchased from a local
hardware store. The studs integrated into
the design served to protect the surface
from being scratched.

STANDARD

golden eagle feathers, cloth, and wood
48 × 8 inches
Osage Tribal Museum

Standards such as this one are known as flags by the Osage.
They were carried in mourning parties as well as in military
campaigns. The shaft, made of Osage orangewood, is covered
in wool broadcloth and cotton fabric. All the tail feathers come
from adult golden eagles, but the red-dyed plumes attached
to the shafts are from the undersides of eagles. The notched
feathers denote specific war honors.

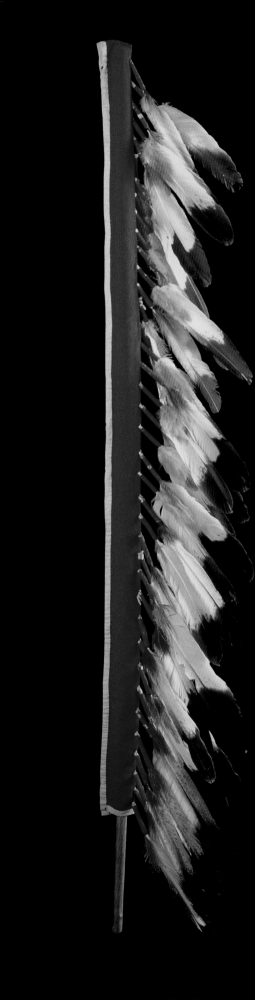

WOMAN'S BLANKET WITH GOURD FOLIAGE MOTIF

cloth with silver ornaments and copper bells
55½ × 66½ inches
Private collection

The horizontal red ribbon appliqué bars on this blanket create a bold composi-
tional statement that echoes the military flair of wedding coats. German silver
medallions add a heightened sense of the military, reminiscent of medals of
honor. In sharp contrast are curvilinear floral motifs that frame the bars. These
motifs represent squash blossoms, one of the traditional staple crops grown
by Osage women. The pairing of military and floral designs conveys the cosmological balance of feminine and masculine so prominent in Osage aesthetics.
The copper bells on the blanket's bottom edge would have produced the sound
of rain during ritual dancing.

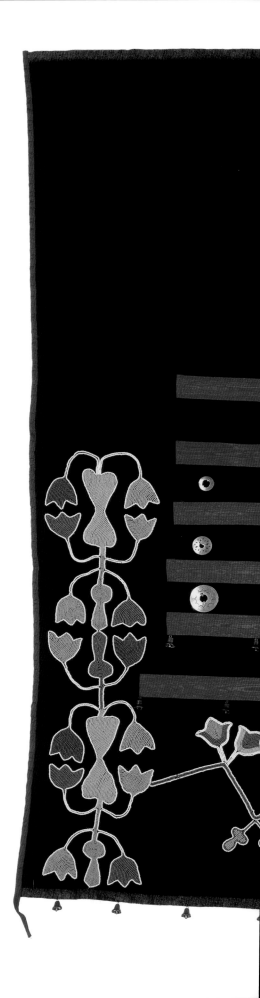

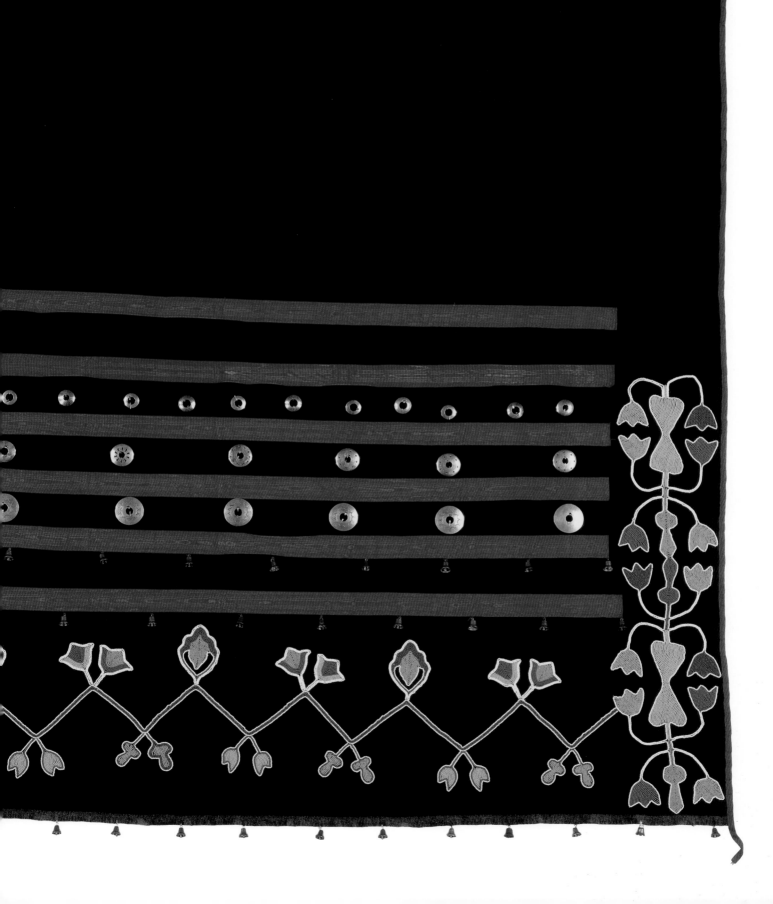

We (humans) . . . have been given hearts and minds to go by. We are ignorant, but have eyes to see with in order to guide ourselves in the ways God wishes us to go. —Edgar McCarthy, Osage religious leader, 1923

Religion and religious beliefs were not merely the core of Osage culture; they *were* Osage culture. There was no separation of the secular from the sacred. Everything that existed in the universe was an expression of an all-controlling invisible force, called *Wakonta;* therefore everything was sacred. Everything the Osage did, whether it was the making of a pipe, the planting of a cornfield, the naming of a child, or the mounting of a war party, was not a reflection of their beliefs but, rather, an expression of their beliefs. Every action involved, as an ancient Osage would have said, putting portions of the cosmos into motion for a specific objective. Sometimes the objective was to produce something tangible: a pair of moccasins or food to eat. Sometimes the objective was more abstract, as in the way a formal ceremony would appeal for the health of an individual or the long life of the community. Regardless of the intended objective and the formality or informality involved, virtually all actions were conceived of symbolically as religious ritual and prayer. To understand why human actions could take no other form, one has to understand how the Osage saw the nature and structure of the cosmos.

According to Osage cosmology, the cosmos was both the conscious creation and the expression of an all-powerful and controlling invisible force, which they called *Wakonta.* Osages considered the cosmos to be an ordered system that was dynamic, ever changing, and logically integrated, with everything in it having meaning and purpose. Although the cosmos was infinitely

complex, it was knowable to humans, to a limited degree, through their powers of empirical observation and logical reasoning. Humans had the responsibility for influencing, as well as the ability to influence, their own destinies. Knowledge of the cosmos was the key to human survival. It was only through such knowledge that Osage people could provide food and shelter for their children and protect them from their enemies. It was only through knowledge of the cosmos that humans could secure and maintain God's blessings. For the Osages, there could be no separation of the secular from the sacred or of science from religion, and in their actions, as in the cosmos, nothing could exist without meaning and purpose.

In the dim past, the ancient priests of the Osage, the *wa-kon-ta-gi* (men of mystery),[1] came to understand the universe as the creation of an all-powerful force. Sometimes they called this force *E-á-wa-won-a-ka,* the "Causer of our Being,"[2] but more commonly they referred to this force as *Wakonta,* a word that refers to something unknown or mysterious.[3] They came to view the cosmos as consisting of two inseparable realms. One realm was the visible world, the world of the living, in which all things took a physical form, breathed, and moved. The other realm was the invisible world, which was the spiritual world of *Wakonta.* Although these two realms were distinct, they were inseparable. As anthropologist Francis La Flesche noted, "This great power [*Wakonta*] resides in the air, the blue sky, the clouds, the stars, the sun, the moon, and the earth. . . . Sometimes the Osage speak of a tree, a rock, or a prominent hill as *Wakonta*, but when asked if his people had a great number of *Wakontas*, he would reply, 'Not so; there is but one God and His presence is in all things and is everywhere. We say a tree is *Wakonta* because in it also *Wakonta* resides.'"[4] Virtually everything, collectively and individually, in the world of the living was a manifestation of *Wakonta*. The visible world was the physical or tangible expression of the invisible world, with birth and death marking the passages between the two worlds.

While *Wakonta* was invisible and revealed little to humans directly, the ancient priests came to the realization that *Wakonta* was at least partially knowable. Although they could not know *Wakonta* directly, they knew that the cosmos was logically integrated and that everything in the cosmos had both meaning and purpose. They concluded that by studying the visible world and everything in it, they could gain greater understanding of this mysterious force that controlled their lives.

Certain aspects of the cosmos were obvious to humans. The universe was divided into earth, which the Osage called *Hunka*, and the sky, which they called *Tsi-zho*. The earth in turn was divided into land, which they also called *Hunka*, and the water, called *Wa-sha-she*. On a clear day, it appeared that the sky extended upward from the surface of the earth, but this was only an illusion. On a partially cloudy day, one could see that humans and other livings things existed neither in the earth nor in the sky but, rather, in a narrow lens situated between earth and sky,[5] which they called the *hó-e-ga*, a word that means "snare or trap" (see cat. 23). All life was the result of the procreative interaction between the forces of sky and the forces of earth. "Life is conceived in the sky and descends to earth to take material form."[6] They came to see the sky as male or masculine, while the earth was perceived as the female or feminine force. After birth, life was held in this lens between earth and sky, like an animal held in a snare. With death, the spirit was released from the snare to escape back into the invisible world.[7]

The priests also determined that the cosmos was dynamic and always changing. The daily changes of day and night and the seasonal changes of spring, summer, fall, and winter were associated with the movements of celestial bodies—the sun, moon, and various stars. It was also apparent to the priests that the sun was the greatest

of the life-giving forces and that the cycle of the day was one of endlessly recurring patterns. The day could be divided into sunrise, midday, sunset, and night. Every day, this cycle was repeated. The sun would rise in the east and travel west to disappear, only to reappear in the east the next morning. They noted a similar pattern with the cycle of the four seasons. In the spring, when it became warm, green plants began to sprout and bloom and leaves appeared on the trees. During the heat of summer, the plants and leaves matured. As the weather cooled in the fall, the plants and leaves began to lose their vigor and color. With the cold air of winter, the plants and leaves died. They noted that humans, animals, birds, and all other living things passed through four stages of life: birth, maturity, old age, and death. The parts of the day, the seasons of the year, and the stages of life presented a series of cycles that all repeated the same pattern. All things of this world passed through the endless cycle of birth (sunrise and spring), maturity (midday and summer), old age (sunset and fall), and death (night and winter). All things born, whether it is the day, the year, a human being, an animal, a bird, a tree, a species of animal, or even a group of people such as the Osage, would die. "Nothing in the cosmos moves backward."[8] All things in the world of the living followed the same relentless path, like that of the sun, from east to west, from birth to death. The ancient priests called this the path of life.[9]

This was the basic structure and direction of the cosmos defined by the ancient priests. There were four major divisions of the cosmos. The sky (male) and the earth (female) were constant, while the day (life) and night (death) divisions were dynamic. The direction of the sky was not up; rather, it formed the symbolic "left side" of the cosmos. It was also considered a symbolic masculine force and associated with the number six. Similarly, the direction of the earth was not down; instead, it formed the symbolic "right side" of the cosmos. The earth was feminine and associated with the number seven. Why the priests made these symbolic associations is not explained.

While sky and earth were associated with the left and right sides, day and night were associated with the directions east and west, respectively. The day was symbolically associated with the sun, life-giving forces, birth,

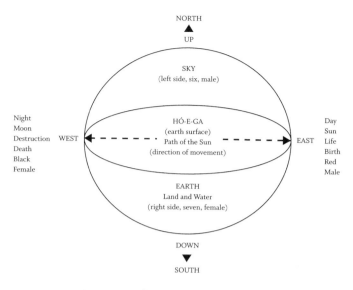

FIGURE 2.1 Structure of the cosmos.

masculine forces, and red, the color of sunrise. Night was symbolically associated with the moon, destruction, death, feminine forces, and the color black.

The symbolic designations of "left side" and "right side" for the sky and earth were significant in the symbolic orientation of the cosmos. The cosmos could face east, which is the direction of birth and the life-giving forces, or the cosmos could face west, the direction of death and destruction. If the cosmos faced toward the east, then the left, or sky, side would be to the north and the earth, or right, side would be to the south. If the cosmos was turned to face toward the west, then the left, or sky, side would be to the south and the earth side to the north.[10]

While these ideas defined the basic structure of the cosmos, they did not explain the meanings and purposes of all the birds, animals, plants, and other things within the world of the living. Thus the priests continued in their search for understanding.

The ancient priests realized that every different plant, animal, bird, fish, and insect, as well as the natural phenomena of rain, clouds, rocks, water, and heavenly bodies, had been created for a specific reason. It was not so simple that each of *Wakonta*'s creations had a single meaning and purpose. Every aspect of their physical being and behavior had significance as well. Birds were unlike most other living things in that they could fly.

Yet a bird was not just a bird. There were many different types of birds, which differed in their physical appearance as well as in their behaviors. Some birds were aggressive or brave, while others were shy or even cowardly. Some were most active at dawn, others at midday or evening, and some at night. Some ate insects, others ate carrion, seeds, or fish, while some hunted living creatures. Some had black feathers, others had blue or red feathers, white or yellow feathers; some even had feathers of several colors. There were birds with sharp, straight, powerful beaks, powerful curved beaks, small delicate beaks, or even bills. Some had feet with sharp talons; some had webbed feet. A bird was not just a bird, and a feather was not just a feather. For example, a hawk, because of its behavior, was symbolic of courage, its talons a symbol of destruction, and, in the case of a red-tailed hawk, its red feathers were symbolic of the sun or life. The same was true of other animals, plants, fish, and all the things in the visible world. There was meaning and purpose within meaning and purpose. The meaning and purpose of a bird, an animal, or any other creation of *Wakonta* depended on the context in which it occurred.

If nothing was created without purpose, then what was the purpose of humans, and of the Osages in particular? The ancient priests noted that humans were different from all other living creatures. Humans had the "capabilities of thinking and of bringing to pass, capabilities not possible to the animals."[11] Only humans were endowed by *Wakonta* with "the powers of reason and speech."[12] Only humans were endowed with *wa-thí-gethon*, the ability to search with the mind and learn.[13] These unique characteristics were a blessing as well as a burden. Humans had the power both to learn and to create. The ability to create meant that humans could give or assign sacred symbolic value to things that did not otherwise have them. An individual or a group of individuals could assume the same symbolic meanings of some element of the sacred world or even the cosmos as a whole. A design or shape could similarly be imbued with the symbolic meaning of some aspect or aspects of the sacred cosmos. Even more important, the ability to create meant that humans could rearrange the elements of the sacred world (what we would call the natural environment) to create something new, with a different symbolic meaning and purpose, that could then be used to meet a particular human need.

Rituals consist of differing arrays of symbolic elements that are brought together and physically moved in different patterns to focus their composite sacred meanings toward a particular objective. This same creative model was found in virtually all aspects of Osage life, including the making of material/art objects. To make an object, different elements, each with a particular symbolic meaning, were fashioned into a new physical form, which could then be used for a purpose that none of the elements could accomplish alone. Because only humans had been given the ability to create by *Wakonta*, humans were responsible for their own actions and their own fate.

Wakonta was invisible and did not directly communicate with humans.[14] There were no direct revelations. Humans had to try and discover what *Wakonta* wished of them, and in order to do that, they had to study the cosmos and all of *Wakonta*'s creations. One aspect of the cosmos that was of critical concern in this pursuit was that nothing in the visible world was permanent. All things born will die. This was true for humans, as well as all other living things. Thus every individual Osage would eventually die, as would every individual buffalo, bear, otter, eagle, blue jay, oak tree, sycamore, cloud, and any other being brought into existence in the visible world. And since this was also true of all collective groups of living things, eventually all of the Osages, the buffalo, bears, otters, eagles, and oak trees would vanish from the world of the living. Why this was true they did not know.[15] Since all individuals and groups were the creations of *Wakonta* and existed only as long as *Wakonta* wished, the maintenance of *Wakonta*'s continued blessings was a primary concern. For an individual Osage, this blessing came in the form of health and long life. However, since every individual would eventually die, the Osages as a whole considered *Wakonta*'s most important blessing to be children. Children were symbolic of *Wakonta*'s desire for the Osage to continue as a people. In addition to children, *Wakonta* gave the Osages and other humans countless other blessings that gave comfort and joy to their lives.[16]

Wakonta created some things for the general benefit of humans and other living things. The sun, certainly the greatest of all of *Wakonta*'s creations, brought life, warmth, and comfort to all creatures. The cloudless day brought a sense of peace. Over these creations, humans

had no direct control. However, *Wakonta* created still other things for the purpose of benefiting humans, over which they could exercise some degree of control.

Wakonta had created a wide range of plants and other things that could ease human suffering and sometimes prolong their lives. The hulls of the black walnut, if boiled in water, made a liquid to treat colic.[17] The green tips of the willow could be used for colds, its roots could be used to treat intestinal worms, and its inner bark could reduce a fever. The roots of the milkweed could treat dysentery, dropsy, or asthma. A powder could be made from the mayapple for use as a purgative. Although dozens of different plants could be used to treat illness, the most important was the "man medicine," ginseng, whose root had many beneficial effects.[18]

Wakonta created many things that could give nourishment to humans. The nuts and fruits of numerous trees, bushes, and other plants could be eaten: walnuts, hickory nuts, pecans, acorns, persimmons, grapes, and pawpaws. There were plants whose roots or bulbs were nourishing, such as the prairie potato and the water lily, and the flesh of deer, elk, bear, and opossum were edible.[19] The two greatest food gifts that *Wakonta* had bestowed on humans were corn and the buffalo.[20]

In the world of the living, *Wakonta* created many things for the use and comfort of humans. The hides of buffalo, deer, elk, and bear could be used to make robes, moccasins, leggings, breechcloths, and dresses. There were rush reeds that could be woven into mats to cover their houses and floors. Osage orange trees yielded wood that was ideal for making bows; the inner bark of other trees could be split into narrow strips and woven into bags; and wood could be carved into bowls or spoons. By far the greatest of *Wakonta*'s gifts was fire, which seemed to them like a piece of the sun.[21] So many things had been created by *Wakonta* for the benefit of humans. The ancient priests realized that they knew of the beneficial qualities of only some of *Wakonta*'s creations and that there were others yet to be discovered.

The priests recognized that not all of *Wakonta*'s creations were beneficial. Sometimes it rained so hard that the rivers flooded and drove people from their villages. There were winters when the snow and ice were so deep and the cold so severe that the people suffered greatly. Sometimes droughts would destroy the crops and drive away the animals so that the hunters could find little game. But the most dangerous of all of *Wakonta*'s creations were other peoples, who competed with the Osages for *Wakonta*'s blessings. What of them? Although they spoke different languages and sometimes differed from the Osages in appearance, they were nonetheless endowed with the same mental abilities as the Osage. From those other peoples, the Osages had to protect their hunting territories, fields, and villages. Most of all, their women and children, the source of future generations and the continuity of the Osage people, had to be protected from any human enemies who might destroy them.[22] To the Osages, "war was regarded . . . as a necessary evil, but only for self-preservation."[23] They realized that "the best of their young men must go and kill and be killed in order that the individual and tribal life might continue."[24]

The ancient priests concluded that to survive as a people, the Osage had to seek the continued blessings of *Wakonta*, while at the same time protecting themselves from their human enemies and competitors. They saw this as an ongoing struggle between the forces of life and death. They had to appeal to *Wakonta* for the preservation of individual life as well as the collective life of the Osage people, even as they were visiting death and destruction on the human enemies who might destroy them. The Osage concluded that the preservation of life often required the taking of life.

How could this best be accomplished? They sought an answer in their knowledge of *Wakonta* or, rather, in the creations of *Wakonta*. The cosmos was the perfect creation. It was integrated, it was ordered, and everything within it had sacred significance. In order to survive as a people, the Osage had to organize themselves along the model of the cosmos: they had to act as one, and in all the things they created and in all their actions, there had to be meaning and purpose. This was no easy task. Every individual had his or her own mind, with his or her own desires and interests. These differing desires and interests had to be controlled and focused toward common goals and objectives. The priests came to realize that they were living in a state of *ga-ní-tha*, a term that refers to something chaotic or without order.[25]

The division into sky (male) and earth (female), which was further divided into water and land, also served as the model for the basic structure of Osage life.

There were, however, innumerable dynamic and secondary expressions of *Wakonta* that had to be integrated into this symbolic model of the cosmos. Of greatest interest were those dynamic and secondary expressions that they came to call *zhó-i-the*, or "life symbols,"[26] or *wa-zhó-i-the* (objects of which our bodies are made). In the formal prayers of the Osage, "life symbols" would symbolically speak to the Osage, saying something such as "make of me your body" and "you will live to see old age." This statement meant that "if you make use of my qualities, it will help you meet the dangers of this world and survive."

The Osage realized that humans came into this world like blank slates. They had minds with a capacity to learn, but nothing else. What should they eat, what should they use, and how should they act? Within the world of the living, there were countless creations of *Wakonta*, each with it own particular set of characteristics and qualities. The question for the Osage was, which of the creations would they choose to use for their purposes and which should they model their behavior after? The life symbols were those creations chosen over time by the Osage to make use of and/or to hold up as models for their own behavior. The Osage also realized that to sustain their lives, they had to take life from others—animals, plants, birds, and even other humans who were their enemies. Life symbols were not only life sustaining, they could be life taking as well. Not all of *Wakonta*'s creations that the Osage made use of were considered life symbols, just the most important.

Many, but not all, of the life symbols of the early Osages are known, although in many cases there is no clear explanation as to the precise reason for which they were chosen. The sun, as the greatest of all the life symbols, was considered the source of life itself. Nothing in the world of the living was more powerful or dominant. Second in importance of life symbols was fire. It was like a piece of the sun on earth. When fire was controlled, as in a fireplace, it was the most beneficial of all *Wakonta*'s creations. It warmed them when they were cold, brought light into the dark of night, and cooked foods that were otherwise inedible. Fire and the fireplace were at the very center of all human actions; in fact, human life could not exist without it. Fire also illustrated to the Osages the dual character of many of *Wakonta*'s creations. Uncontrolled fire, as in a prairie fire, could be the most dangerous and destructive of all *Wakonta's* creations. In fire, the forces of life and the forces of death were present within a single creation.[27]

The Osage had other life symbols that fell into the generally beneficial category: the morning star, the sun's rays, the cloudless day (or peaceful day), the moon, the night, and various stars and constellations. All these life symbols were in a general sense associated with birth, life, and death.

The Osage desired long life, even everlasting life, and there were life symbols associated with those pursuits. Every part of the body of a pelican—its feet, head, muscles, and skin—was wrinkled and folded like that of an old person. The pelican looked like what every individual wished to become—aged. The aged eagle also looked elderly, and it, like the pelican, was made a life symbol, because it had the quality of long life that the Osage desired.[28] Shellfish, too, were thought to live for a long time, so they were also made a life symbol.[29] The spider could weave a web to trap and ensnare other insects, so it became a life symbol representing the earth and the ability to hold life in the world of the living.[30]

Cedar trees and sedge grass were life symbols that represented everlasting life. Unlike other trees, cedars did not lose their leaves during winter but remained green when all other trees "died." Sedge grass, too, remained green throughout the year.[31] Even though individual humans could not live forever, everlasting life was desirable for the Osage people as a whole. Several life symbols were associated with health. The "man medicine," or ginseng root, was a life symbol, as were a number of other healing plants.[32]

Some life symbols had to do with food and nourishment. Buffalo and corn were the two most important life symbols among Osage foods. They were so important that both were actually divided into several different life symbols. In addition to the generic buffalo life symbol, there were also life symbols for the buffalo bull, buffalo back, and buffalo tail. Similarly, there were several distinct life symbols associated with corn: the generic corn life symbol was supplemented with life symbols of red corn, yellow corn, blue corn, speckled corn, and flint corn. Of the other plants cultivated by the Osages, only squash is known to have been a life symbol. Elk, bear, and deer were important sources of meat for the Osages,

and all three were life symbols.[33] However, these three animals also had other qualities that made them important to the Osages, so it is difficult to determine whether it was one particular quality or a number of factors that caused them to be life symbols. Although the Osages collected a wide range of wild food plants, only the water lily was taken as a life symbol.

Many birds and animals had qualities that were generally desirable to the Osage and that Osage warriors, in particular, needed. The most significant was the little hawk. The little hawk (the term actually refers to several different species of small hawks) would, at times, risk certain death in fighting larger birds to protect its young and its nest. To the Osage, the hawk was the most courageous of all *Wakonta's* creations and came to symbolize the ideal behavior of the warrior.[34] Eagles, variously termed golden eagles, sacred eagles, and red eagles (see cat. 15), as well as the black bear and the puma, were made life symbols to be associated with warriors. Because of its strength and endurance, the swan was made a life symbol, not just for the warriors, but for others as well. Otters and beavers could swim as well as move on land, a versatility that humans, too, needed to survive, and so these animals were also made life symbols.[35]

Although the "little pipe" and the "peace pipe" were not *Wakonta's* creations, the Osage made them life symbols also. The pipe symbolized humans, unity, and singleness of purpose (see cats. 20 and 21), particularly in relation to *Wakonta*.[36]

We speak of life symbols as if they had a single meaning and purpose to the Osage, but that is only because our knowledge concerning most of these symbols is very limited. Since the Osage realized that every creation of *Wakonta* had multiple attributes, each with its own more specific function, the symbolic significance of a particular life symbol could change with the context in which it was used. The black bear life symbol is an example of multiple symbolic meanings. Because of its courage, the black bear was used as a general symbol of the warrior. More specifically, however, its claws were a symbol of courage and its black fur was associated with the fire that shows no mercy, both attributes of the warrior (see cat. 18). Beyond that, the entire body of the bear could be taken to symbolize long life and old age,[37] or it could be seen as a metaphor for the life-giving sun, a reference drawn from the white spot on the bear's chest.[38]

Creating the Symbolic Cosmos

Osage knowledge of the cosmos developed over a long time, and tribal structure evolved accordingly. What emerged was a structure of moieties, phratries, and clans that symbolically represented the various forces of the cosmos. There were twenty-four clans, or *ton-won-gthon*,[39] that served as the basic units. Clans were also called *u-dsé-the*, a term referring to the hearth or fireplace. Nine of these clans, the *Tsi-zho* or Sky moiety or division, were representative of the Sky forces. The Sky clans were further divided into two groupings. A group of seven clans made up the *Tsi-zho* or Sky people or phratry. According to Osage myths, the people of these seven clans were the original Sky people. Later, two other clans joined the Osages. These two clans were not true Sky people, but in order to maintain the balance of the tribal structure, they were symbolically placed with the Sky division. They were distinguished from the other seven clans by being placed in their own separate two-clan phratry, called the *Tsi-ha-shi*, meaning "last to come."

Fifteen clans made up the *Hunka* or Earth moiety. Just as the earth consists of both land and water, so were these fifteen clans divided. The seven clans that symbolically represent the water portions of the earth were collectively called the *Wa-sha-she*, or Water people or phratry. The seven clans of people associated with the land were grouped as the *Hunka* people or phratry, which referred to the "land" and not the earth as a whole. Later, another

people joined the Osage. These people were also of the earth, so they joined the Water people and the Land people as an isolated clan within the Earth division; they were called the "Isolated *Hunka*" clan.[40]

Each of the twenty-four clans was symbolically associated with a different portion of the cosmos. The life symbols associated with that portion of the cosmos were the life symbols of the clan. Each clan had an origin story that defined most of the life symbols associated with it. The life symbol in the origin stories was often referred to as "grandfather" or "grandmother." The use of kinship terms did not imply any biological relationship; rather, they were used as a manner of showing respect. As one Osage said, "We do not believe that our ancestors were really animals, birds, etc., as told in the traditions. These things are only *wa-wé-ku-ska-ye*, symbols of something higher."[41] Clan members symbolically represented that portion of the cosmos associated with their life symbols, and they were both responsible for and had authority over that portion of the cosmos.

Collectively, the clans of a particular phratry symbolically represented that portion of the cosmos. Some life symbols appear to have been associated with a particular phratry, and the clans of that phratry had collective responsibility for them and authority over their ritual use. Still other life symbols belonged collectively to all of the clans of one or another of the two great divisions or moieties, the Sky and Earth peoples. Finally, there were some life symbols that served as general tribal life symbols.

Since the Osage did not communicate with *Wakonta* directly, all they could do was to appeal indirectly or to

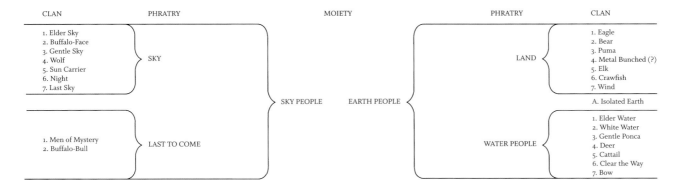

FIGURE 2.2 Organization of Osage clans.

FIGURE 2.3 Arrangement of an Osage House of Mystery.

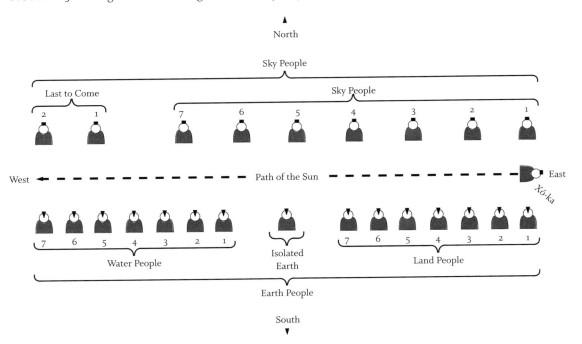

some particular manifestation of *Wakonta* for assistance or guidance. There were general appeals for *Wakonta's* continued blessings for the tribe and their endeavors, while other appeals were made to some particular manifestation of *Wakonta* for help in specific undertakings, such as a war or a hunt or with the weather.

Osage rituals fell into two categories: important rituals that were said to be "inside the house of mystery," and minor rituals that were "outside the house of mystery."[42] A "House of Mystery," or *tsi-wa-kon-da-gi*, was a symbolic reconstruction of the cosmos. Each of the twenty-four clans had its own formally initiated and trained priests, called *non-hón-zhin-ga*, or "little old men." Only these men had the knowledge of clan ritual procedures, the authority to perform them, and the right to represent their clan in religious rituals.[43] A House of Mystery was a symbolic re-creation of the cosmos, with the clan priests representing the various parts of the cosmos. The term *tsi* or "house" is misleading in that these rituals may not have actually been performed in a house or dwelling. In many ceremonies, the priests were seated outside on the open ground.

In a House of Mystery, the priests representing the nine clans of the Sky division were seated on the north side. At the east end of this line of priests were those of the Sky people, in clan order. At the west end of the line were the priests of the Last to Come people. The priests representing the fifteen clans of the Earth division were seated in a line on the south side. At the east end of the line, in clan order, were the priests of the Land people. The priests of the Water people sat, in clan order, at the west end of the line. The priests of the Isolated *Hunka* clan sat in the middle of the line, between the Land and Water priests. The rectangular area between the two facing lines of priests, which served to symbolize the earth's surface as well as the path of the sun and path of life, was the space where all action and movement in the ritual would occur. The east end, the place of the rising sun, was the end from which action would be initiated. The official in charge of the ritual would variously stand, move, or be seated at the east end.

Every House of Mystery ritual consisted of three elements: human participants, each representing some aspect of the cosmos; ritual items of symbolic importance; and songs, prayers, and ritual actions that involved particular participants and the use of ritual items.

The priests from the twenty-four clans represented their clans' portions of the cosmos. For some, possibly

FIGURE 2.4 Method for painting a face, adapted from the *Bureau of American Ethnology, Thirty-ninth Annual Report*, Smithsonian Institution.

all, rituals, the clan priests painted themselves. The lower portions of their faces, chins, and jaws were blackened with moist black soil, symbolic of the Earth portion of the cosmos. White eagle down spread over the tops of their heads symbolically represented the sky. Using black soil, stylized figures were drawn at the edges of both eyes, and two lines were drawn downward across the cheeks. A red circle was painted in the middle of the forehead to represent the sun. Each priest wrapped himself in a buffalo robe, hair side out.[44]

The focal point of the ritual was the figure of the *Xó-ka*. At the beginning of the ritual, the *Xó-ka* usually represented the symbolic sun, but during the course of the ritual the role of the *Xó-ka* shifted to that of the symbolic man. The symbolic man, who represented "a man, perfect in physical form, possessed of mental powers and the ability to express thought," was able to represent both Sky and Earth forces and was a metaphor for the Osage people as a whole.[45]

The dress of the *Xó-ka* accorded with his symbolic role and varied according to the ritual and/or clan involved. The general pattern was that the *Xó-ka*'s face and body were painted red, as a prayer to the sun that his life would be fruitful and that he would be blessed with a long line of descendants. The dark line drawn across his forehead with lines drawn down to both his cheeks was symbolic of the *hó-e-ga*, or snare, that held life in the visible world. The four additional lines descending from this forehead

FIGURE 2.5 Painting of a *Xó-ka*, adapted from the *Bureau of American Ethnology, Thirty-ninth Annual Report*, Smithsonian Institution.

line down to the eyebrows represented the four winds, that is, the breath of life. Finally, the figure of a man that symbolically represented his soul or spirit was painted on the *Xó-ka*'s right side.[46] He wore in his hair a white downy plume from the underwing of an eagle, representing the two shafts of light from the sun seen at sunrise, which was symbolic of the life of a warrior. A shell gorget symbolizing the sun was hung around his neck (see cats. 16 and 22). Two narrow woven bands tied around his wrists were called "spirits," and they referred to the fact that his body and his spirit were held captive to the earth. Around his waist was tied a woven belt that was associated with words for both "captive" and "spirit" and probably had the same symbolic meaning as the wristbands. Finally, a puma-skin robe that symbolized destruction was placed on his back.[47] In other ceremonies, the *Xó-ka* wore a buffalo robe, which symbolized the sustaining of life.[48]

Ritual ceremonies of the early Osages required the use of items that included sacred bundles, tally sticks, rattles, pipes, war standards, war clubs, and sacred bows and arrows. The use of ritual items varied with the purpose of the ritual.

There were three categories of sacred bundles: clan bundles, which belonged to specific clans; great bundles, which were tribal bundles associated with the Sky division; and great medicine bundles, which were tribal bundles associated with the Earth division. Every part of these bundles had symbolic meaning and purpose.

All clan bundles were basically the same. The most sacred object contained in a clan bundle was a hawk skin that had been painted blue and symbolized the courage of the warriors.[49] It was placed inside a rush bag that had been woven as one piece, with the lower third brought up to form a pocket. The designs woven into the bag used the symbols for earth and sky, day and night, to represent the cosmos. The pocket of the bag was the symbolic space between sky and earth, the *hó-e-ga*, or snare of life. There were seven knots in the left side of the pocket, the side that would face the clans of the Earth division in a ritual, and there were six knots in the right side of the pocket, which would face the clans of the Sky division. When placed in the pocket, the head of the hawk would face toward the end with seven knots. The rush mat and the rituals associated with it were the symbolic and collective property of the seven clans of the Water people. The ritual responsibility for supplying the rushes to weave these bags fell to the Elder Water and Cattail clans.[50]

A rope of buffalo hide was used to close the rush bag. The rope symbolized the rope used by warriors to bind the hands of captives. The members of the Buffalo Face clan supplied the hide for these ropes.[51] The closed rush bag was placed inside a deer-hide bag furnished by the Deer clan.[52] The deer-hide bag and its contents were in turn placed in a bag of woven buffalo hair supplied by the Buffalo Bull clan. If the bag was to be made for a bundle belonging to the Sky division clans, the hair had to be picked from the left shoulder of the buffalo, but if it was for a bundle belonging to an Earth division clan, it had to be picked from the right shoulder. "This prescribed rule for gathering the materials for the case also teaches that when hunting the buffalo, a food animal, the people must arrive at their decisions as with one mind and act as with a single body."[53] Finally, the entire bag was wrapped with a hide-hanging strap furnished by the Elder Sky and Wolf clans. A scalp provided by the Bear and Puma clans and an eagle leg from the Winged *Hunka* clan was attached to the strap.[54]

Tally sticks were sticks with clusters of notches. Every priest had his own tally sticks, which he used to keep track of the song sequence. Every notch represented a song. Considered to be sacred, tally sticks were made of a willow branch, symbolic of everlasting life.[55]

A gourd rattle was frequently the only musical instrument used in ceremonial rituals (cat. 17). The gourd itself symbolized a head. In some contexts, the rattle was said to be the head of a puma and symbolized the relentless fire. In other contexts, the rattle represented the head of the leader of the Isolated Earth clan. The "stones" inside the rattle were said to symbolize the teeth of either a puma or a man, while the wooden handle represented the forearm of either a puma or a man.[56]

The war standard was a wooden pole about six feet long and curved at the top to form a so-called shepherd's crook. The pole was first encased in deerskin, then entirely covered in long strips of swan skin, whose large feathers had all been removed, leaving only the down. Attached to the staff in three bunches of four each were eagle feathers. In some rituals, the feathers were the tail feathers of an adult golden eagle, which are white with a black tip. In other rituals, the feathers were the tail feathers of an immature golden eagle, which are dark and mottled in appearance.[57] Attached to the top of the standard was a deerskin. Priests of the Bow and Bear clans jointly made the standard, while the Deer clan furnished the deerskin. Some rituals required only one standard, while others required two, one for the Earth division and one for the Sky division.[58]

The war club was a slightly curved, heavy wooden club. It represented indestructible life, the desire to maintain tribal existence, and the striking of the enemy.[59] The Elder Sky clan served as the symbolic custodian of the war club.[60]

A sacred bow and two arrows were required for some rituals. The flat, inside surface of the bow was painted red, referring to the recurrent day, while the back side of the bow was painted black for the night. Similarly, one of the arrows was painted red and the other black, also symbolizing day and night.[61]

Every ritual required the use of pipes at different points in the ceremony. The Osages made use of several distinct types of pipes. Although the particular meanings and uses of each are not always known, it is clear that they all were expressions of the same basic meaning, namely, that "the pipe was a symbol of unity of purpose and . . . [through its smoke] a symbolic prayer to *Wakonta* for compassion and help."[62]

Every ritual required the singing of specific songs, the reciting of formal prayers, and the acting out of particular events. Songs were grouped into a number of standardized sets and addressed particular issues or subjects. While the names for these song sets were basically the same for all clans, individual clans frequently had their own versions of the songs. In some rituals, there might be close to a hundred individual songs sung, not even counting all of the clan variations.[63]

Every ritual included a varying number of formal prayers or recitations in which the text "set forth the relation in which the tribe stood to nature in all its various forms."[64] In highly metaphorical terms, the recited poems told of the various life symbols of the Osage and how those symbols related to specific clans, the grouping of clans, and most aspects of Osage life. Recitation of the prayers was actually the core element in the rituals. All

prayers were the exclusive property of specific clans, groups of clans, or one of the two divisions, and only members of certain priesthoods could recite them. Most prayers contained several hundred lines of text, although Francis La Flesche recorded one having 1,542 lines of text.[65]

Finally, every ritual included one or more ritual dramatizations. These short skits involved symbolic actions by the participants and the use of the ritual items to the accompaniment of songs and prayers. The Osage considered these dramatizations necessary because they thought that words were not adequate to express certain ideas or concepts.[66]

When all the priests and other participants assumed their positions in the ceremony, the singing would start and the Osages would symbolically begin to put the cosmos into motion. According to La Flesche, the "songs with their . . . symbols and dramatic action are supplicatory in character: they are expressions of a craving for divine aid toward the perpetuity of the tribal existence and the continuity of the life of the individual by an unbroken lineage."[67] All rituals were general appeals for *Wakonta*'s continued blessings, but each type of ritual directed these appeals toward different expressions (life symbols) of *Wakonta*, ones that the Osage felt relevant to the issue at hand. In rituals symbolically structured to face "east," the appeals were directed toward various life-giving and life-sustaining expressions of *Wakonta*. In rituals symbolically facing "west," the appeals were directed toward the destructive expressions of *Wakonta*.

In speaking of these rituals and the sacred objects used in them, La Flesche noted that "the [men] who formulated these intricate rites, and many of the men of the succeeding generations through whom these rites were transmitted, knew that the various articles dedicated for ceremonial use, together with their prescribed forms, were intended to be employed as aids in conveying certain fundamental ideas that could not be adequately expressed by words alone. They also knew that there resided in the articles thus dedicated no mystical power to excite fear or to be adored."[68] The Osage recognized that the rituals and the sacred objects used in them were the creations of humans, not *Wakonta*. They were treated with reverence, not out of fear but out of respect for what they represented. To show respect for the sacred objects was to show respect for *Wakonta* and all of *Wakonta*'s creations. Only in this way could they hope to continue to receive the bounty of *Wakonta*'s blessings.

The rituals also served to emphasize two critical concepts important to the Osage. One concept was that every feature of the ritual had meaning and purpose. The ritual itself was performed for a particular purpose, such as war, health, or hunting. But within the ritual, every participant, every ritual item, every song, every prayer, and every act had its own specific meaning and purpose. Every adornment of the participants and ritual items and every movement in the ritual acts had symbolic meaning and purpose. Every feather, every color, and every hide had meaning and purpose. If one used a hawk feather in place of an owl feather, if the color was black instead of white, if the hide was buffalo instead of bear, if the movement was to the right side instead of to the left, if the participants faced east instead of west, then the meaning and purpose changed. In the rituals, as in the cosmos, nothing was without meaning and purpose.

The rituals served to emphasize the unity of the cosmos, which was the second important concept. Each song, each prayer, each ritual act, and each ritual item was the property of a particular clan or group of clans. Only the priests of a particular clan or group of clans had the authority to sing a particular song, recite a particular prayer, perform a particular ritual act, or make a particular ritual item. In major rituals, every clan had a role, which its priests alone could fill. If the priests of any clan were missing, then the ritual would be incomplete and could not be performed. *Wakonta* assumed many different expressions and manifestations, yet *Wakonta* was a single integrated and unified force. In their rituals, the Osage people also had to act as a single unified force, and they had to act with meaning and purpose.

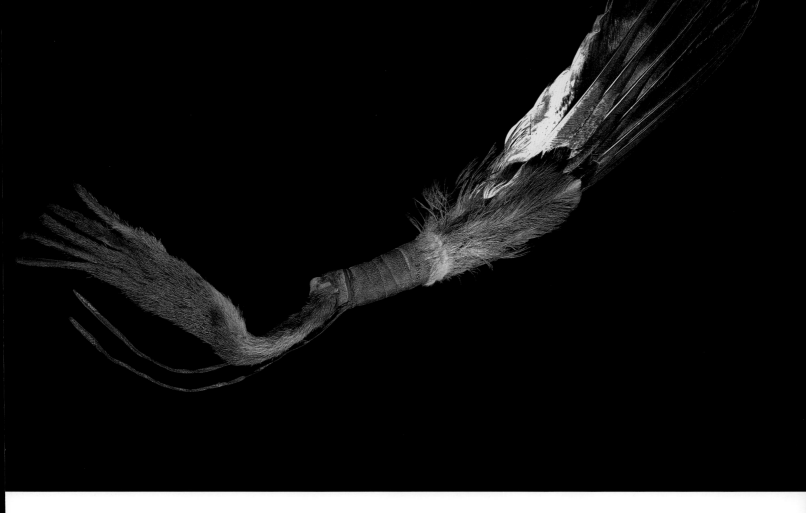

EAGLE WING FAN

feathers, bone, and hide
36½ × 6½ × 2½ inches
Department of Anthropology, Smithsonian Institution

Chief Bacon Rind, also known as Star That Travels, used this golden-eagle-wing fan primarily for personal prayer. As an Osage clan priest, Chief Bacon Rind was well versed in the Black Bear clan traditions. The fan is decorated with dyed red plumes that come from the underside of the golden eagle's tail, and the handle is wrapped with otter fur that is split and consecrated with paint. The wind produced by the motion of the fan re-creates the sacred breath of *Wakonta*.

CHOKER

glass beads, shell, leather, and pigment
16 × 2 × ½ inches
Department of Anthropology, Smithsonian Institution

Shell gorgets—ornamental pendants suspended about the throat—were one of
the few universally shared sacred objects
among the Osage. Worn only by males,
the gorgets carried a symbolism that was
constant throughout the tribe. The freshwater mussel shell represents the sun and
the red tint painted between the incised
lines portrays the blood of life. The lines
themselves are suggestive of the sun's rays.
Young Osage warriors would have been
inspired with courage upon seeing the color
red, which represents life's blood and the
energy of the sun. The imported Dutch
beads are arranged in blue and white pairs,
the meaning of which is not clear. The
wrinkles on the back of the shell represent
the skin of old age to the Osage, who aspire
to not only achieve old age but also acquire
the signs of it. The shell of the mussel,
admired for its ability to travel upstream
against the current, represents strength
and stamina.

CAT. **17**

RATTLE

gourd, wood, and wool
7½ × 3⁹⁄₁₆ inches
The Field Museum of Natural History, Chicago

Sacred rattles like this were used in ritual
observances in which their sound and
rhythm accompanied the chanting of
the priests of the ancient *non-hón-zhin-ga*
society. The rattling sounds would increase
and decrease in volume to give greater
emphasis to the songs that sometimes
contained hundreds of lines. The gourd
itself represents a male human head or
a puma head, and contained within it are
the rattling agents—the literal or symbolic
teeth from the right jaw of either a human
or an adult male puma.

CAT. 19

HATCHET PIPE

metal and wood
20 1/16 × 10 1/16 × 1 inches
National Museum of the American Indian, Smithsonian Institution

This commercial combination of pipe and ax was of European origin, but it was modified to suit Osage purposes. An artifact such as this seldom made it west of the Mississippi River and, as such, was extremely coveted by the Osage for both its rarity and its dual function. An Osage would have had a blacksmith cut out the crude yet powerful heart motif, which may represent the leaf of the redbud tree. Wood from the redbud tree is considered sacred, and the charcoal produced from it was used to paint the body of a warrior, who was then transformed into an agent of destruction, symbolically as devastating as a prairie fire.

CAT. 18

BEAR CLAW NECKLACE
WITH TRAILER

bear claws, otter fur, silk, hide, cloth, glass beads,
and feathers
77 1/2 × 11 inches
Brooklyn Museum of Art, Museum Expedition 1911, Museum Collection Fund

A distinctive sign of valor, bear-claw necklaces were worn exclusively by those who earned the right by winning war honors in the defense of the people. This necklace has a circular hide pouch at the top of the trailer, which is the strip that would hang down from the necklace at the back of the neck. The pouch would contain personal medicine, which served as a protective force for the wearer. The fringelike lightning motif attached to the medicine pouch imbued it with additional power. The claws of the bear symbolize deadly flames of fire. Despite its warlike association, the animal had many peacetime uses as well: bear fur was used for bedding and saddle padding, and bear fat served as a base for perfume and hair dressing.

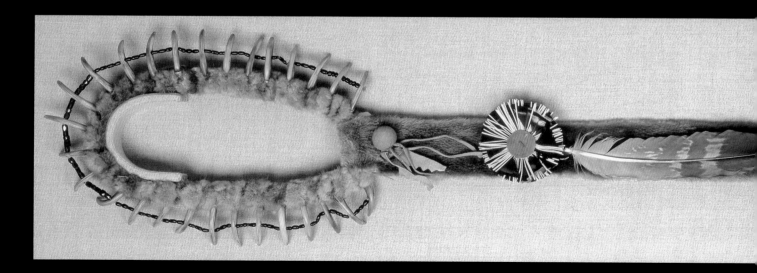

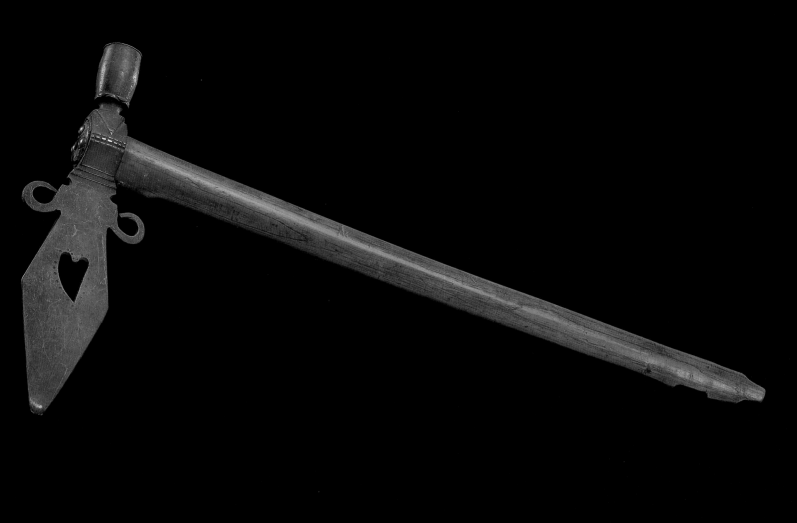

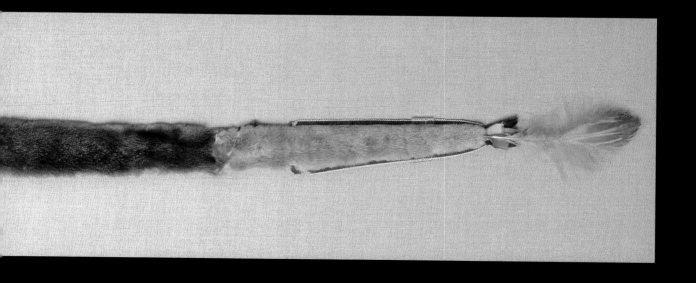

CAT. 20

HEAD EFFIGY PIPE BOWL

catlinite
3¾ × 1³⁄₁₆ × 2⅜ inches
National Museum of the American Indian,
Smithsonian Institution

This catlinite pipe, which was made for personal use, features an outstanding portrayal of the human head. His status as a warrior is indicated by the fully displayed roach on the top of his head. Traces of red paint still remain on the lips. Near the place where the pipe stem is inserted is an incised figure that illustrates a man wearing a split-horn headdress—an image unique to pipe iconography. The incised floral image is of an unidentified plant. The bisecting converging triangles may represent dragonflies, which are an important life symbol to many Osage clans.

PIPE BOWL WITH CORNCOB STEM

catlinite, leather, corncob, and wood
stem: 1 × 1 × 10¹³⁄₁₆ inches
bowl: 4¾ × 2⁹⁄₁₆ × 1 inches
National Museum of the American Indian, Smithsonian Institution

This pipe has a corncob stem with a hollow wooden shaft running through its center.
Designs have been filed into the surface, now burnished through years of use to a shiny,
rich, dark brown patina. The lead inlay was created by pouring molten metal into the
carved beveled grooves while the pipe rested in its earthen mold. After the metal cooled,
the excess material was removed with a metal file or a piece of sandstone until it was flush
with the pipe. This pipe was intended for personal, rather than ritual, use.

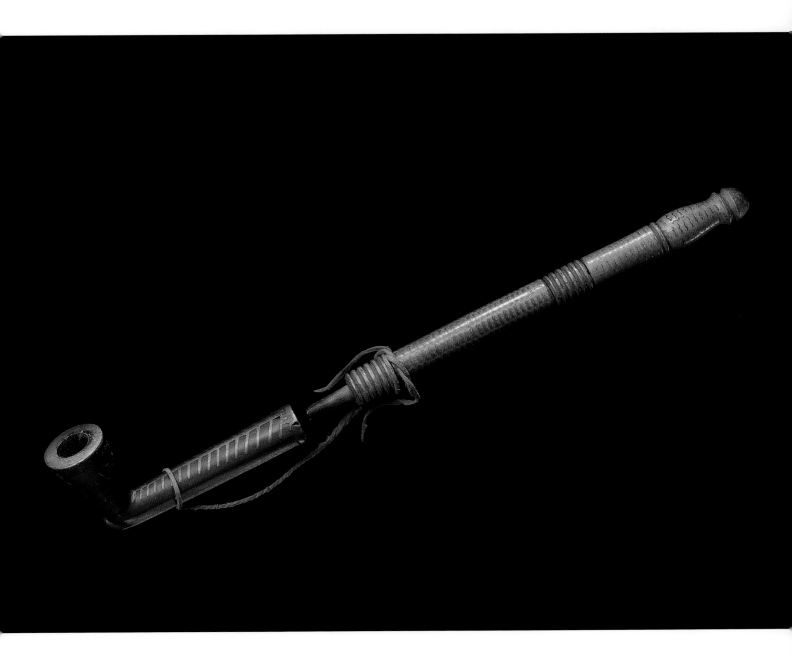

SHELL GORGET WITH CRESCENT TACKS

shell and metal
2¾ × 2¾ × ¹³⁄₁₆ inches
National Museum of the American Indian, Smithsonian Institution

This gorget was made from the outer chamber of the hairpipe shell found in seawater. This particular shell came from the Gulf Coast. Mississippian peoples used hairpipe shells for gorgets, pendants, and sacred masks. A hide thong would have attached this gorget around the wearer's neck. A crescent formed by brass tacks symbolizes the vault of the sky. After the morning prayers, Osage men held pendants like this up to the sun to receive the blessings of *Wakonta*. After the prayers were concluded and the sun had risen above the horizon, the men hung the shells from their necks and rested them on their chests.

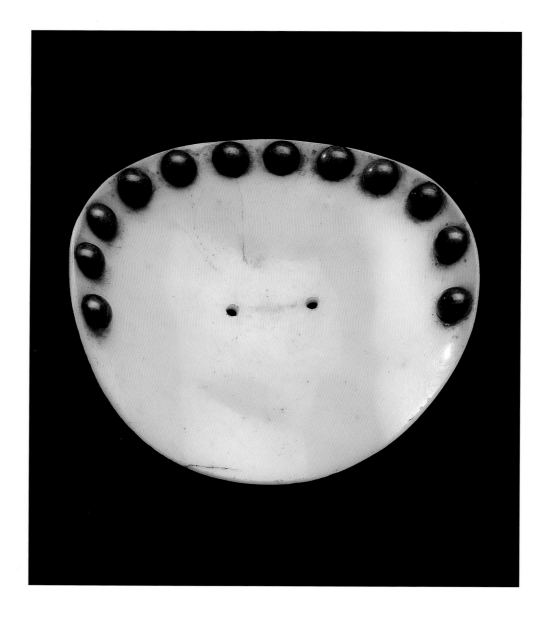

CAT. 23
MIRROR BOARD
wood, glass, and metal
2 × 6 × 10 inches
Milwaukee Public Museum, James Howard Collection

Mirror boards are held by men as they dance during the E-Lon-schka dances in June. A young man angles the mirror to reflect sunlight onto a girlfriend or potential mate in order to catch her attention. The mirror itself is in the shape of the *hó-e-ga*, the hunting snare. The wind, symbolizing the breath of life, freely passes through the upside-down Romanesque arches that form the "fingers" of this object. Mirrors are also used by the dancers when grooming before the dances begin. The tacks protect the surface of the mirror from getting scratched or broken. In earlier times, mirrors were used to communicate over long distances in a signaling technique the Osage learned from the French.

Before sunrise in the morning following the first night of our visit, I was awakened by the noise of a great wailing. I arose and went out. As far as I could see, men, women, and children were standing in front of the doors of their houses weeping. —Francis La Flesche, 1921
(speaking of his visit to the Osage as a boy in the 1870s)

The Osages attempted to show their respect for *Wakonta* and all of *Wakonta*'s creations by organizing themselves in such a manner as to present a mirror image of the cosmos. Just as the cosmos had a unity among all its many parts, so did the Osages have to act as one in all activities, and every event in their lives had to have meaning and purpose. To this end, their daily lives were structured as a symbolic ritual and a continuous prayer thanking *Wakonta* for the blessings they had received.

Every morning, shortly before dawn, the entire village arose. As they dressed, the women would comb their hair and in the part they would paint a red line as a symbol of the path of the sun and a prayer for continued life. Going outside and placing moist earth on their foreheads, the men, women, and children of the village greeted the rising sun with prayers of thanks. This ritual, called the Rite of Vigil, was repeated at midday and at sunset. Longer versions of this rite, some for four days and some for seven days, were used at other times.

The Villages

According to their oral traditions, the Osages had originally lived in a single village on the banks of a large river when a great flood forced them to flee and scatter in the direction of a large hill.[1] The families who took refuge on top of the hill became known as the Dwellers-Upon-the-Hilltop, or simply the Big Hills. Other families who stopped in the forests on the flanks of the hill became

known as the Dwellers-in-the-Upland-Forest. One group of families got caught in a patch of thorny trees and bushes and came to be called the Thorny Thicket people. The families who stopped at the base of the hill were called the Dwellers Below, or sometimes the Little Osage.[2] The families who remained near the old village were called the Heart-Stays.[3] After the flood, the Osage families who took refuge together remained apart and formed five separate villages. During the late eighteenth century, Europeans began referring to the Osages as either the Great Osages or the Little Osages. The Little Osages were the village of the Dwellers Below, while the Great Osages were the other four villages.

In terms of political and religious organization, each of the villages appears to have been identical to the others, each having its own complete set of chiefs, priests, and clans. With that arrangement, any tribal ritual could be performed by any of the villages independently of the others. In the early days, every village may have had its own separate hunting territory. While the existence of a formal overarching tribal political structure cannot be conclusively shown, there was at least a strong sense of Osage identity uniting the villages, particularly in regard to their unity in the face of other peoples. If one village organized a war party to attack an enemy, men from the other villages joined them. When going on buffalo hunts on the plains, the chiefs of the different villages would meet to coordinate the hunting. The Peace Ceremony (see "The Osage Year" later in this chapter) appears to have played an important role in maintaining unity among the villages. Regardless of which village they belonged to, the Osages always thought of themselves as, and acted as, one.

Authority within the Osage villages was invested in the chiefs and the priests. The chiefs were concerned with the internal harmony of the village and the general well-being of its members. The priests, on the other hand, were concerned with external matters, such as relationships with neighboring peoples and the supernatural world of *Wakonta*.

Each village had two chiefs—a Sky chief and an Earth chief—symbolically representing the two major forces of the cosmos. The position of chief was hereditary within specific clans as well as within families or lineages. The Sky chief was chosen from the Gentle Sky clan, while the Earth chief was from the Gentle Ponca clan. Within each village, specific lineages or families of these clans filled the positions.[4]

Oral traditions tell that after the ancient priests created these two positions, the newly appointed chiefs undertook the Rite of Vigil to seek the approval of *Wakonta*. Going alone and separately into the forest, for seven days and nights the Sky chief and the Earth chief prayed and fasted. Showing approval, *Wakonta* revealed to the Sky chief the great healing root shaped like a man and called it "man medicine." At the same time, *Wakonta* revealed to him its companion, a similar root shaped like a woman. These two roots were made into a new sacred bundle called the Great Medicine Bundle. Again showing approval for what the priests had created, *Wakonta* revealed to the Earth chief the Aged Pelican, with its powers to live to see old age. The pelican was also made sacred and combined with an existing sacred bundle used for tattooing. This new bundle was then known as the Great Bundle.[5]

Although there were two chiefs, the village was a single unit. Just as the cosmos consisted of both earth and sky but was still one, so it was with the village. The chiefs were like the left and right sides of a person. Either the two chiefs acted together or they alternated in leading the village. Only in the absence of one would the other act alone.

The houses of the chiefs were sacred, symbolically representing the Earth and the Sky. They had two doors, one facing east toward the rising sun and the other facing west toward the setting sun, symbolizing the continuous flow of life. The fireplace in the middle of the house symbolized the sun. All of the family fireplaces in the village were kindled from coals taken from the chiefs' fireplaces, which in turn made all the fireplaces sacred. The houses of the chiefs also served as houses of refuge. Even an enemy who took refuge in the house of a chief could not be harmed.[6]

The chiefs were entrusted with a wide range of responsibilities. One of their major roles was to maintain harmony and peaceful relations among the families of the village. While the chiefs always attempted to resolve disputes between individuals and families in such a manner as to restore harmony, they did have the authority to expel or, in extreme cases, even to execute members of the village.[7]

The chiefs had joint responsibility for the overall well-being of the village and its people. As discussed in "The Osage Year" later in this chapter, the two chiefs served as the leaders of the summer and fall buffalo hunts, and so they were entitled to a part of every animal killed. They were also responsible for the safety of the hunting party. If enemy raiders killed an individual or stole his horses during the hunt, the chiefs had to compensate the family.[8] They were responsible for commissioning the priests to perform important seasonal rituals. And it was the chiefs who had the authority to grant life to captive prisoners and have them adopted into the tribe.

To assist them in their duties, each chief had ten *Á-ki-da*, a term usually translated as "soldier," but it might also be translated as "police." Each chief had to choose his soldiers from specific clans, five from the Earth division and five from the Sky division.[9] Their primary purpose was to enforce the chief's orders within the village as well as on the hunts. Each soldier carried a whip or quirt, not just as an indication of his office but also as a weapon of enforcement if necessary (see cats. 6 and 36). However, the soldiers had another important function as well. After the death of a chief, it fell to his ten soldiers to choose his successor.[10] While any male member of the family was eligible, ideally the eldest son of the deceased chief was chosen.[11]

While the two chiefs were the most public of the leaders, the real power in the village rested in the collective hands of the priests. There were four distinct priesthoods among the Osages. By far the largest of the priesthoods were the clan priests, known as the Little Old Men. In every village, there was a full complement of twenty-four clans, each of which had its own sacred bundles and associated priests. As the most important ritual items of a clan, the sacred bundles were called Little Sacred Objects. In their basic form and meaning, all of these bundles were identical regardless of clan. There was no set number of bundles. Each clan in the village had multiple bundles, and periodically new clan bundles were made, sanctified, and added. Although some particular bundles had historical significance and even names, ritually they all had the same significance.[12] Although not actually part of the bundle, a pipe was kept with each bundle (see cat. 42).

The clan priests formed what was a de facto village council. Almost every morning, they met at the House of the Keeper of the Little Old Men (*Non-hón-zhin-ga Wa-thin Tsi*). No particular house was established or maintained for this purpose, and the home of any of the clan priests might be used. The priest in whose home they met was given the title Keeper of the Little Old Men. The Keeper presided over the meetings.[13]

The clan priests had exclusive authority over issues and decisions about war. Neither the chiefs nor their soldiers played any formal role in decisions relating to war. Any act of war against an enemy had to be sanctioned by the clan priests, and in some cases they had to be led by a clan priest. As discussed in "Growing Up Osage" later in this chapter, war was as much a religious ritual as a military action.

The clan priests had numerous other ritual responsibilities, including the giving of formal names to all of the children of their clan.[14] Some rituals had to be performed by a priest from a specific clan. For example, at burials a priest of the Wind clan would ritually release the spirit of the dead and burn cedar to purify the people attending,[15] while a priest of the Deer clan performed the ritual that opened the hunting season for bear and deer.[16]

In addition to the clan priesthoods, there were three different tribal priesthoods: the Great Bundle priests, the Great Medicine Bundle priests, and the Peace, or Pipe, priests. The Great Bundle priests were responsible for the rituals associated with that particular bundle.

Although these bundles were associated with the Earth chief and although the Gentle Ponca clan acted as the symbolic keepers of the bundles, the Great Bundle priests themselves could belong to any of the twenty-four clans.[17] The Great Bundles contained a cormorant skin, a pelican skin, eight tattooing instruments, ten to twelve scalp locks, seven weasel skins, and half a mussel shell, among other items. The items were all placed together inside a rush mat, which was placed inside a woven buffalo hair bag.[18]

The Great Bundle priests were called the "guardians of the village" and had several ritual responsibilities. They controlled the tattooing ritual, actually performing the sacred tattooing themselves, and they performed the Spring Rite. Only five Great Bundles are known to have existed, which corresponds to the number of Osage villages, so it may well have been that there was only one Great Bundle per village.[19] Unlike clan bundles, Great Bundles were very rarely transferred. A Great Bundle priest continued to perform his rituals until he became too elderly or too blind to perform the tattooing. Only at that time would he initiate and transfer the bundle to a younger priest. Great Bundle priests would retire after transferring the bundle, since without the bundle they could not perform the required rituals.[20]

The Great Medicine Bundle priests were the men with ritual authority over the Great Medicine Bundle. Although this bundle was associated with the Sky chief, and although the Gentle Sky clan served as the symbolic keepers of this particular bundle, a man from any of the twenty-four clans could serve as a priest of this bundle that was associated with the sacred "man medicine" and its counterpart, the "woman medicine." The rituals associated with these bundles are thought to have been concerned with healing. None were in existence at the turn of the twentieth century, and Osages living at that time could recall the past existence of only one of these bundles.[21]

The Peace, or Pipe, priests were associated with the sacred pipe ceremony, which was frequently called the "calumet dance." There was no bundle associated with this priesthood. Instead, the sacred object used was a pipe decorated with feathers. Two pipes were assembled by the priests from a number of different clans as part of the ritual itself. There was no initiation ceremony as

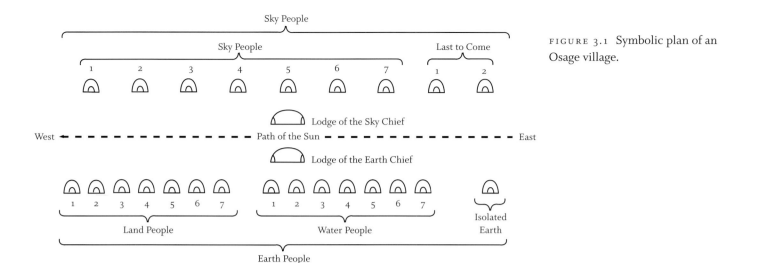

FIGURE 3.1 Symbolic plan of an Osage village.

such for this priesthood. A candidate for this priesthood had to sponsor four sacred pipe ceremonies, under the sponsorship of an existing pipe priest. After these four ceremonies, the new priest assumed the title of *ni-ka don-he,* or Honored Man, and could himself act as a sponsor for new candidates.[22] The real authority of these priests appears to have been the ability to issue a formal order or summons to the clan priests, who then had to appear for the ceremony.

All of the Osage villages were physically arranged in the same manner. There was a long east-west street with dwellings constructed along both sides. Arranged along the north side of the street, in a specific clan order, were the houses of the Sky division families. Along the south side of the street, also in order of clans, were those of the Earth division families.

In the middle of the village, directly across the street from each other, were the houses of the two village chiefs, the house of the Sky chief to the north and that of the Earth chief to the south. Next to the houses of the chiefs were those of the families of the ten men who served as *Á-ki-da* or "soldiers" for each of the chiefs.[23]

The village, as a symbolic reconstruction of the cosmos, faced east, toward the rising sun. The Sky families lived on the north side of the village, or symbolic left side of the cosmos, while the Earth families lived on the south, or symbolic right side of the cosmos. The east-west street was the symbolic path of the sun, or path of life, and also served as the symbolic *hó-e-ga,* the earth's surface.[24]

The most common type of Osage dwelling was a long-house, or *wa-sha-tsi.*[25] These were rectangular dwellings made from poles stuck into the ground, bent over, and tied together to form a domed frame. The frame was covered with woven cattail mats, bark, hides, or some combination of these materials. They were usually about twenty feet wide, forty to fifty feet long, and fifteen to eighteen feet high and oriented along an east-west axis. Unlike the houses of the chiefs, the longhouses of common people had two doors opening on the south side, one toward the east end and the other toward the west. Houses generally had two interior fireplaces, each with its own smoke hole in the roof. Along part of the interior wall of the house was a low bench, about two feet off the ground, which could be used for sleeping as well as seating.[26]

Osage dwellings were well furnished, with hides and robes usually covering both the interior benches and the floors for use as seating and bedding. There was also a range of domestic goods. In the early days, Osage women made utilitarian pottery jars and bowls that were used primarily to prepare food, but by the late 1700s brass trade buckets had replaced pottery for cooking.[27] Carved wooden bowls of various sizes were used for serving food, and spoons carved from wood and buffalo horns were used for eating (see cats. 26 and 56).

Most likely, the Osages made plaited basketry at the time of European contact, but no examples have survived and no mention of them is found in the early literature. What have survived are various types of bags that were used for the storage of food, clothing, sacred items, and other small objects. Traditionally, Osage women wove a range of flat, two-sided bags in a variety of materials, using both loom- and finger-weaving techniques.

Some of these bags were woven out of buffalo hair. In the nineteenth century, only bags for holding sacred items were woven from buffalo hair, but during earlier times they may have been woven for more utilitarian purposes as well. Although the hair in these bags was natural in color, the weave was varied to make designs. More utilitarian bags were woven using thin twisted strips of the inner bark of trees and other plant fibers. Some of the plant materials were dyed for designs, and in some cases buffalo hair was used to add color. During the middle of the eighteenth century, after trade blankets had become more common, women began unraveling the yarn from blankets and using it to weave bags of yarn. By the early nineteenth century, skeins of different-colored wool yarns had become available from traders, and plant-fiber bags were replaced with yarn bags. Although these bags were frequently decorated with intricate designs woven from different-colored yarns, they continued to be used primarily as storage bags. Most loom bags were rectangular in shape and measured about two feet by one and one-half feet in size (see cats. 47, 48, 49, 50). Smaller bags were usually made using the finger-weaving technique.[28]

Leather bags and rawhide containers also served for storage. Special-purpose bags made from soft tanned leather were also made. Some, such as those used in the medicine bundles, were left undecorated. Traditionally, leather bags used for domestic purposes were decorated with paint (see cat. 41) or quillwork (see cat. 29), but by the early nineteenth century they were decorated in beadwork (see cat. 38).

Storage bags, too, could be made from rawhide. Most were simple, flat, envelope-type parfleche bags that were tied with leather thongs. These bags held everything from dried meat to extra clothing and smaller items. Most often, designs were painted on these bags (see cat. 40).[29] Larger storage bags that could hold dried food and heavier items were usually piled at either end of the longhouse or under the bench. Smaller bags and those containing sacred or delicate items were hung on the walls.

The Osage Year

The Osage began their new year in April, the month they called "when the deer give birth." They saw spring as symbolic of birth and considered that it was to the year as the sunrise was to the day. When spring arrived, the priests of the Gentle Sky and Gentle Ponca clans (in this case representing the two great divisions of the tribe) assembled at the house of the Sky chief. The Sky chief addressed them, saying that the time had arrived for them to ask the assistance of certain forces of *Wakonta* to give them another year of tranquility and happiness. The clan priests then donated clothing, weapons, household goods, and horses to pay the Overseer of the Village to perform the necessary New Year ceremony. From the house of the Sky chief, the clan priests and the Sky chief walked in formal procession to the house of the Overseer. Seated on a buffalo robe with the hair side out and wearing in his hair feathers from the wings of a pelican—a symbol of long life—the Overseer began reciting the Prayer of the Overseer. In this prayer, he appealed to the forces of the cloudless day, the night, the upper reaches of the day, and the earth for their blessings on the people.[30]

After the New Year ceremony, families began clearing and planting their fields with corn, beans, and squash along the creeks and rivers near their villages. Every family had its own field or fields, generally only a few acres in size. Men did most of the clearing, while planting the crops was done by the women.[31]

The planting of each field began with a short ritual. Beginning at sunrise, the woman prepared seven small mounds, called the Mysterious Hills. She used her digging stick to make a hole in the center of the first mound, in which she placed a single grain of corn that she tamped in with her foot. In the second mound she placed two grains of corn, continuing to increase the number of grains of corn until she placed seven grains in the seventh mound. This ceremonial planting of the seven mounds constituted a prayer for three things: the maturity of the corn, the success of the hunters in finding game, and the success of the warriors in protecting the village. After planting these mounds, the woman continued her planting without any additional ritual.[32] The fields were weeded only until the sprouts were large enough not to be choked out by weeds.[33]

As soon as the fields had been planted and the crops started to grow, preparations began for the summer buffalo hunt. The winter food supplies would have begun to run short, and game was always scarce near the villages. The Sky and Earth chiefs from the different villages would meet and agree on the hunting areas to which each village would proceed. They did not wish to compete with one another. Depending on conditions, some of the villages might have a joint hunt.[34] There were undoubtedly rituals associated with the buffalo hunts, but nothing is known about them, when they were held, or what they involved (see cats. 3, 34, 37, 39, and 57).[35]

While the chiefs were meeting, the families in the villages began the rather elaborate preparations for the hunt. All mats, bark, and hides were removed from the houses, leaving only the pole frameworks standing. The house coverings were piled at one end of the village, covered, and tied down with poles. Other items were tied into bundles and placed in trees. Some men left their guns and other valued personal belongings cached in hidden pits near the village. Buffalo were hunted only with bows and arrows. Not all the Osages of the village went on these hunts: some individuals too old or sick to travel, women with babies or young children, and poorer families who lacked horses and hunting equipment would stay behind. Most of these individuals continued to occupy their dwellings within the village itself; however, some moved to smaller camps hidden in the woods some distance from the village.[36] With virtually all of the younger able-bodied men away on the hunt, the village would be extremely vulnerable to enemy raiding parties.[37]

The village hunting party traveled west toward the buffalo plains along one of several well-defined trails. Moving in two parallel columns, the party was led by one of the two chiefs, who alternated leadership daily. The chiefs' soldiers scouted for the column, looking for the signs of enemy raiders who might steal horses or attack straggling families.[38]

Every ten to twelve miles along these trails, there were regularly used and named campsites, each of which had pole frames standing from earlier trips.[39] At night

the hunting party would cover these frameworks with five or more buffalo hides, leaving them open at either end.[40] These were simple long frameworks, about fifteen feet long, seven feet wide, and four and one-half feet high. The camp was organized like the permanent village: the Sky division clans were in their regular order on the north, while the Earth division families camped in clan order on the south side.[41]

In the early 1800s, it took a hunting party about two weeks to reach the Arkansas River. Before entering the grasslands west of the Arkansas, every family cut poles to be carried on their horses and used later for their tent frames. Beyond this point, there were no regular hunting trails or campsites. West of the Arkansas, there were just vast grasslands, scattered herds of buffalo, and the hunting camps of other tribes, many of whom were hostile to the Osages. As a result, the nature of the caravan changed. As the Osage entered the grasslands, scouts were sent ahead to locate herds of buffalo and look for enemy war parties. A large group of warriors preceded the caravan itself. If signs of hostile tribes were found, a war party would be organized, not necessarily to attack them but, rather, to frighten them out of the area.[42]

After the scouts located the herds, the party moved to a nearby sheltered valley and established a camp. The soldiers were responsible for policing both the camp and the hunt. No individual was allowed to hunt or discharge guns for fear of disturbing the herds. The soldiers regularly went through the camp, carrying their whips and announcing the orders of the day.[43]

Osage buffalo hunting strategies were quite different from those of the Plains tribes. There was no attempt to surround or control the movements of the herds. Starting in the morning and led by the soldiers, the hunters moved as close as possible to the herd. Only when the soldiers gave the signal could the hunters charge into the herd. Each hunter could then act independently in pursuing and shooting the animals as they scattered. The hunters did not attempt to kill the animals outright. Rather, they shot them in the loins to disable them, while they continued to chase and shoot other animals. After they had disabled a sufficient number of animals, they stopped the shooting and returned to kill, skin, and butcher the animals they had wounded (see cats. 27 and 35). Sometimes a hunter would be forced to spend the night beside an animal he was butchering and return to camp the next day.[44]

The purpose of the summer hunt was to secure meat and tallow. However, that task took only two to three weeks of work. After the hunt was over, the party remained in the hunting camp on the plains, with individuals and families free to pursue other interests. With the hunts over and the food abundant, individuals, families, and sometimes whole hunting camps would visit other Osage camps and even the hunting camps of friendly tribes, such as the Kansa. These visits were frequently highlighted by the performance of the Peace Ceremony. Although the Peace Ceremony could be performed at any time of the year, the time in the summer after the hunt appears to have been the most common. Since all of the families and hunting camps were abundantly supplied with food, it was an ideal time for the people of different Osage villages to visit one another.

The Peace Ceremony had a very different character from most Osage ceremonies in that it was public and virtually everyone participated in one manner or another. In contrast to the seriousness of other ceremonies, joking and buffoonery were part of this ceremony. It started with the clan priests and organizing officials gathering in a house to prepare the two sacred pipes (see cat. 30). The priests were seated in clan order, Sky clan priests in a line on the north side and Earth clan priests on the south. Nine symbolic articles, supplied by the sponsor, had to be placed in front of the priests of nine specific clans as indicated:

1. Elder Sky clan priest: Two head skins, with the maxilla attached, of ivory-billed woodpeckers.
2. Eagle clan priest: Tail feathers of a golden eagle.
3. Gentle Sky clan priest: Fluffy white feathers from under the tail of an eagle, which have been dyed red.
4. Crawfish clan priests: Two forked-stick rests for the pipes.
5. Buffalo Bull clan priest: Fat taken from the back of a buffalo.
6. Isolated Earth clan priest: Two large, fluffy white feathers taken from under the tail of a yellow-tailed hawk.
7. Cattail clan priest: Cattail leaves.
8. Sole Possessors of the Bow clan priest: Two straight sticks for the pipe stems.
9. Deer clan priest: Owl feathers.

After the nine articles had been placed in front of the appropriate priests, all to the accompaniment of songs and ritual acts, the nine priests assembled the two necessary pipes. After this part of the ceremony, the clan priests left, since their part in the ceremony was completed.

The Peace Pipe party then made a public procession to the house of a man designated as *Hunka* for the ceremony. At his house, the party was joined by their invited guests, sacred songs were sung, and prayers recited. Finally, a Ceremonial War Leader was chosen. Once again in a formal procession, the party then moved to the house of the Ceremonial War Leader, where several things occurred. Charcoal was prepared to the accompaniment of singing and recitation of prayers. After an intermission, the songs of Weeping were sung and a call was made to all of the families in mourning in the village to terminate their period of mourning. The mourners in the village then threw away the old blankets they had been wearing. The first day of the ceremony ended with the arrival of two men, disguised as members of an alien tribe, who warned that the village would be attacked. A crier was sent through the village with warnings that two great enemy war parties were going to attack them in the morning.

That night the young men and boys who were going to act as the attacking enemy war parties went to their maternal uncles for new names. Their uncles gave the "enemies" humorous names such as "He-who-is-always-being-jilted" or "Last-to-get-up-in-the-morning," or "Sore-back" (referring to his poor horse).

In the early morning, the young men and boys with black-painted faces assembled on their horses about a mile from the village. They charged toward the village in a sham attack on the house of the man who was *Hunka* for the ceremony. The attackers were given blankets and other gifts, which they in turn gave to the Ceremonial War Leader. As they handed the gifts to the War Leader, he would call out their new names so the spectators could hear.

An open rack of poles, about seven feet high and thirty feet long, was then constructed. A pole with a shield on it was placed near one end of the rack. The first gifts placed on the rack were those given by the honored warriors. While the man's wife stood next to a horse packed with gifts, the warrior recited his war honors, striking the shield with a club for each honor. When he had finished, his wife tied the horse to the rack and placed the gifts on the crossbars. As the warriors were reciting their honors and presenting their gifts, the village clowns would stage short skits mimicking fights, quarrels, and other embarrassing activities of certain individuals and families in the village. Along with their buffoonery, they went from house to house asking for gifts to be placed on the rack. The ceremony ended with these gifts being given to the Peace Pipe party. The purpose of the ceremony was to promote peace and friendly relations not just between the clans and the villages of the Osage but with other tribes as well.[45]

By the middle of August, the families returned to their permanent villages and preparations began for the harvest of the crops. Harvest commenced with the Green Corn Ceremony. This one-day ceremony was performed before any of the fresh corn was eaten and concluded with a feast of specially prepared green corn. Other than these bare facts, little is known of the actual ritual. It appears that there was no sacrifice or emetic used in the Osage ritual, unlike those of the tribes farther east and south.[46]

The harvesting and preparation of the crops for storage was time consuming. Corn had to be picked, shelled, and dried. Beans were collected and dried. Squash and pumpkins were cut into long strips, braided, and dried. Wild food plants such as chinquapins (water-lily roots), prairie potatoes, and persimmons were dug or gathered in large quantities and cooked or dried and prepared for storage. The work of harvesting, preparing, and storing food for winter lasted through the month of September.

Toward the end of September, the preparations for the fall buffalo hunt began. Once again, the chiefs of the different villages met to decide on hunting areas, and once again the houses in the village were stripped of their mat and bark coverings. However, there were some important differences in the nature of, and the preparations for, the fall hunt. By the autumn, the buffalo had their thicker winter coats, which were ideal for making robes, so the fall hunt was primarily for skins, not food.[47]

Families had already prepared most of their winter food supply for storage. This food supply was too heavy and bulky to carry with them on the hunt and its loss would be disastrous, so some of the winter food was cached in pits. Osage families also established smaller camps, hidden in the woods some distance from the village. There they could hide additional stores of dried crops and other winter foods.[48]

The fall hunting party would leave their villages around the first part of October. Under the alternating leadership of the two chiefs, they followed the same trails westward to the plains. They were able to travel somewhat lighter than the summer party and returned to the village about the first of December.[49]

Growing Up Osage

All Osage families wanted children. The birth of a child was an important event since it was one of the most tangible indications of *Wakonta*'s blessings. A child was a member of his or her father's clan. The relative status of an individual was mostly determined by order of birth within the family. There were three birth rankings for each gender. The eldest son was *in-gthon*, the second *kshón-ga*, and the third and all additional sons were termed *ká-zhin-ga*. With daughters, the first daughter was called *mí-na*, the second *wí-he*, and the third and all subsequent daughters were termed *ci-ge*.

Naming was a critical event in a child's life. Until they were formally named, children were not considered to be clan members and thus not Osage or even human beings. Each clan had its own form of the naming ceremony. A priest from the child's clan filled the position of *Xó-ka*, or leader. Priests from other clans, in some cases as many as eleven, were formally invited to the naming. In this ceremony, ritual prayers were recited. First the *Xó-ka* blessed the child by touching one bowl of water containing red cedar and another of cornmeal and then touching the child's lips, head, arms, and body. Each of the other clan priests repeated this process of blessings. If this was the mother's first child, she would receive instructions as to the care of the child. If not her first child, then the *Xó-ka* would proceed with the actual naming. Each clan had it own set of names, associated with the clan's symbolic history. Some of these names could be given only to the eldest son, others to the second son, and still others to the third son. There was a fourth set of names that could be given only to the fourth and all subsequent sons. Similarly, there were four sets of names for daughters. The *Xó-ka* would choose the appropriate name for the child. These naming rites were held only for the first three children of each sex. The ritual for the third son and third daughter sufficed for the subsequent children of their gender.[50]

An infant slept at night with its mother, wrapped in a specially marked buffalo robe. During the day, the child was placed on a baby board about three feet in length and a foot wide. The top portion of the board was decorated with carved and painted designs that were frequently highlighted with brass tacks. Such designs appear to have been related to the clan and family of the child. A U-shaped wooden bow attached to the front of the board and covered in ribbon work or beadwork served to protect the child if the board fell over. The baby was wrapped in swaddling and secured to the board with a very wide finger-woven belt (see cats. 24 and 25).

Every clan had its own distinctive style of haircuts for children. Haircuts were symbolic of a particular life symbol of the clan and served as an appeal for the life of the child. While still a baby, the child would have its hair cut in the appropriate manner.[51]

The eldest sons and daughters occupied privileged positions. It was assumed that the eldest son would eventually be a leader, and he was trained by his father from birth for his future role. His younger brothers and sisters were conditioned to defer to his wishes. Later, as a young man, the eldest son assumed the position of the head of the family in the absence of his father. Eldest sons usually filled hereditary offices, and clan priests were also usually eldest sons.

Similarly, the eldest daughter in the family received the greatest attention. The term for the eldest daughter means "the favorite" or "the favored." The eldest daughter was often said to be spoiled by her family: less-demanding work was usually required of her, and she received more gifts and attention from her family than did her younger sisters.

Regardless of their relative birth order, all children were desired by Osage families. After being taken from their cradleboards, most wore little more than a blanket for the first few years. As they grew older, they were dressed in miniature versions of the clothes their parents wore: boys wore moccasins, leggings, and breechcloths, and girls wore moccasins and skirts. Small blankets were worn by both (see cats. 59 and 60).

Children's play usually copied adult behavior. Girls had dolls and miniature cradleboards (see cats. 61, 62, 63) and imitated their mothers in caring for their "babies." Boys had toy bows and arrows and played at hunting and war. Both girls and boys had a variety of other types of toys as well (see cat. 64).

Since girls were considered eligible for marriage after they reached puberty, many were married by the time they were thirteen or fourteen years old. A boy, on the

FIGURE 3.2 Mother and child with clan haircut. Photograph by Drum; courtesy Osage Tribal Museum.

FIGURE 3.3 Osage wedding near Fairfax, Oklahoma, 1918. Photographer Vince Dillon; courtesy Osage Tribal Museum.

other hand, was not considered eligible for marriage until he was in his late teens or early twenties. Marriage was an important event, and the type of marriage engaged in affected the status of the parents as well as of the couple.

An ideal marriage that had the highest status was called a *mí-zhin*. This was an arranged marriage between two previously unmarried individuals. Since adolescent boys and girls were not allowed to speak to or socialize with each other, it was the responsibility of the boy's parents and relatives to find him a suitable wife. Frequently the boy's family would initiate a marriage unbeknownst to the boy himself. After a suitable girl had been selected, the family asked four men of good character to negotiate the marriage. For this service, these men were paid with gifts.

The four men visited the girl's family and presented the marriage proposal. There were several important considerations. Ideally, the families were from different villages and thus not well acquainted. The girl's family would be concerned about the relative social status of the boy's family. Was the marriage of his parents a *mí-zhin* marriage? Was the boy an eldest son? Marriages had to be between individuals whose clans were from opposite moieties, and they could not marry a person who

belonged to any of the four clans to which their grandparents belonged. Once these issues had been satisfactorily resolved, the four men negotiated the number and value of the gifts to be presented by the boy's family and then reached a tentative agreement.

The girl's parents then contacted their relatives to discuss the proposed agreement. Of particular importance were the girl's maternal uncles. If they agreed, the other members of the extended family would concur. Once the extended family agreed, word was sent to the boy's parents that the gifts should be brought to the home of the girl's parents on a particular day.

The groom, his parents, and their relatives went to the home of the girl on the day set for the beginning of the ceremony. Each relative of the groom brought a gift of a horse or a blanket for a member of the bride's family. After the gifts were distributed, the groom and his family returned home.

On the second day of the ceremony, a prominent man led a procession of the bride on horseback and her family to the home of the groom. The bride was dressed in special wedding clothes, which included a "wedding coat": a military-style, three-quarter-length topcoat of red and blue wool decorated with ribbon-work panels, braid trim, epaulettes, large brass buttons, and silver brooches (see cat. 28). The coat was secured with a wide, finger-woven yarn sash. Her wedding outfit was completed with a felt top hat whose brim and crown were decorated with feather plumes and sometimes a silver brow band. The bride's family also brought gifts of horses, blankets, and clothes to be given to the members of the groom's family. The bride's family then returned home, leaving the bride to spend the night with the groom and his family. On the third day, the bride and groom, accompanied by his family, returned to the home of the bride's family to complete the marriage.

The new couple lived with the wife's family. The husband "at once . . . [became] the possessor of the entire wealth of his father-in-law, master of the family lodge and all the household."[52] In fact, the new son-in-law now became the head of the household and was responsible for not only his wife and parents-in-law but also for his wife's unmarried siblings. The father-in-law could now concern himself with things other than the day-to-day subsistence needs of the family. It was now the son-in-law's job to hunt to provide meat for the family. Not surprisingly, the husband of the eldest daughter in the family had the right to marry her younger sisters as they came of age.[53]

Both the husband and wife had rights and obligations to each other. If his wife proved unfaithful, the husband could, and in some cases did, kill her and her lover.[54] However, a husband who killed his wife without reason could himself be executed.[55] A wife could divorce her husband and remarry, if she had a good reason.[56]

It is frequently difficult for individuals with a Western cultural perspective to fully comprehend the true nature of gender roles in societies such as the Osages'. Western peoples tend to judge gender role differences in terms of social inequalities, so in viewing societies in which husbands were the public figures in the family, they tend to think in terms of male dominance. Osage people judged the male/female or husband/wife role from a very different perspective. Just like the village, the family was structured as a symbolic mirror image of the cosmos. Every individual had to marry a person from one of the clans of the opposite division, so that every marriage was the symbolic joining of Earth and Sky. The Osages even took this symbolic structuring one step further. Every marriage symbolically brought together the masculine and feminine forces of the cosmos, regardless of which spouse was Earth and which was Sky. Certain aspects of the cosmos were masculine and thus defined the husband's role in the family, while other aspects of the cosmos were feminine and served to define the wife's role.

Masculine forces were associated primarily with death and destruction. To Osages, the destruction of life was necessary to sustain life, so two of the major roles of the husband were those of the warrior and the hunter. As the warrior, the husband was the destroyer of the human enemies of his family and community. As the hunter, he was the destroyer of animal enemies and the provider of food for his family and community. In contrast, feminine forces were primarily associated with bringing life into the world and nurturing it. The survival of the Osages depended on their children and future generations, so the primary roles of the wife were mother and gardener. In Osage religious rituals, the wife's role as the bearer of children was equated with her husband's role as the warrior. Just as the husband risked his life and suffered pain to protect his wife and family, so the wife risked her life and suffered pain to bring new life into the world. In the rituals, the role of the wife as the cultivator of corn was equated to the husband's role as the hunter of buffalo.

Formal honors were bestowed on men in Osage society because they were the public representatives of the family. In reality, these honors were bestowed on the family and reflected on the wife as much as the husband. The relative status of a family in Osage society was as much dependent on the qualities of the wife as they were on those of the husband.

Osage society was one in which status was greatly emphasized. The relative status of an individual was determined only partly by relative birth order and family. Through their own actions and abilities, individuals could increase the respect and esteem in which other members of the community held them. For a man, there were three basic areas in which he could excel: as a husband and father, as a warrior, and as a religious leader.

An Osage male first had to excel in his duties as husband and father. When a man moved in with his in-laws and became head of the household, he had to be not just an adequate provider but someone who provided well for his family. The Osages placed great emphasis on appearance, so it was important that a man's family be well fed, well dressed, and well provisioned with horses, metal tools, and other items. As a hunter, the man could not merely secure sufficient game to feed and clothe his family; rather, he had to acquire surplus food to feed and entertain guests and secure horses, hides, and other goods that could be used as "gifts"—usually horses or clothing—to pay individuals to perform certain ritual acts for his family. A man hunted not only to secure meat for his family, but also to secure hides and pelts that could be traded for other goods or made into clothing.

The way a man was able to provide for his children as they were growing up was important, but the final indication of a man's success as a father was in the marriages of his children. *Mí-zhin* marriages not only proved the father's ability to pay but, even more important, demonstrated that he had raised his children to respect the social norms and values of the society.[57]

Only after all his children had been properly married and had children of their own could a man be called *dón-he*, which means "decent," or "clean" or "of good character." Like the title "sir," given to an elder member of the society, the designation did not mean that the man had lived a perfect life, but that he had overcome his early failures to live an exemplary life. He had become the type of man that young men should model themselves after.[58]

The second arena of achieved status for an Osage man was that of warrior. In contrast to many of their neighbors, the Osage did not glorify war, but they did greatly honor their warriors. An early missionary once wrote that "the Osages are remarkable for always being at war, without being a war-like people."[59] They saw war as a necessary evil in that if they could not protect themselves, their enemies would destroy them.

To the Osage, war had to be rational: it had to have an objective. The purpose of war was to protect the community, particularly the women and the children who were their future. Men whose bravery caused them to excel in warfare were to be publicly acknowledged. However, warlike actions had to serve the greater purpose of protecting the community. Purposeless acts of individual bravado were not to be acknowledged. To make certain that acts of warfare were focused and purposeful, control of warfare was given to the clan priests. Only they could authorize the organization of a war party, and only the

clan priests had the authority to publicly acknowledge the achievements of the warriors.

The authorizing and organizing of a tribal war party was the collective decision of the clan priests.[60] The chiefs and their soldiers played no role in either initiating or leading the war party. After meeting and agreeing that an attack on a particular enemy was necessary, the clan priests first chose one of their members to act as the Sacred Leader for the party. The Sacred Leader then went into seclusion for the Rite of Vigil for four to seven days. During this time, he prayed and fasted and asked *Wakonta* for guidance. On his return, he did not speak of what he had learned.

The clan priests then selected two priests, one from the Earth division and one from the Sky division, to act as "ceremonial leaders." Those two men then chose eight priests, four from the Earth division and four from the Sky division, to be "captains." It was the eight captains who would actually lead the attack. From among these eight, two would be chosen, one from the Earth and one from the Sky division, to be the "head captains." After those selections had been made, one clan priest from each of the twenty-four clans would volunteer to lead the warriors of his clan in battle, carrying one of his clan's bundles on his back.

As the rituals related to the selection of the leaders of the party were coming to a close, the two ceremonial leaders left to take down their houses and rebuild them at the west edge of the village. However, in doing this, they switched directions. The house of the Earth leader was rebuilt on the north side of the east-west street, while the house of the Sky leader was rebuilt on the south side. These two houses would serve as the ritual centers for their respective divisions, and their movement was the signal to all the families in the village that they should begin tearing down their own houses and moving them to the opposite side of the street. The Sky people would now be on the south side, the Earth people on the north, and the village itself would "face" west, the symbolic direction of the forces of death and destruction.

In the Earth and Sky houses, the sacred charcoal was prepared and the two sacred war standards constructed. Priests of the Bear (Earth) and Night (Sky) clans prepared the sacred charcoal from branches of redbud or willow trees, both considered sacred and symbolic of

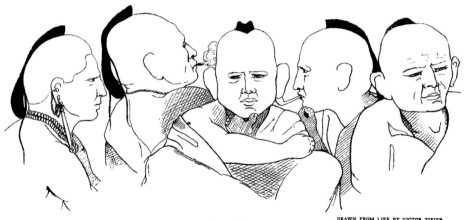

Osage Warriors
Chonkêh, Man-chap-ché-mani, La Grosse Tête,
Kansé-Tanga, Ta-ouan-li

DRAWN FROM LIFE BY VICTOR TIXIER

FIGURE 3.4 Osage warriors Chonkêh, Man-chap-ché-mani, La Grosse Tête, Kansé-Tanga, and Ta-ouan-li, 1844, from *Tixier's Travels on the Osage Prairies*, edited by John Francis McDermott, 1940. Reprinted with permission from the University of Oklahoma Press.

The Charcoal Dance (Médecine du charbon)

DRAWN FROM LIFE BY VICTOR TIXIER

FIGURE 3.5 The Charcoal Dance, or War Ritual, 1844. From *Tixier's Travels on the Osage Prairies*, edited by John Francis McDermott, 1940. Reprinted with permission from the University of Oklahoma Press.

long life. Priests of the Bear clan and Bow clan then prepared the two war standards, each of which was about six feet long with a top that looked like a shepherd's crook. The staff was covered in deerskin and wrapped in a long strip of swan skin plucked of its feathers. Twelve eagle feathers, in three bunches of four feathers each, were attached to the staff. Finally, a dressed deerskin was attached to the top. As rituals continued in the Earth and Sky houses, the leaders of the war party, with their standards and other sacred items, began ritual singing and dancing in public together with the warriors who were to follow them.

During this ceremony and the public rituals that followed, the dancers dressed in various ways. Some men carried war standards (cat. 13) while others carried pipes, rattles, clubs, and other sacred items. Men who had distinguished themselves in battle wore crow belts. Made of crow feathers, which are symbolic of death and the field of battle, the belt was constructed in such a manner that when the man danced, its feathers waved and bells on four projecting branches tinkled.[61] Still other men wore deer-tail roaches or bands of bird beaks on their heads. The meanings of these deer tails and bird-beak crowns are not known. Dances continued through the first day until midnight.

The rituals on the second day, similar to those on the first day, lasted until about midnight. On the third day, each warrior was given a bag of sacred charcoal. At the end of four days, the war party left the village in search of the enemy.

Osage warriors traveled light, carrying little more than some dried food, their bag of charcoal, and weapons. Most men carried a shield (see cats. 32, 43, 44, 46), and every man had a bow and arrows or a gun. Other weapons appear to have been a matter of personal choice. Since wet weather could render bows and guns ineffective, a spear (see cat. 58), a tomahawk, or a war club (see cats. 31 and 54) was usually also taken. War clubs shaped like gunstocks with large steel blades were the most effective for hand-to-hand combat (see cat. 45).

During the war party's march toward the enemy, the Sacred Leader traveled separately, with a clan war bundle on his back.[62] Although he was in contact with the party, the Sacred Leader kept to himself, even at night. As the party prepared for attack, the chief commander came to the Sacred Leader and had his bundle placed around his neck. This bundle was the emblem of his command. At the same time, the warriors prepared themselves by painting their faces black with charcoal, signifying that they were setting aside their normal human feelings of pity and compassion and instead becoming like the merciless fire consuming all before them. As the eight commanders led the men into battle, the Sacred Leader stayed in seclusion, praying for the success of the party.

Osage tribal war parties were terrifying to their enemies. Their tactics were simple. They moved as close to an enemy camp or village as possible without being discovered, then they charged in a straight line, killing all before them.

The return of the war party to the village was filled with ritual, too. One of the most important events was the claiming of war honors, called *o-dón*. Each man publicly announced the war honor (or honors) he had earned and then claimed it by placing a red stick on one of the clan bundles.[63]

The types of war honors given reflect, more than any other factor, the Osage attitude toward warfare. There were thirteen named war honors, which were divided into a grouping of seven and a grouping of six.[64] While many questions concerning war honors cannot be answered, one thing is clear: twelve of the thirteen could be earned only on a formally organized war party that had been sanctioned by the priests. However, the thirteenth, and

FIGURE 3.6 Chief Bacon Rind (Wah-she-hah) with tattoos, 1900. Photographer Delancy Gill; courtesy Osage Tribal Museum.

most esteemed, war honor was the one earned for killing an enemy warrior found in the camp or village itself. The defense of the women and children was the primary responsibility of the warrior, and enemy raiders attacking either the camp or village were a direct threat to them. The war honor for defending an Osage camp or village was the only one that did not require that the man be a member of a war party authorized by either a clan priest or by the clan priests collectively. It was also the only war honor that did not require the warrior to have black charcoal on his face at the time of his action. The Osage believed that, except in times of extreme peril, the aggressive nature of the warriors had to be controlled and focused toward a specific purpose or objective. In other words, war honors were given only to men who acted for the collective good of the people.

To the Osages, the sheer quantity of a man's war honors was irrelevant. It was considered more important to earn one of all thirteen types. While any man could strive to gain some war honors, only a man who was also a clan priest could gain all thirteen, because one of the honors was for serving as the Sacred Leader of a tribal war party, and only a clan priest could fill this position.

There was great status attached to having achieved all thirteen honors. This accomplishment allowed the man to be tattooed. The priest of the Great Medicine Bundle did the tattooing. The design consisted of thirteen rays, representing the thirteen rays of the sun as well as his thirteen war honors, emanating from his neck. A knife symbolizing war was tattooed on one shoulder and a pipe, symbolic of peace, on the other. Other designs were also used, the meanings of which are unknown. The man could also pay to have his wife, or wives, and daughters tattooed.[65]

While every Osage man became the head of a family and at times served as a warrior, not every man became a member of one of the priesthoods. In fact, only a minority of men ever became priests. Priesthood among the Osage was for the serious minded, and priests formed the intellectual elite of the community. Not only did they learn the long ritual prayers and songs, they also had to try to understand the complex meanings embedded in these teachings. It was mentally and intellectually challenging to be a priest, and it was extremely costly to the family.

The decision to join the clan priesthood was as much a family decision as an individual one. To become a priest brought honor, status, and responsibilities not only to the man but to his family as well. However, the process of becoming a clan priest was long and expensive. It required years of sacrifice by the family to collect the vast amount of gifts necessary to pay the priests who would participate in the initiation, as well as the food required to feed both them and their families during the initiation.

Becoming a candidate for priesthood was a serious matter. After the man took a vow that he would be initiated, he had seven years to collect the gifts, food, and sacred skins necessary for the ceremony. If during this period he failed to collect all the required items or if, even due to adverse circumstances, he used part of the

food or goods set aside for his initiation, supernatural forces would punish him.

Although the Osages were a patrilineal society and males were the most conspicuous public figures in the family, the important role of women was regularly noted. To the Osages, the roles of men and women were complementary, not superior or inferior. In fact, the Osage saw the role of wife as more central to the family than that of husband. The primary roles of a wife were those of a mother and keeper of the hearth. The actions and achievements of the wife were as important in determining the relative status of the family as were those of the husband.

Children were the greatest of *Wakonta*'s blessings. In Osage oral traditions, the "good" women usually had many children, while the "bad" women and "bad" families usually had few or no children. Since children were considered the most precious of all creations in that they represented the future, mothers were entrusted with their care and with bringing them to maturity. To accomplish this, the mother needed *Wakonta*, whose help she sought with three things: a sacred robe and the sacred foods of corn and water-lily roots.

The mother had to make a sacred robe for her children. With her own hands she had to dress the skin of an old male buffalo that had been killed by the child's father. Once the skin had been dressed, she then painted it. With red paint she drew a straight, narrow line from the head through the body to the tip of the tail. This line represented the power of day that lives forever. Midway in the line she painted a red disk, which represented the sun at midday. She then painted the buffalo skin's four legs. The painting on these legs represented the dawn, the force of day and of life. The very act of painting the robe served as a prayer for a long and fruitful life both for herself and for her child. For four nights she would take her baby in her arms with the robe drawn over them. In this context the robe symbolically represented the sky from which all life came, and her action was an appeal for protection.[66]

The mother also had to nourish her children with two sacred life-giving foods, corn and water-lily roots, which she had to grow or collect herself. Both were thought to be especially nourishing for children.[67]

As a wife, the woman was the keeper of the fireplace. The Osage word for fireplace, *u-dsé-the*, refers to the

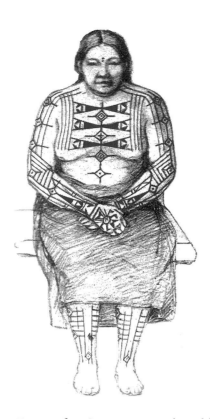

FIGURE 3.7 Tattoos of an Osage woman, adapted from drawings by Francis La Flesche in "Researches Among the Osages," 1918. *Smithsonian Miscellaneous Collections.*

attempted to make and decorate clothes as finely as she could. A wife not only made clothing for her own family members, but she also made items of clothing for gifts that had to be publicly given to priests at rituals and at the Peace Ceremony. It was critical that these items be as fine as the wife could make.

The full significance of the tattooing of Osage women is not clear. Some sources suggest that only a warrior who had earned all thirteen *o-dón* could publicly honor his wife and daughters by having them tattooed.[70] However, one early source noted that "nearly all the female Osage have their bodies tattooed."[71] It is known that tattoos on women were far more elaborate and extensive than those on men. Women's tattoos covered most of their hands, arms, legs, chests, and backs, making their tattoos far more expensive, in terms of gifts to the Great Bundle priests who performed the tattooing, and far more painful than those applied to a man.

The tattooing was, in essence, a prayer for long life. The tattoos on a woman's face, chest, and back symbolized the sun, stars, and various elements of the sky. The designs running from her shoulders down her arms to her wrists symbolized the "paths of animals," the "path of life." The design on the back of her hand was associated with the spider, symbolizing the earth or the snare of life.[72]

The tattooing ritual involved the reciting of prayers and the singing of sacred songs. The prayer was not just for the individual being tattooed but for the whole Osage community. Tattooing a woman publicly was important because it demonstrated that she, like her husband, had personally undergone pain and suffering for the good of the people. She had sacrificed of herself in a symbolic prayer for everyone.[73]

When a man was initiated into one of the priesthoods, the duties of his priesthood fell upon his wife or wives and family as well. The wife of a priest who had custody of one of the bundles had her own ritual duties. During the initiation ritual for her husband, the wife was brought into the ritual and formally instructed in these duties. Every war party required that the leaders take with them clan bundles, which had to be formally borrowed from the clan priests. When it came time for the war leader to come to the house of the clan priest to borrow the bundle, the priest's wife prepared herself. She dressed

hearth as in a house, but it also refers to the clans.[68] Fire was one of *Wakonta*'s gifts to humans and was sacred. Every fire in the village was kindled with coals taken from the sacred fireplaces of the two chiefs. Thus it was that the fire in every home was also sacred. It was the sacred object that symbolized the unity of the family. As a result, the fire and fireplace had to be treated with the respect accorded a sacred object. It was the role of the wife to maintain the fireplace and keep it clean. A woman who kept her fireplace clean was honored, for it was a sign of "her reverence for things sacred, her kindliness and her hospitality."[69]

The keeping of the fireplace was only one aspect of domestic life. A good woman wanted her family to be well dressed. If they were not, it reflected poorly on her, in the same way as her husband being a poor hunter would reflect badly on him. Status was attached to the quality of clothing the family wore. The making of clothing was the responsibility of the wife, and every woman in becoming clothes and painted a red line in the part of her hair, which represented the path of the sun and the path of life. If she had one, she would seat herself on a bearskin robe, the symbol of strength and courage, with the bundle in her lap. The war leader took the bundle from her lap, without her touching it, and left the house. After he left, she would then remove the red paint from her head, saying, "My grandfather bade me to say, when I do this act, 'I remove this symbol from my head and wipe my hands upon the bodies of the enemy.'"

On the first morning following the departure of the war party and just as the sun rose, the wife would again paint the red line in her hair and also paint a blue line on her forehead and on each of her cheeks. This act symbolized the sending of courage and the wish for success to the warriors. Before the sun reached midday, the wife had to remove the paint while saying, "My grandfather bade me to say, when I do this act, 'I remove these symbols from my head and face and wipe my hands upon the body of the chief of the enemy.'"

On the morning of the second day, she repeated these acts, adding a red line with the three blue lines. On the third morning, she again repeated these acts, adding another blue line on her head and cheeks. On the following four mornings, she again repeated these acts, each time adding another line on her head and cheeks. Having completed this, her duty to the war leader was complete.[74]

While women were not directly initiated into the clan priesthoods, the widow of a priest could take her husband's position by going to one of the leading clan priests and asking to be installed. If he agreed, then during a pause at the next initiation ceremony, the sponsoring priest would present the widow's request to the clan priests. If they approved, then the sponsoring priest would recite the prayer for the installation of a widow in the priesthood. All references to killing and the destruction of life were omitted in this prayer. The prayer reflects why women, under normal circumstances, could not be priests. The clan bundles were associated with war, killing, and destruction. Women, on the other hand, were symbolically associated with birth and continuance of life.[75]

After a woman was accepted into the priesthood, she, like all the male priests, was required to attend rituals when formally called. Women priests were seated behind the male priests of the clan, which was actually the clan of their deceased husbands and not their own clans. During parts of the ceremony, the women priests would wail in unison. In initiation ceremonies, the wailing sometimes served as a call to the clan priests to perform their parts without reservation or prejudice,[76] while at other times it was in remembrance of their husbands, whose places they were filling.[77]

Of the many Osage women who had supernatural powers, the most important were the prophets who warned the people of events to come. One of the most famous of these women in oral traditions was *Wa-zhí-xa-win*. In the middle of the night, *Wa-zhí-xa-win* began to sob and cry in grief. Her crying continued until sunrise, and it was so loud that it awakened much of the village. When asked by the men why she had wept in the night, *Wa-zhí-xa-win* replied, "Bring to me a pipe filled with tobacco and light it for me, and I will find out for you the cause of my grief." A pipe was brought to her and she took four whiffs. She then said, "Spare me the pain of telling that which will bring sorrow to all the people; bear with patience your eagerness to know till tomorrow when the sun rises. On the brow of the hill, a man will appear; hasten to him and he will tell you."

The next morning a man appeared on the hill and the people of the village rushed toward him. He was the sole survivor of a war party of ten men from the village, who had been ambushed and killed by the enemy. This was only one of the dreams of *Wa-zhí-xa-win* that proved true, and she became a highly respected prophet.[78]

Death was the natural passage from the visible world of the living into the invisible world of *Wakonta*. The Osages had no clear ideas as to what happened to the individual's spirit after death, but there were stories told of certain individuals whose ghosts stayed behind and had contact with living people.[79]

Burials were an important ritual, and the relative status and wealth of the individual's family affected the form of burial rite. Normally the Osages buried the person who had died in a rock cairn at noon of the fourth day after death. It was thought that there was an opening between the visible and invisible worlds at noon that allowed for the passage of the spirit of the individual. The cairn was usually on a high hill. The individual was

FIGURE 3.8 Osage Mourning Dance. Photographer unknown; courtesy Osage Tribal Museum.

seated in the cairn so as to face east. Food and some of the person's most treasured possessions were also placed in the grave. Sometimes a favorite horse was killed at the gravesite to accompany the deceased. A priest from the Wind clan burned cedar fronds that symbolically released the spirit of the deceased so it could be borne away on the winds. The mourners took the smoldering cedar fronds and pulled them over their bodies and heads so that the smoke would cleanse them from their contact with the dead. The burial ended with a special feast that was meant to be the symbolic last gift of the deceased to the living, and the family gave gifts to the mourners.[80]

The formal mourning by family members varied. Wives and husbands frequently went into the woods and performed the Rite of Vigil, placing moist earth on their foreheads, fasting, and praying. The Rite of Vigil lasted four or seven days, although their mourning usually continued even after family members returned to the village. The women cut their hair, while the men allowed their hair to grow out. They wore their old clothes and would not take part in rituals or social activities. There was no set period for how long this period of mourning would continue; in fact, some families were said to have mourned for as long as two years. However, as mentioned in "The Osage Year" earlier in this chapter, at one

point during the Peace Ceremony the leader would call on all the families in mourning to end their grieving and rejoin the community.

The mourning by relatives formally ended the burial. However, if a family wished to further honor a deceased relative, and if they could afford the additional expense, they could request the "Mourning Dance."[81] Rather than an actual dance, however, it was the organizing of a war party to kill an enemy so that the spirit of the enemy could accompany that of the deceased Osage. The mourner first asked a priest of his clan to act as *Xó-ka* for the ceremony. The *Xó-ka* then summoned the clan priests of his division to ask their consent. If they agreed, a man from the opposite division was chosen to be the Ceremonial Mourner, who would then gather the clan priests from his division to ask their consent. Only with the formal consent of all of the priests could the ritual be held. The ritual itself was an abbreviated version of the tribal war ceremony. Just as in a tribal war party, a man was chosen to be the Sacred Leader. He in turn chose two men from each division to serve him, and four men from each division were chosen to be the Commanders to lead the men. However, in contrast to the tribal war ceremony, the dwellings in the village were not moved in the Mourning Dance. After the charcoal had been prepared and the other ritual preparations were completed, the war party left the village and traveled westward in search of an enemy, meaning any non-Osage. Usually it was a lone hunter or traveler who was discovered and killed. The party returned home immediately after taking the scalp that would be attached to a war standard and planted in the ground at the head of the deceased's grave. The Ceremonial Mourner then had to mourn the death of the slain enemy, since at the time he was killed, they had no evil intent toward him.

The Collapse of Osage Traditional Life

In 1871 the Osage abandoned their reservation in Kansas and by 1872 had been settled on their new reservation in Indian Territory in present-day Oklahoma. The treaty they had signed with the federal government in which they agreed to this move was unlike any treaty signed by the government with any other tribe. The Osage did not cede their Kansas reservation but, rather, allowed the government to sell their land for them to white farmers and ranchers. Part of the money received from this sale was to be used to purchase their new 1.5-million-acre reservation, with title in fee simple, from the Cherokee. The remainder of the money was to be placed in an Osage trust account invested in government bonds paying 5 percent interest a year. By the 1890s, the funds in this trust account amounted to more than $8 million.[82]

In 1872 the life of the Osages was still very much like it had been a hundred or more years earlier. Twice a year they traveled to the plains to hunt buffalo, and the women still planted their fields of corn, beans, and squash. Their social institutions were still intact and their religious institutions and priesthoods were still fully operative. At the time, few observers would have guessed that in little more than a decade their hunting economy would have vanished, their religious institutions would have collapsed, and their social institutions would be in chaos.

In the summer of 1876, the Osage held their last buffalo hunt. The hunters found nothing, because the southern herd of buffalo was virtually extinct. Messengers were sent to the Osage Agency to tell officials that the people in the hunting camps were on the verge of starvation. Rations from government stores were rushed to the camps to feed the starving people so they could go home.[83] At first, the agency used funds from the interest payments on their trust account to purchase rations to issue to hungry Osage families. Later, the government began making quarterly per-capita payments in cash, which brought the Osage into the regional cash economy and allowed them to purchase goods at local stores.[84]

This economic change was the least of the problems for the Osage. For reasons that are not fully clear, the members of full-blood families began dying in unbelievable numbers. More than 3,600 full-blood Osages made the move to Indian Territory in 1872. In the following seven years, their population declined by almost half, numbering fewer than 1,900 by 1879. By 1892 there were only 1,003 living full-bloods remaining.[85]

The collapse in population wrought havoc with Osage religious institutions. The elderly seem to have died in disproportionate numbers. Clan priests and tribal priests died without passing on their sacred bundles and ritual knowledge. Very quickly, some clans lost all their priests, and with them vanished both their ritual knowledge

and authority. In order to get the full representation of clans needed for rituals, the Osage resorted to placing an uninitiated male member of the clan in the ceremonies. While the clan part of the ritual might not be included, at least the clan could be symbolically represented. Eventually, they began to use female members of some clans to create a full representation. Finally, some of the clans became extinct, and with their passing the major rituals could no longer be performed. Only minor rituals continued to be performed. In 1911 the last traditional public ritual was held. It was a Mourning Dance, a ritual that did not require the full representation of all twenty-four clans.[86]

Although full-bloods continued to live in their traditional longhouses and wear Osage clothes, without their religious institutions, Osage life became little more than an empty shell. They desperately sought something to fill the void. In 1884 the Kansa people of the Kaw River brought an E-Lon-schka drum to the Thorny Thicket people living at Pawhuska. Later they would give another drum to the Upland Forest people at Hominy, and the Ponca would give a third drum to the Big Hills people at Gray Horse. The Osage took these drums and their associated songs and dances, mixing them together with pieces of their traditional rituals in what proved to be a futile attempt to create a new spiritual core.[87] The E-Lon-schka dance was later adopted and continues today, but in its greatly modified form it is more of a social dance.

There were other attempts to revitalize Osage religion and spirituality. In 1890 Sitting Bull, an Arapahoe, brought the Ghost Dance to the Osage, who danced it once or twice but abandoned it. A few years later, William Faw Faw, an Oto, had a vision of everlasting life. About 1894 he brought a drum and his new ritual to the people at Hominy. They dug out a special circular dance ground and in the middle placed a cedar tree, a symbol of everlasting life, with a buffalo skull on top. They danced his dance and listened to his vision, and then they rejected it.[88] Finally, in 1898, John Wilson, a Caddo-Delaware called Moon Head, brought his new Peyote Religion to the Osage. It turned out to be what they had been searching for.

CAT. 24

CRADLEBOARD

ca. 19th century
wood, glass beads, felt, trade cloth, brass tacks,
leather string, and brass bells
42 × 13 × 11 inches
Jackson County Parks and Recreation

CAT. 25

CRADLEBOARD

1930–1940
wood, brass, beads, brass bells, yarn, and cloth
40½ × 12 × 11 inches
Gilcrease Museum, Tulsa, Oklahoma

Osage cradleboards consist of a foundation board to which the infant is strapped
securely. A cloth is draped over a wooden
bow to protect the baby from insects, sun-
burn, and other harmful elements. The
attached bells, which make a light sound
when brushed, were used by the mother to
soothe her baby and to keep it from crying,
a critical factor when tribal warfare was
intense. The vertical straps are examples
of loom beadwork. The patterns of the
bead field represent converging arrows.
Unlike other American Indian cradleboards, Osage boards were not strapped
to the mother's back; rather, they were
carried or propped up.

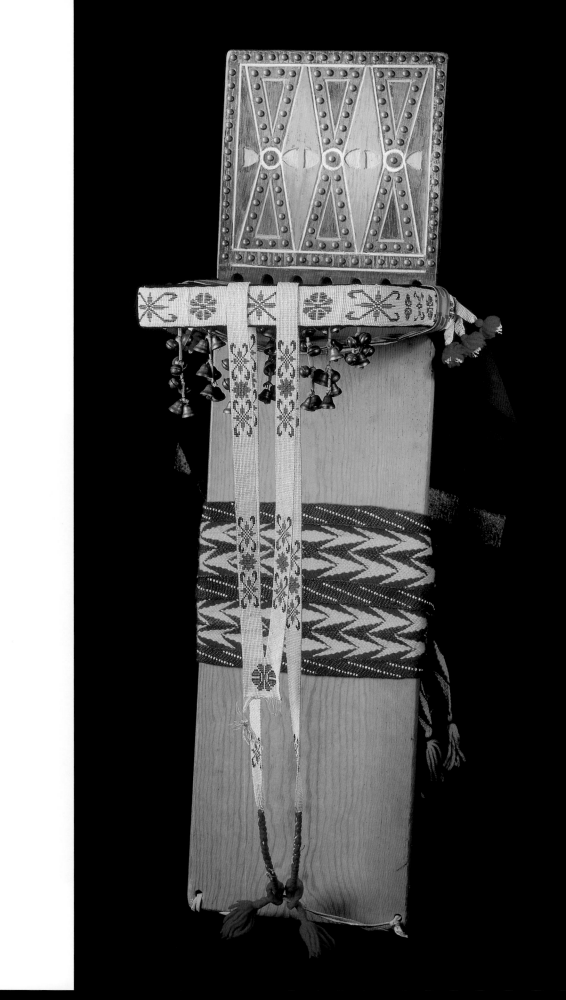

BOWL WITH FIGURES

ca. 19th century
wood
5½ × 16⅛ inches
National Museum of the American Indian,
Smithsonian Institution

This serving bowl was made from the
protruding knot of a red oak tree. After
the knot was removed, the cut side of the
knot was sealed with beeswax. The outer
bark was removed to allow the wood to
dry from the outside inward to avoid crack-
ing. The figures depicted around the rim
include a hog, a bird, and a human head
with roached hair. Made for everyday use,
the bowl has a flange on the rim opposite
the head that serves as a hand grip.

CAT. 27
BOW

wood, leather, fur, and quill
56⅛ × 2³⁄₁₆ × 1¾ inches
Collection of Nordamerika Native Museum,
Zurich, Switzerland

This is a traditional longbow used by the
Osage to hunt elk and deer or to kill a
wounded bison. Longbows were considered
very personal items, and the owner would
frequently incise the weapon with scenes of
the hunt and warfare, creating his own auto-
biography. Represented here are a hunter
with a bow, the sun, and a deer. The four-
pronged abstraction may refer to the snare
of life, the *hó-e-ga*, which has the power to
ensnare a life on its sacred path and return
its essence to the visible world.

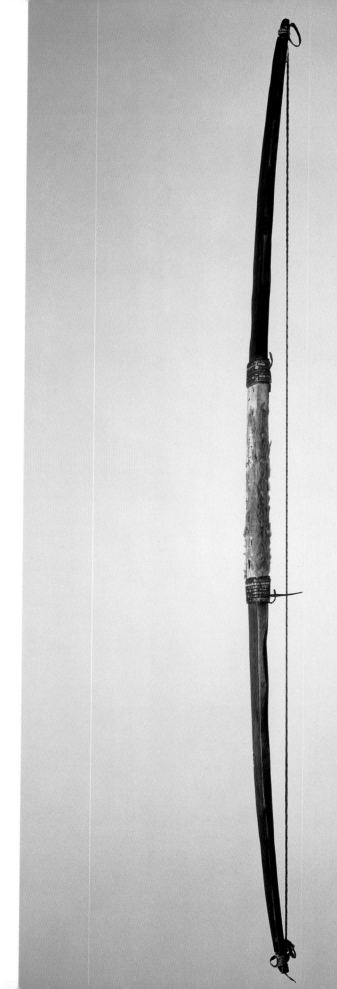

CAT. 28

WEDDING COAT

20th century
cloth, silk, and ribbon
42 × 61 inches
Denver Art Museum Collection, Native Arts Acquisition
funds, 1963.157

Osage women have worn military-style
coats in their weddings since the nineteenth century. According to oral tradition,
Osage men were given U.S. military coats
during their visits to Washington, D.C., at
that time. Since most Osage men were too
large for the coats, they gave them to Osage
women, who adopted them for wedding
rituals. The use of ribbon work appliqué
gives an Osage look to an otherwise Western style of clothing.

CAT. 29

SCISSORS CASE

ca. 1885
hide with quillwork
5 × 2 inches
Department of Anthropology, Smithsonian Institution

This personal scissors case is adorned with dyed and flattened porcupine quills. Scissors were used to complete fine and delicate work and to cut silk ribbon. As Osage women took great pride in their work, they coveted fine tools and stored them in beautiful containers. The red and green floral patterns on this case appear to be roses. Catholic nuns introduced floral motifs such as these to Osage girls at the boarding schools they attended in the mid-nineteenth century.

CAT. 30

CALUMET

ca. 1870
wood, feathers, hair, and hide
53 × 17 × 2 inches
Department of Anthropology, Smithsonian Institution

Calumets are often mistaken for personal smoking pipes, but they are actually sacred prayer pipes that have no bowls or hollow stems. An appointed clan priest would hold the sacred pipe in his left hand with the mouthpiece pointing toward the sky. With outstretched arms, he would turn in a circle with the calumet, addressing the four cardinal points, and wave the pipe from side to side to accentuate the rhythm of the songs. This ritual action fulfilled many purposes, including controlling the weather and promoting peace in and outside the tribe. The black and white feathers suspended below the pipe stem are from a mature golden eagle, while the cluster of split and pithed, brown, two-toned feathers attached horizontally to the top of the shaft are from a great horned owl. In response to the call of the owls, *Wakonta* would bless them and their offspring, enabling them to be raised in safety without fear, a life also desired by the Osage.

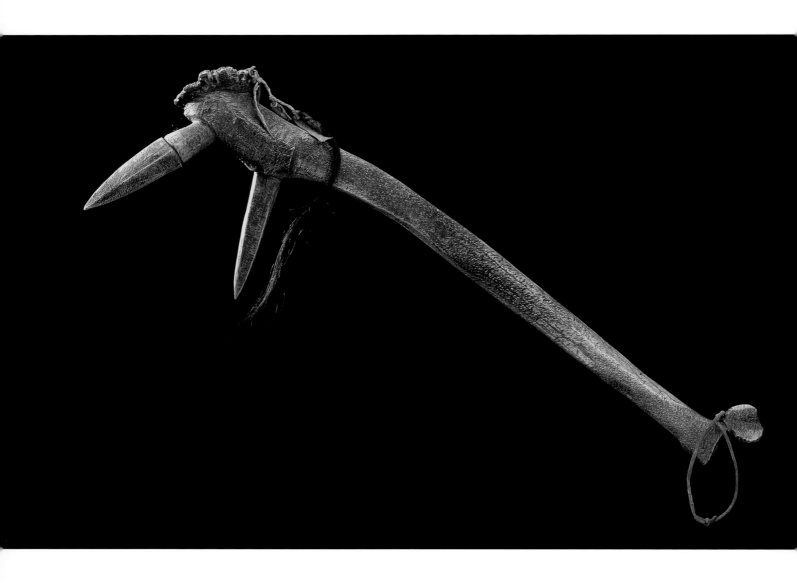

CAT. 31
ELK ANTLER CLUB

wood, elk antler, horsehair, and paint
30½ × 10 × 3¾ inches
Department of Anthropology, Smithsonian Institution

This club is the only known example of such a weapon found among the Osage. The club
has been consecrated with blue and red paint, colors that are associated with a corpse and
the deathblow of lightning, respectively. The weight of the club suggests that a large and
formidable man carried it into battle. Its tines have been altered so that the victim would
receive a diamond-shaped wound when struck. The club's design and its balance of weight
made it an extremely efficient tool of death. Remnants of scalp and hair are evidence that
it was used on a successful war expedition.

SHIELD

hide, glass beads, iron, and steel
33 × 19½ inches
Department of Anthropology, Smithsonian Institution

This shield not only protected its owner, but its design and decoration were intended to project an intimidating energy. The enemy would have immediately recognized the human hair adorning the perimeter of the shield as evidence that the warrior bearing this shield was a veteran of many successful battles. The shield's central decoration conveys strength and endurance, symbolized by the horsehair attached to the beadwork, composed in concentric circles. The configuration of the five-pointed stars suggests a constellation personally significant to the owner.

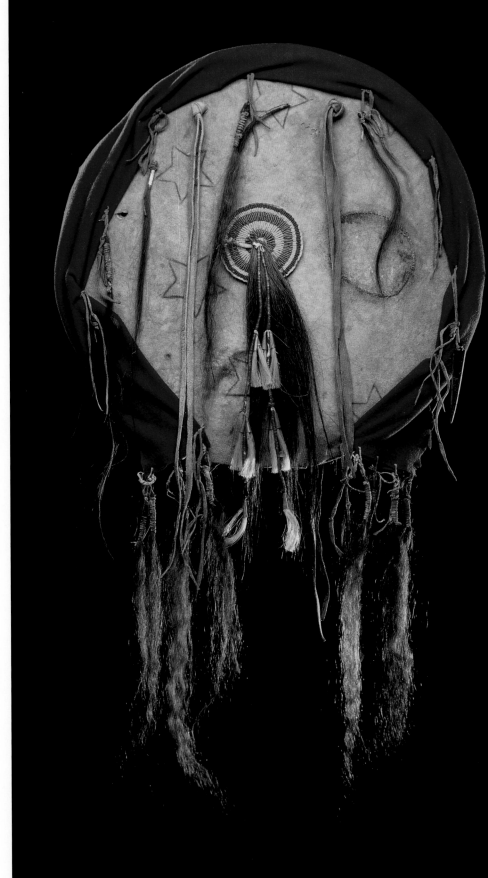

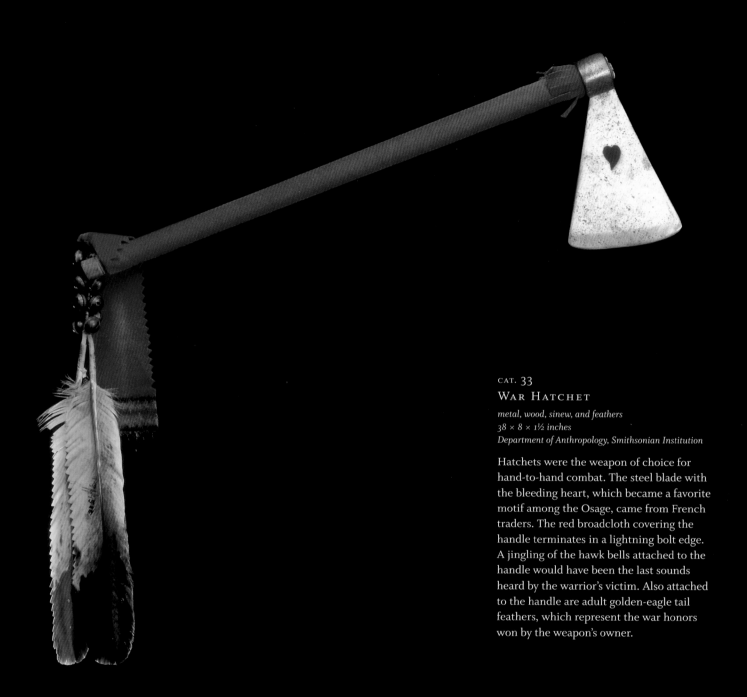

CAT. 33
WAR HATCHET

metal, wood, sinew, and feathers
38 × 8 × 1½ inches
Department of Anthropology, Smithsonian Institution

Hatchets were the weapon of choice for
hand-to-hand combat. The steel blade with
the bleeding heart, which became a favorite
motif among the Osage, came from French
traders. The red broadcloth covering the
handle terminates in a lightning bolt edge.
A jingling of the hawk bells attached to the
handle would have been the last sounds
heard by the warrior's victim. Also attached
to the handle are adult golden-eagle tail
feathers, which represent the war honors
won by the weapon's owner.

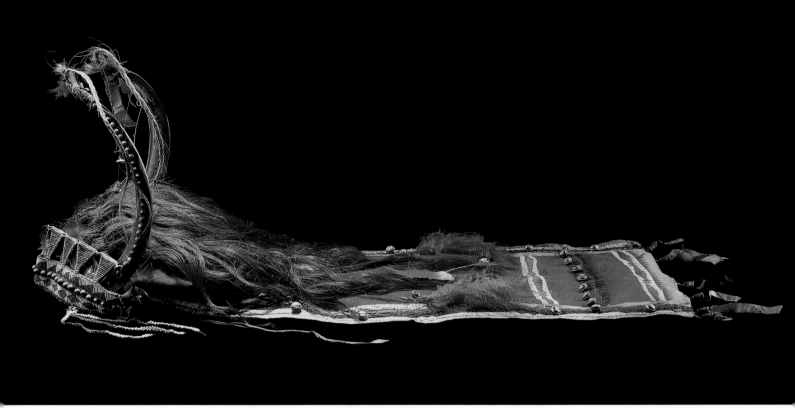

CAT. 34
SPLIT-HORN HEADDRESS

plant fiber, animal hair, cloth, feathers, metal,
glass beads, and dye
35¹⁄₁₆ × 10¹⁄₄ × 14¹⁵⁄₁₆ inches
The Field Museum of Natural History, Chicago

This magnificent headdress is uniquely decorated with glass beads, brass tacks, hawk
bells, silk ribbon, red wool broadcloth, dyed
horsehair, and painted steer horns. Dyed
eagle plumes, tips of peacock tail feathers,
and crow feathers also adorn the headdress.
These decorative ornaments suggest the
incredible spirit and power of this work.
The crow feathers attached to the beaded
cylinder represent death, as the crow not
only is the first beneficiary of the slain but
also is a bird associated with night. The
gathering of these diverse sacred materials
in this headdress would bring together the
combined forces of the universe to ensure
the well-being of the community, success
of the hunt, and protection of the hunters
from rival nations.

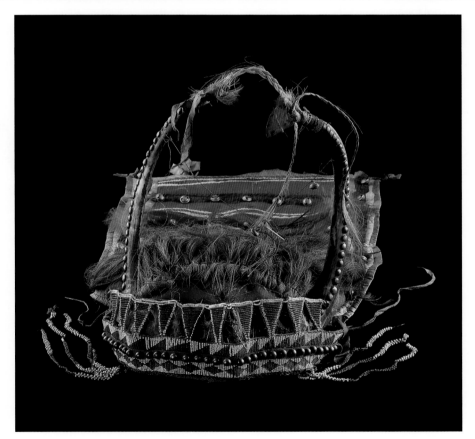

CURVED BOW

wood, animal tendon, and cotton
39⅛ × ¹¹⁄₁₆ × ¾ inches
The Spurlock Museum, University of Illinois at
Urbana-Champaign

Curved bows were used by hunters on horseback in the pursuit of bison. Cotton cloth running the entire length of the front of the bow was glued to the surface and lashed down by sinew. This was a common method for reinforcing the spring action of the weapon. Osage orange is a wood known for its incredible tensile strength, a quality particularly suitable for making bows, and for the way it retains its weight when dry. Interestingly, this bow lacks the end notches that usually hold the string. Instead, the string is secured with wrapped cotton cords. Hunters would aim for the flanks of the animals in order to make them limp and cause them to move in a circular pattern. This allowed the hunters on the ground to use longbows and war clubs to mortally wound the animal.

CAT. 36
QUIRT

ca. 1850
engraved elk antler with buffalo rawhide
13⅝₆ × 2½ × 1½ inches
The Detroit Institute of Arts, Founders Society Purchase with funds from Flint Ink Corporation,
Robert H. Tannahill Foundation Fund, and the Benson and Edith Ford Fund

The pointed end of a mature elk antler was used to make the handle of this quirt, or riding
whip. The pierced, interlaced rawhide thong is held in place by a brass upholstery tack.
Traces of red paint can be found on the fringe secured at the handle. At the base of the
grip is an empty hole, which is missing the loop that would be used for securing the quirt
around the wrist. The incised pictographic images tell the owner's personal stories that
involve two horses and two warriors. The larger horse at the center has an eagle feather
attached to its tail, a trade blanket on its back, and an image of a splayed figure on its flank.
Based on dress and hairstyle, the two warriors appear to be from different tribes. The top
figure seems to be leading, or perhaps stealing, the large horse.

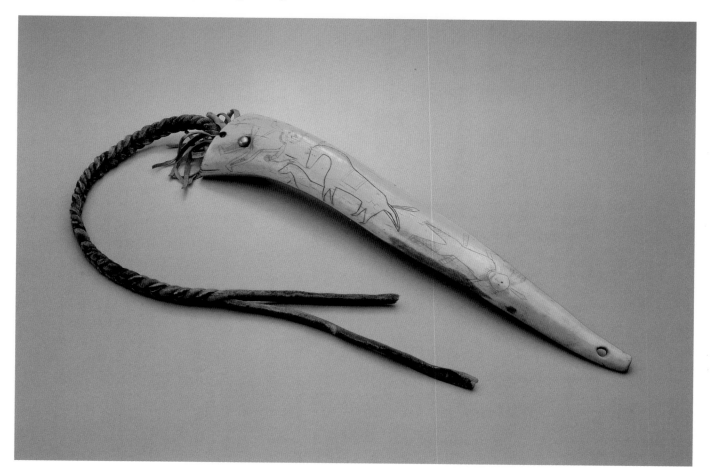

SPLIT-HORN HEADDRESS

ca. 1890
steer horn, horse hair, deer hair, wool, cotton, and hide
38 × 18 inches
Missouri Historical Society

This elaborate headdress is constructed of three main parts: the long red broadcloth covered with horsehair; the split horns of a steer; and the appliqué beaded band that would fit over the forehead of a dancer. The two yellow lozenges on the band might represent the eyes of the animal, but they might also refer to lightning and the sun. The tacks that decorate the split horns would reflect the sunlight and give the dancer a special radiance while he was praying for *Wakonta*'s blessings. Hourglass shapes are outlined by the white beads on the band, and they, in turn, frame dark blue bead lozenges. Seen over time, the foreground-background relationship reverses.

CAT. 38

HORSE REGALIA

buffalo hide, cloth, and beads
41¾ × 11¹³⁄₁₆ inches
Brooklyn Museum of Art, Museum Expedition 1911,
Museum Collection Fund

This ceremonial regalia from the early
twentieth century once decorated the hind
flanks of a horse. The ingenious use of red
broadcloth to enhance the design is superbly
executed. The red lozenge-shaped motif
may be related to female tattoo patterns
associated with lightning and other cosmic
entities, including stars and constellations,
clouds, and wind. A horse adorned with
this regalia would have been given away
at public ceremonies and festive occasions,
such as weddings, E-Lon-schka dances,
birthdays, and graduations. The thick
fringe would have swept by and touched
the horse's flanks, having a calming effect
on the young animal that had to endure the
many sights and sounds of the ceremony.

CAT. 39

BISON HEADDRESS

bison hide, horn, feathers, beads, and brass
28⅜ × 15¾ × 7⅞ inches
National Museum of the American Indian,
Smithsonian Institution

Unlike other headdresses of this kind, the
bison horns on this headdress face forward.
It is crowned on top with the feathers of
the red- and yellow-shafted flickers of the
woodpecker family; these types of feathers
are believed to be imbued with great power
and are still used by Osage people today.
Trailing down the back of the headdress
are feathers from the underside of an adult
golden eagle, along with two dyed red
plumes and one of natural color. The wing
feathers from the flicker are wrapped in
blue glass beads. The foundation of hide
and fur comes from the head of a bison.
Round beaded medallions with German
silver domes on the front of the headdress
represent the eyes of a bull bison. The
meaning of the design in the beaded front
section is not known.

PARFLECHE

hide, beads, and pigment
11⅝ × 8¹¹⁄₁₆ × ¹³⁄₁₆ inches
National Museum of the American Indian,
Smithsonian Institution

Osage people have used rawhide containers, or parfleches, to store precious items as well as everyday prepared foods, including dried meat, dried pumpkin strips, dried persimmons, and corn. After the hide has been scraped clean of all hair, membrane, and flesh, it is allowed to dry. Next, it is soaked in water, which softens the hide enough that it can be molded into a permanent form. Rawhide thongs are used to lace the parts of these very sturdy envelopes together. The term *parfleche* comes from the French *parer,* "to ward off," and *flêche,* "arrow." The colorful individual designs, usually geometric, are highly personalized to denote ownership. The designs on the sides have actually been split in half; the viewer uses the mind's eye to reassemble the parts. One unique feature of this parfleche is the beaded edge, which adds another aesthetic dimension to the work.

PAINTED BAG

hide and pigment
18¹¹⁄₁₆ × 28½ × 3¹⁵⁄₁₆ inches
National Museum of the American Indian, Smithsonian Institution

The shape and style of this painted bag were particularly well suited for storing scalps.
It was considered a vessel that contained portions of the victim's soul. Sturdy enough to
ward off arrows, these containers were sometimes carried into battle. The strikingly symmetrical design must have had a meaning and purpose that were best appreciated by the
owner. The addition of the long fringe underscores the importance of the painted bag as
a personal possession, serving to represent the hair of a vanquished enemy and to perform
the functional task of leading rainwater away from the seams.

PIPE BOWL WITH STEM

stone, wood, and pigment
stem: 20 1/16 × 7/8 × 7/8 inches
bowl: 8 × 2 1/2 × 17 inches
National Museum of the American Indian, Smithsonian Institution

The opposing bison hooves carved in relief in the center of the pipe stem suggest that this pipe may be from one of the Buffalo clans. The red on the painted hooves symbolizes life, since the bison itself is a designated life force. An overhead view of this type of pipe also refers to an ancient disc-platform pipe unique to the Osage. Dark edges on its stem indicate that it was passed through a flame during the consecration process. The T-shaped bowl is made of red catlinite, a hard, rocklike clay. Pipes such as this would be offered to hostile parties within the tribe in an attempt to make peace. If they refused to accept the pipe and all it represented, they would be banished forever.

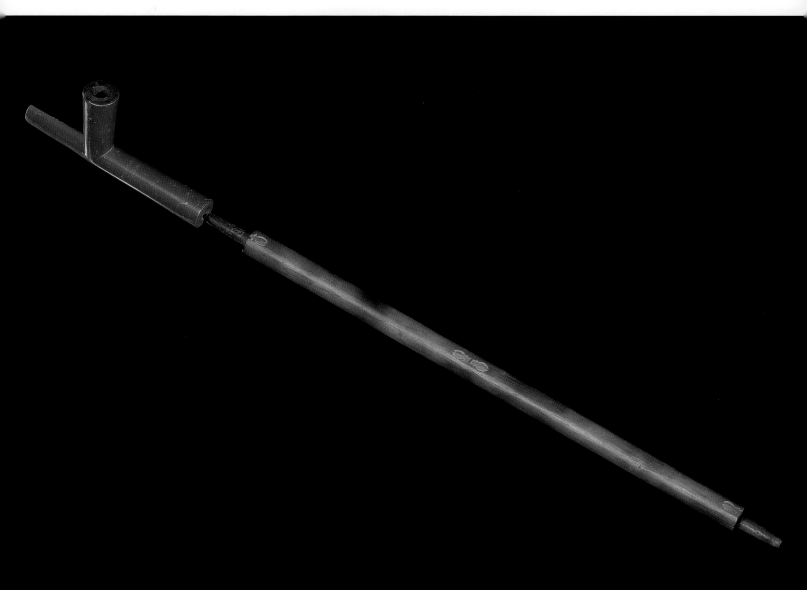

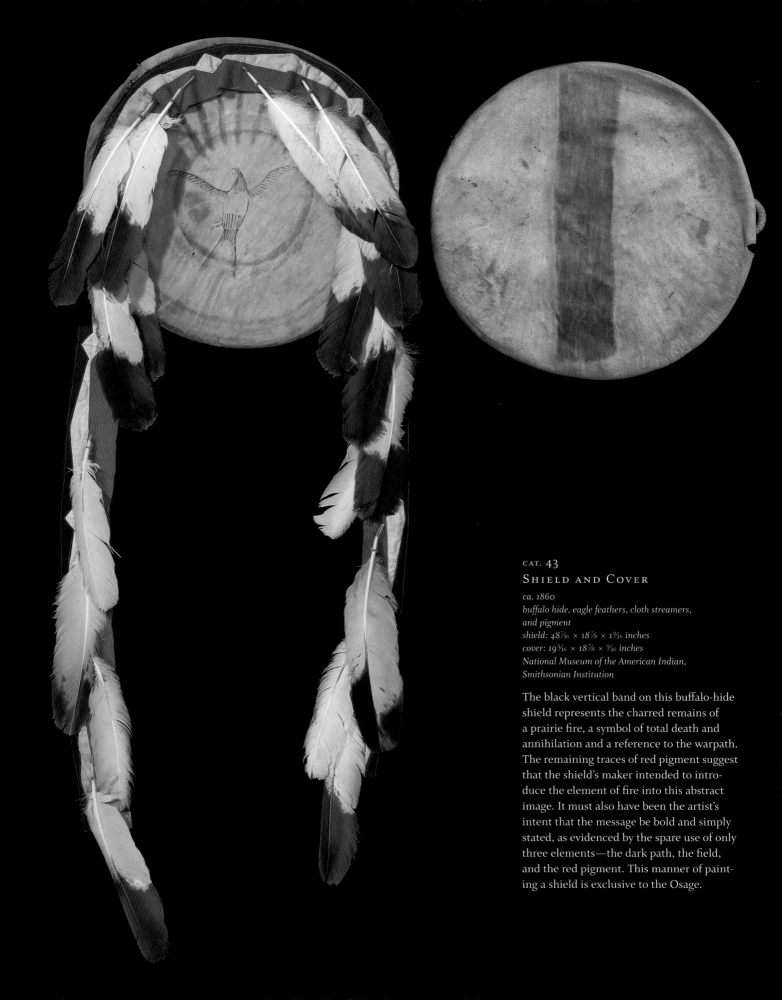

CAT. 43

SHIELD AND COVER

ca. 1860
buffalo hide, eagle feathers, cloth streamers,
and pigment
shield: 48⁷⁄₁₆ × 18⁷⁄₈ × 1⁹⁄₁₆ inches
cover: 19³⁄₁₆ × 18⁷⁄₈ × ⁹⁄₁₆ inches
National Museum of the American Indian,
Smithsonian Institution

The black vertical band on this buffalo-hide
shield represents the charred remains of
a prairie fire, a symbol of total death and
annihilation and a reference to the warpath.
The remaining traces of red pigment suggest
that the shield's maker intended to intro-
duce the element of fire into this abstract
image. It must also have been the artist's
intent that the message be bold and simply
stated, as evidenced by the spare use of only
three elements—the dark path, the field,
and the red pigment. This manner of painting a shield is exclusive to the Osage.

SHIELD

hide, eagle feathers, wool, brass, and pigment
42½ × 20¹⁄₁₆ × 1¹⁵⁄₁₆ inches
National Museum of the American Indian,
Smithsonian Institution

This shield features a soft yellow ground surrounded by a dark band. At its center is a group of concentric circles meant to emanate power. A warpath spreads out from the bottom of the outer circle. The central motif of a zigzag line suggests the destructive force of lightning. Both the cut yellow hawk feather suspended from the top of the shield and the bunch of purple hawk feathers attached to the bells in the middle represent war honors. The black and white feathers hanging from the outer band come from the lower wing section of a golden eagle.

CAT. 45
GUNSTOCK CLUB

wood, metal, feathers, and leather
33¹⁄₁₆ × 13¾ × ¹³⁄₁₆ inches
National Museum of the American Indian,
Smithsonian Institution

Clubs like this one were widely used among warring nations. The stylized crescent at the top represents the butt end of the rifle, thus the name "gunstock." A hand-forged steel blade was inserted into a slot and cushioned with a hide gasket. A fragment of hair at the top may have been the owner's share of a successful mourning party. Brass tack designs include the cross, symbolizing the evening star and the coming of night, and circles, which represent the moon. The red color of the club may be associated with the destructive force of lightning.

SHIELD

hide, feathers, cloth, metal, and pigment
diameter: 24 inches
Osage Tribal Museum

This war shield belonged to Chief Black Dog,
who met and was sketched by the American
artist George Catlin in 1834. Black Dog was
a hereditary chief, as opposed to one who
was elected. An arm loop and a smaller
finger loop on the back of his shield enabled
Black Dog to firmly grip his reins with one
hand while freeing the other for battle. The
feathers on the broadcloth flap below the
shield are from immature bald eagles, and a
crescent of golden-eagle feathers adorns the
front edge of the upper flap. Hawk feathers
hang from either end. Several smaller feathers, possibly from the wing of a woodpecker,
are attached to the center of the shield along
with a silver disc at its center. The loop at
the top of the cloth may once have held a
sacred object. While many interpretations
of the shield's painted surface have been
offered, the original intent of the paintings
was to strike fear in the heart of the enemy,
and in this regard, the shield could be said
to emanate the face of death itself.

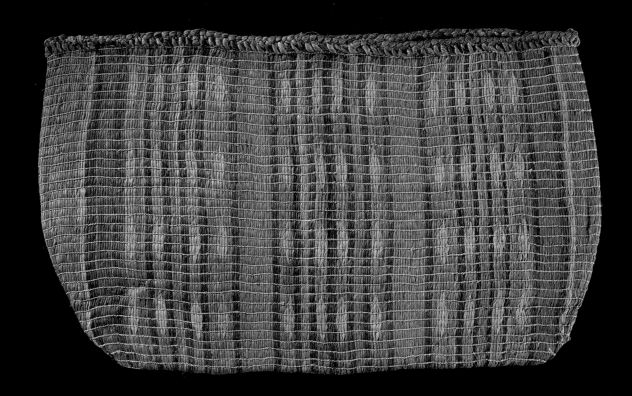

CAT. 47
FIBER FEAST BAG
wool, beads, and pigment
13¾ × 33¹⁄₁₆ × ¹³⁄₁₆ inches
National Museum of the American Indian,
Smithsonian Institution

CAT. 48
FIBER FEAST BAG
wool, beads, and pigment
18⅛ × 20¹¹⁄₁₆ × 1³⁄₁₆ inches
National Museum of the American Indian,
Smithsonian Institution

CAT. 49
FIBER FEAST BAG
wool, beads, and pigment
15¾ × 16⁹⁄₁₆ × ⅜ inches
National Museum of the American Indian,
Smithsonian Institution

CAT. 50
FIBER FEAST BAG
wool and pigment
19¹¹⁄₁₆ × 23¼ × ¹³⁄₁₆ inches
National Museum of the American Indian,
Smithsonian Institution

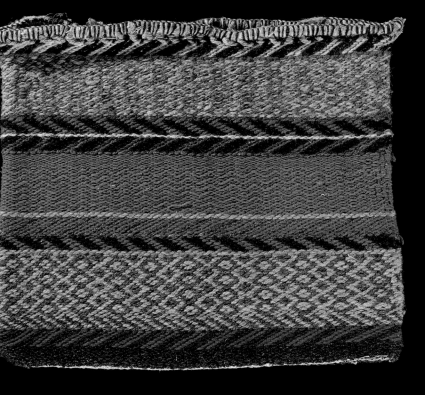

Only women who had been initiated
into the clan priesthood wove these kinds
of bags. The women owned looms made
from red oak poles that were stuck into
the ground. Warp spreaders made of Osage
orangewood were tied to the frame and
hung horizontally. The women sang ceremonial chants while weaving, which served
to infuse their work with sacred power. The
bags were intended to be vessels containing
the ritual fees paid by initiates seeking ad-
vancement in the priesthood. All twenty-
four of the Osage clans received fees that
included red-handled knives, brass kettles,
bison or buffalo fat for anointing sacred
objects, sinews, and ceremonial foods.

The shape of these bags represents a
pregnant bison. The symbolic tail is located
at the top end of each opening. Composi-
tionally, three of the bags are divided into
horizontal bands of various widths, each
of which presents a variation of a repeated
lightning pattern. The pattern and brillant
color combine to create an eye-dazzling
effect. The shimmering surface is meant
to transfer awesome regenerative powers
to the metaphorical bison.

CAT. 51

STANDARD

wool and owl, hawk, and eagle feathers
101⁹⁄₁₆ × 15¾ × 1³⁄₁₆ inches
National Museum of the American Indian,
Smithsonian Institution

A standard such as this one would be sup-
ported by a wooden pole and carried on
horseback by an officer of the hunt known
as the *Á-ki-da*. Acting like a policeman, the
officer carried out his duties of keeping
order among the bison hunters, prevent-
ing stampedes, resolving disputes of ownership, and enforcing the will of the chiefs.
The white tail feathers of the trumpeter
swan are a primary war symbol, as are
the feathers of the crow and golden eagle.
The full tail of a male great horned owl
at the top of the standard represents death
and destruction.

CAT. 52
PIPE

ca. 1850
wood and catlinite stone
3⅜ × 16⅛ × ⅞ inches
Roberta Campbell Lawson Collection, Gift of Mr. and Mrs. Edward C. Lawson,
Philbrook Museum of Art, Tulsa, Oklahoma

This pipe was made for personal rather than ritual use. It features a warrior with a roached-hair headdress seated in a saddle riding a horse. The swirling spiral motif of the stem may refer to lightning or the powerful force of a tornado. The edges of the spiral have been fire-engraved and decorated with incised striations. An image of an unidentified three-leaf plant has been incised at the base of the spiral. This pipe was purchased from a Cheyenne Indian in 1890 and later was acquired by the Philbrook Museum.

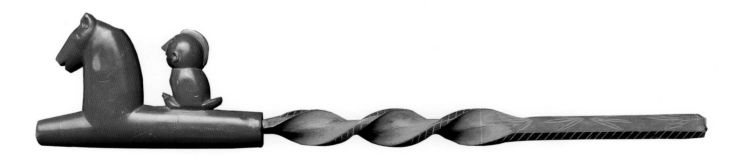

CAT. 53

SHIELD

ca. 1850–1870
buffalo hide, hair, feathers, golden eagle feather, and sinew
diameter: 19⅛ inches
Courtesy of Beloit College, Logan Museum of Anthropology, 31207.1

Osage shields were used exclusively in war. When not in use, they were stored on tripod stands or suspended at heights sufficient to protect them from the village dogs, which loved to gnaw on leather. Made from the right side of the hump of a male bison, this shield is even bullet resistant. The braided white hair may be from a white bison. A feather from a golden eagle is attached at its center, while the banded feathers from a horned owl hang above. It is believed that the golden eagle brought the Osage people down from the sky at the beginning of creation. The owl, on the other hand, hunts at night and is considered to be a harbinger of death. The black discs placed around the rim of the shield may refer to the death of enemies.

CAT. 54

CLUB

ca. 1883
wood, paint, iron, brass, hide, and glass beads
26 × 7⅞ × 2¾ inches
Linden-Museum Stuttgart

Hand-to-hand combat was central to traditional Osage warfare, and the warrior's
success depended on highly developed
skills, particularly those associated with
the war club. This club is in the shape of
a blue heron. The blade, ball, thorn growth
marks, and long handle represent the heron's beak, head, eyes, and neck and body,
respectively. As a stealthy hunter with great
vision, the heron embodies qualities suited
to Osage warfare. With its long, serrated
tail positioned on the top of the ball, the
image of the alligator snapping turtle further enhances the powers of the warrior
and his weapon. Known as the "pit bull"
of the turtle family, this animal has great
strength and a powerful snout that can
strike with lightning speed. The incised
triangles on the bottom edge of the weapon
are studded with tacks to symbolize a lightning bolt. The remarkable capabilities of
both animals combine to provide the warrior with the skills as well as the confidence
to overcome his enemy.

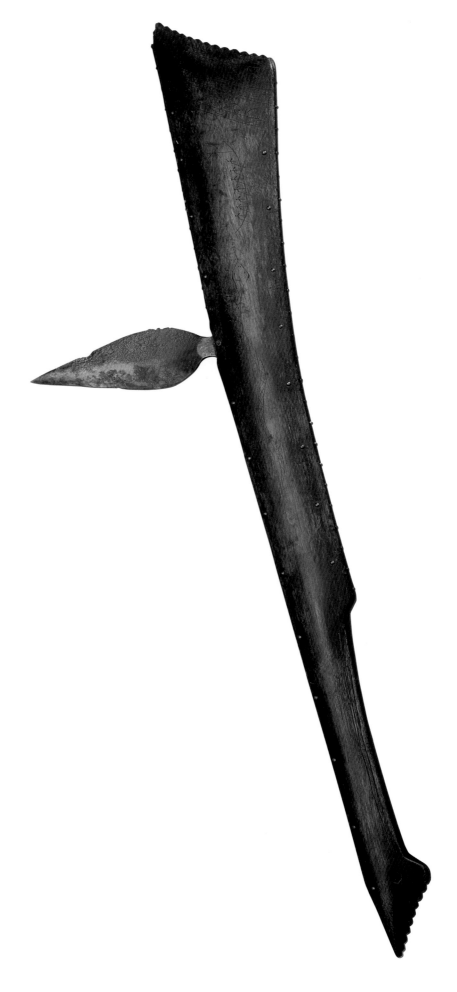

CAT. 55
Gunstock Club

ca. 1750–1775
wood and metal
24 × 7 inches
Collection of Mr. and Mrs. Timothy L. Drone,
Saint Louis, Missouri

This remarkable weapon was used in hand-to-hand combat. Although small, its weight and balance would have aided a veteran warrior to quickly dispatch an opponent. The lightning bolt design of the serrated edges at the top and bottom is symbolic of deadly speed. The designs on the weapon narrate a familiar scene in Osage life during the eighteenth and early nineteenth centuries. On one side of the weapon is a flat-bottom boat, a French pirogue, that could carry seven warriors, who propel the boat with poles. Placed on a stand at the front of the vessel is a calumet, a highly ornamented ceremonial pipe that conveys the peaceful nature of the journey. The diamondback rattlesnake on the same side suggests the ability of this party to strike a quick and lethal blow. The remainder of the story is told on the reverse by the arrow of death and three headless corpses. These victims were either fooled by the "peaceful" mission of the party or could not come to friendly terms with the emissaries. The much larger figure on top appears to be a mythical bird-man.

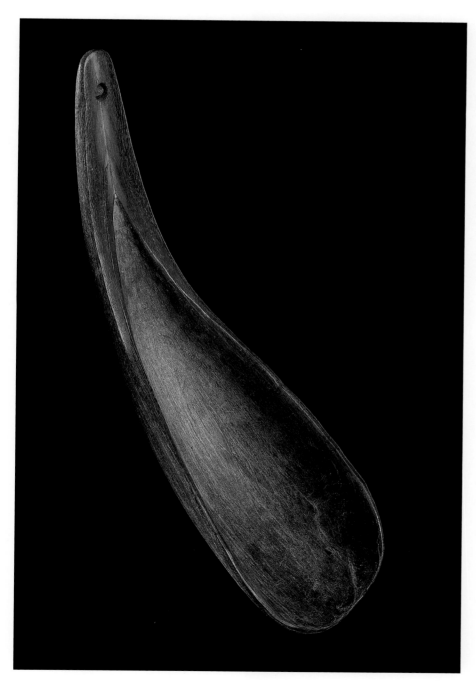

CAT. 56

BISON HORN SPOON

horn
6⅛ × 1¾ × 1/16 inches
National Museum of the American Indian,
Smithsonian Institution

Elegantly contoured, this is a rare example of a horn spoon made for personal use. Most spoons are much larger and were used as serving spoons. The burnished edges of the handle suggest that the spoon was used frequently. The simplicity of form and line is an Osage aesthetic. This small spoon is best appreciated when held, so that its functional balance and weight can be experienced.

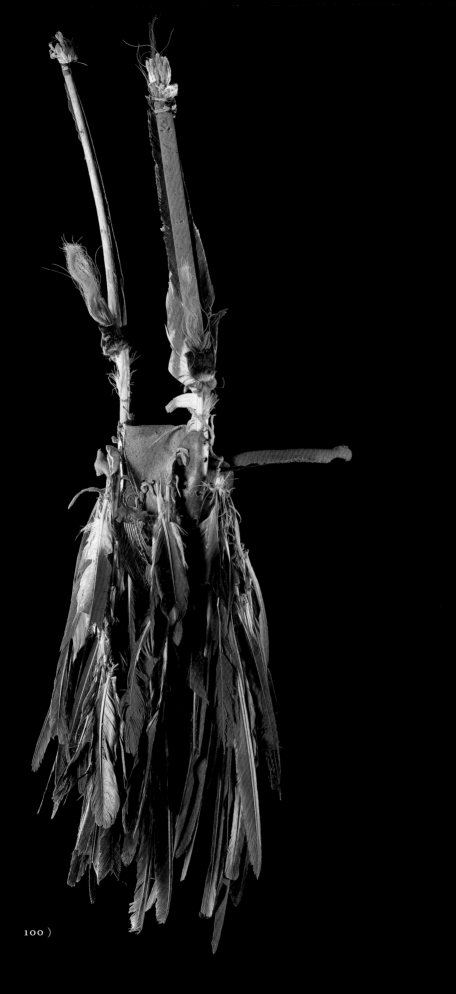

CAT. 57

STYLIZED SPLIT-HORN HEADDRESS

feathers, hide, painted wood, and brass
41¾ × 8¼ × 4¾ inches
National Museum of the American Indian,
Smithsonian Institution

This headdress is so stylized, it was once classified as a bustle. Dyed red horsehair tufts were used to attach the throat sections of male mallard ducks to the carved and painted wood horns. All the elements, including the horns, are attached to the fitted rawhide cap that fastened under the chin with a red broadcloth strip. Crow and eagle wing feathers radiate from the cap. The bell attached at the top has a dramatic and resonant tone.

CAT. 58
LANCE

wood, metal, otter fur, bear claw, glass beads, turkey feathers, owl feathers, and pigment
24½ × 61 × 1¾ inches
Missouri Historical Society

The materials used in making this lance show how dependent the Osage came to be on items of commercial trade. The iron blade, brass bells, and brass wire used to attach the golden-eagle tail feathers, as well as the red paint and metal buttons, were all products of trade. The painted Osage orangewood nodule at the opposite end of the blade resembles the head of a bear, while the otter tail near the base of the blade is probably a personal insignia. The bundle is made of painted otter fur, which was also used to wrap the shaft. The striped bundle of feathers comes from a great horned owl, a bird that symbolizes destruction.

CAT. 59
CHILD'S BLANKET
ca. 1850
cloth with embroidery and glass beads
42 × 42 inches
Osage Tribal Museum

This blanket once belonged to the grandson of Chief Nopapawalla, who was a chief of the
Little Osage during the 1850s. The human figure at the center of the blanket may represen
the symbolic man. He wears fringed leggings, a bone breastplate, armbands and bracelets,
a bead necklace, and earrings. His roached hair is adorned with an eagle feather. Flags on
either side of the figure may represent the grand division of the tribe, namely peace and
war, or sky and earth. The five- and six-pointed stars on the flags may refer to the morning
and the evening stars, respectively, and, in a broader sense, life and death. The horse with
a feedbag on its mouth above the figure is a symbol of prosperity. Above the horse, a cedar
tree, which stands for everlasting life, is depicted with a bird on top; flanking the sides of
the tree are two stylized fleurs-de-lis. Images of sacred plants decorate the corners of the
blanket, and ribbon work patterns of lightning bolts frame this cosmological scene.

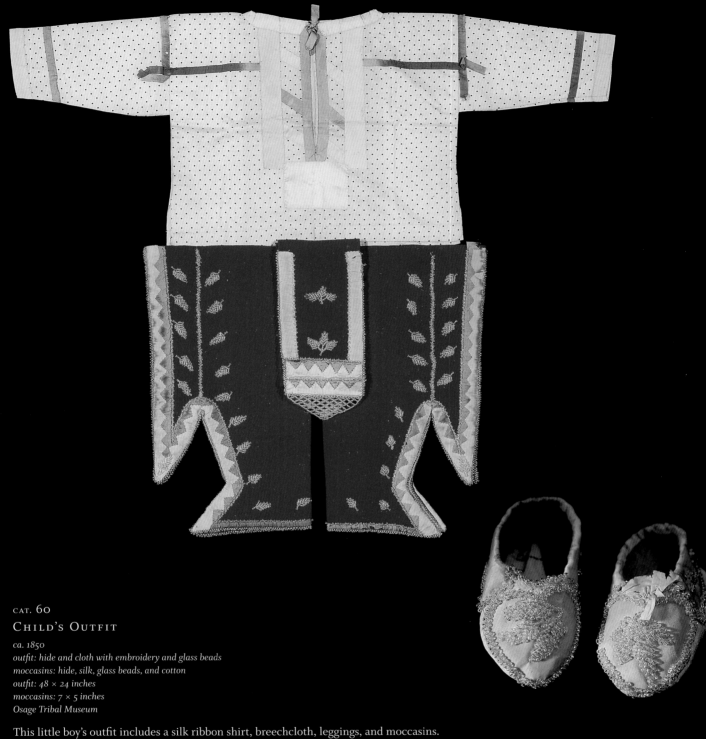

CAT. 60

CHILD'S OUTFIT

ca. 1850
outfit: hide and cloth with embroidery and glass beads
moccasins: hide, silk, glass beads, and cotton
outfit: 48 × 24 inches
moccasins: 7 × 5 inches
Osage Tribal Museum

This little boy's outfit includes a silk ribbon shirt, breechcloth, leggings, and moccasins.
The blanket on the facing page (cat. 59) was made for the same child and beaded by the
same hand. The ribbons placed diagonally across the front yoke of the shirt present a
unique fashion statement among the Osage. The edge of the shirt has a remarkable translucent bead netting on the breechcloth. Floral motifs surrounded by hearts on fields of
silk decorate the moccasins. The artistic attention devoted to this child's outfit speaks
to the importance of a male heir in the family.

CAT. 61

WOMAN DOLL

ca. 1850
cloth, ceramic, wood, and metal
height: 17 inches
Osage Tribal Museum

Wearing ritual dress typical of the late nineteenth century, this doll is clothed in short
leggings that were tied above the knee. The
ribbon-work strip on the doll's skirt is on
the left side, which is a unique feature of
Osage female dress even today. German
silver brooches hold the shirt closed. The
white discoloration on the skirt was caused
by clips that held the wool during the dye-
ing process. The dramatic tension in the
doll's appearance results from the combination of a young girl's figure with the face
of a wise and older woman.

CAT. 62

MAN DOLL

ca. 1850
wood, cloth, metal, bone, and feathers
height: 22 inches
Osage Tribal Museum

This powerfully rendered male figure with
an ominous expression was actually an
Osage girl's play doll. But it was also useful
as a tool to teach children the proper order
of dress for an adult male. The hairstyle indicates a particular clan affiliation, and the
pattern on the ribbon-work strip attached
to the flaps of the leggings signifies a specific family. The intricately fashioned breastplate replicates a piece of armor from earlier
times. However, the porcelain hands of this
late-nineteenth-century doll were taken
from a commercially made European doll.

CAT. 63

TOY CRADLEBOARD

wood and cloth with yarn, beads, bells, brass tacks, and paint
12 × 4 inches
Osage Tribal Museum

The little girl who played with this cradleboard most likely placed a baby doll in it as she imitated her mother and other female relatives. It is a complete cradleboard with all the elements, including the bow and cover, chest ties, bedding, a foot stop, and bells to entertain and calm an infant. The swastika motif at the top of the board may represent an eagle or the overhead view of a tornado and refers to clan affiliation.

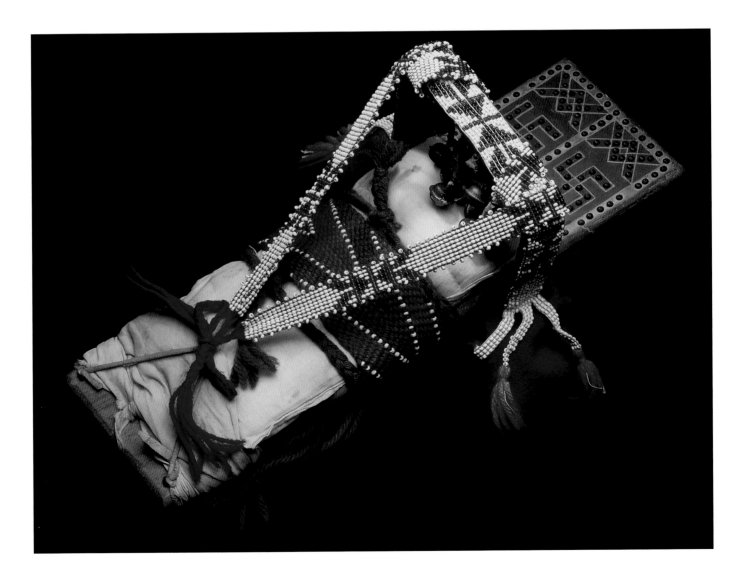

CAT. 64

TURTLE TOY

ca. 1937
turtle shell, cloth, and metal
5 × 6 inches
Osage Tribal Museum

This pull toy features the box turtle or land terrapin shell commonly found in Osage County. Figures of a mother and child are seated on a bedroll on top of the shell. As a child pulled the toy, the curvature of the shell caused a rocking motion. The toy was originally owned by Mr. and Mrs. Paul Pitts and acquired by the Osage Tribal Museum in 1947. The Osage Tribal Museum, the very first tribal museum in the United States, opened in 1938.

*Moon Head said that our father Wakonta talked to him. . . . Moon Head said that our Father and Mother
are in heaven. The Father would love and pity us as he wants us to pity one another in this world. . . .
Moon Head said that he would go to be with Wakonta and he would be there when we came to join him.
We must change our lives for better lives. We are pitiful people and we should not be proud, but live simple
and humble lives. If you want to see the Father and be with him, we must change to a Christian life.
Someday we would be with him in Wakonta's land. —Humpahtokah, ca. 1949*

The only extant, first-person account of the origin of the Peyote Religion among the Osage people is provided by Humpahtokah, daughter of the Osage leader and prophet Watianka. Born in 1856, she was forty-two years old when she witnessed Moon Head's introduction of Peyotism to the Osage people. The story of Osage Peyotism tells of the structural change that facilitated spiritual continuity amid the disruptions and dislocations the Osages experienced at the close of the nineteenth century.

Peyote (*Lophophora williamsii*) is a small, spineless cactus that has been an important component of the pharmacopoeias of native peoples of the Western Hemisphere for thousands of years. In Mexico, peyote played an important role in the social and ceremonial lives of many Indian communities. North of the Rio Grande, the Lipan Apache, Carrizzo, Tonkawa, Karankawa, Mescalero Apache, and various Caddoan groups all knew of peyote and used it as a spiritual and physical medicine. In the 1870s, a new religious movement emerged on the southern plains that focused on the ritual consumption of peyote. A number of the elements in the modern Peyote Religion of the nineteenth century were present in earlier Mexican ceremonies, including the use of drums and rattles, cornhusk cigarettes, a ritual fire, ceremonial foods, and, most important, peyote as a sacrament.[1]

By 1880 the ceremonial structure, ritual instruments, and core theology of Peyotism became more uniform and the religion spread to tribes within present-day Oklahoma. The growth of Peyotism was influenced by the development of a trade system that ensured a dependable and affordable supply of peyote, increased knowledge of English as a common language, new forms of intertribal contact through prisoner of war camps and boarding schools, and increased exposure to Christianity.[2] By 1900 the Peyote Religion had spread to the majority of Oklahoma tribes, greatly facilitated by long-standing patterns of intertribal visiting and intermarriage. And by the 1930s, the Peyote Religion had spread from its birthplace in Oklahoma to surrounding states, northward through the plains into Canada, and to footholds in the more conservative Southwest.

The ceremonies of the modern Peyote Religion, which are called "meetings," generally consist of the following

FIGURE 4.1 Peyote plant in bloom, Starr County, Texas, 1998. Courtesy Daniel C. Swan.

elements: an all-night ceremony; the use of peyote as a holy sacrament; an earthen, crescent-shaped altar; a ritually maintained fire; and rounds of individual singing. The ceremony, its officials, and its ritual instruments have remained amazingly consistent over both time and space. Although there is some opportunity to accommodate local customs and practices, the basic structure and content of the religious service are remarkably similar throughout North America.

Big Moon Peyotism

In the seventeenth century, Caddo Indians were settled in villages along the eastern fringe of the southern plains, adjacent to the natural habitat of peyote in the Rio Grande Valley of south Texas and the northern plains of Mexico, and their use of peyote in the ceremonial dancing of harvest celebrations is well documented as early as the eighteenth century.[3] The Caddo have been identified as the major innovators of the Peyote ceremony. This tradition of innovation is best seen in the

expansion of the ritual altar, including an elongation of the arms of the crescent altar, the addition of a small circular mound to the east of the crescent, a line connecting the tips, another line from the mound to the crescent, and a heart where the two lines intersect.

John Wilson, a Caddo-Delaware Indian with some French ancestry, is the individual most associated with continued changes in the altar and ceremony of the Peyote Religion. Wilson, also known as Moon Head, seems to have been a religious specialist for much of his adult life, participating in traditional Delaware ceremonialism, shamanistic doctoring, and prophecy, and he was an early leader of the Ghost Dance movement in Oklahoma.[4] Wilson claimed to have received instructions for his Big Moon and its associated ceremony

FIGURE 4.2 John Wilson. Courtesy University of Oklahoma Library, Western History Collections, Phillips Collection.

FIGURE 4.3 Osage Big Moon altar, Pawhuska, Oklahoma. Photo by Chaz Vandiver; courtesy Andrew Gray.

FIGURE 4.4 Osage church house. Courtesy Smithsonian Institution, National Anthropological Archives.

through divine revelation. He is credited with coining the phrases "Big Moon" and "Little Moon" to distinguish his Peyote altar and ceremony from those of the more standard form used by the Kiowa and Comanche. Wilson also learned from peyote the duties of the officers and the rules necessary to conduct the religious service, a code of moral teachings, exact instructions for the construction and symbolism of the ritual equipment, and a number of the songs used in the ceremony. Following his revelation, Wilson immediately set out to find converts to his variant of the Peyote Religion.[5]

The Big Moon altar has a sunken area for the fire that is surrounded by an apron approximately two feet wide. Most Osage altars are approximately eight feet wide and ten feet long. Hearts are drawn at the head of the altar, at the point where the Peyote Road intersects the Cross Roads, and on the small mound at the end of the altar. The time and effort necessary to construct a Big Moon altar led to the use of more durable construction materials, such as commercial concrete instead of pond clay and soil. In some cases, a wood-frame octagonal "church house" was constructed over the altar, replacing the

tepee as the place of worship and providing protection from the elements that might erode the altar.

Osage Society and the Adoption of Peyotism

In the 1880s, the Osage people were living in residence bands (a term for social units that reside together) scattered throughout their Oklahoma Reservation. The bands were geographically clustered into the five traditional physical divisions of the tribe. Relative to their Native American neighbors, the Osage were politically advantaged, having purchased their reservation with the proceeds from the sale of their former reservation in Kansas. Osage economy revolved around quarterly per-capita payments from interest on the tribe's considerable government trust account and revenues from the leasing of grazing rights to the rich pastures of the reservation. Additional income was available through farming and ranching. The majority of tribal members continued a communal lifestyle and augmented their household economies with hunting, gathering, and gardening. Despite relative affluence, the Osage community faced serious challenges to its social order and spiritual direction; both were precious tenets of Osage society that had always been reinforced by the theology of the Osage Tribal Religion.

In the 1880s, Osage religious leaders were confronted with additional evidence that the structure and ideology of the Osage Tribal Religion held little relevance to the material and social conditions around them. Rapid population decline in the eighteenth and nineteenth centuries compounded the situation so that a number of clans faced ceremonial extinction: their number of initiated elders and native speakers had been dramatically reduced in a short period of time, and it was difficult to motivate individuals to dedicate the time and energy necessary to memorize the complex narratives associated with the tribal ceremonies. This combination of factors created a situation in which it became impossible to observe the ceremonial division of labor dictated by the teachings of the Osage Tribal Religion, and the religious content was omitted or reduced so that the ceremonies of the Osage Tribal Religion became increasingly secularized.[6]

These conditions, compounded by the ready availability of liquor, created a crisis in Osage society in the

1890s. With the traditional mechanisms for social and moral conduct no longer effective, it was a time of disintegration and disruption. The Osage people were living in material comfort but spiritual confusion.[7] Into this situation, John Wilson brought the "teachings" that Humpahtoka and her contemporaries came to view as divinely inspired intervention in the lives of the Osage people.

A History of Osage Peyotism

John Wilson became active in the Osage community in 1897–1898, having already established his Big Moon among the Delaware and Quapaw communities in northeastern Oklahoma. A small band of Quapaw led by Tall Chief assumed residence in the southeastern region of the Osage Reservation in 1874. Tall Chief and many other Quapaw people intermarried with the Osage and remained in their settlements near the modern-day town of Skiatook, Oklahoma. The Osage gained their first exposure to the Wilson Big Moon at Tall Chief's and soon wanted to establish the new religion in their home bands.

The first Big Moon altar established by John Wilson among the Osage was at the camp of Francis Claremore, east of the present-day town of Hominy, Oklahoma. Wilson's early meetings there generated tremendous excitement and enthusiasm among the Osage. As news of Wilson's activities spread throughout the reservation, different bands of Osage traveled to Claremore's camp to observe Wilson and his religion.

The decision to adopt Peyotism involved a large segment of the community, who decided en masse to turn away from the practice of the Tribal Religion and follow John Wilson's Big Moon Peyote Religion. The Osage provide a rare instance in which the decision to adopt Peyotism was conducted at the community level. The arrival of John Wilson as a missionary of Big Moon Peyotism provided the Osage religious leaders with both the opportunity and the means to effect a radical reorganization of Osage religious practice while preserving its ancient ideological foundation. Osage history is replete with stories of the various "tests" of Wilson and his claim that he was a messenger of the word of God. Modern Peyotists have great faith in the truthfulness

of Wilson's message and in their ancestors' decision to embrace it as such.[8]

It was customary for John Wilson to supervise the construction of Big Moon altars and to either create or arrange for the construction of the ritual instruments used in the ceremony. He would then conduct a series of meetings at the new altar to facilitate their consecration and to instruct and commission the new Roadman with the authority to lead religious services (see "Osage Peyote Ceremonies" later in this chapter). A series of negotiations took place between John Wilson and the Osage leaders regarding certain aspects of the Big Moon ceremony and the altar. Among the most stringent of Wilson's requirements was the complete cessation of any practice of the ceremonies of the Osage Tribal Religion following conversion to Big Moon Peyotism. With the guidance of the remaining leaders from the Osage Tribal Religion, the first generation of Osage Peyotists abandoned their previous religious activities abruptly and completely. This prohibition was so strong that even discussion of the Tribal Religion was discouraged in the households of Osage Peyotists, and all attempts to learn anything of the "old ways" were sharply rebuked.[9]

The negotiation of the form and structure that Big Moon Peyotism would assume among the Osage was more flexible. The most important development to result from this process was the introduction of a "West Moon" altar. In the Little Moon form of the religion and in the majority of Big Moon churches, the opening of the altar faces east, with the Roadman sitting at the head of the altar in the west. In the West Moon variant, the leader's position is in the east, with the altar opening to the west. Contemporary Osage Peyotists generally acknowledge Chief Black Dog as the originator of the West Moon altar.[10]

Contemporary Osage Peyotists continue the tradition of philosophical and historical discourse, and they devote considerable dialogue to the decision of their ancestors to adopt Big Moon Peyotism. Much of this dialogue focuses on both the impact that John Wilson had on the Osage leaders of the day and the rapid abandonment of their prior religious activities. Osage oral tradition embraces the conclusion that Big Moon Peyotism provided both the catalyst and the theological charter for the major reorganization of Osage society.

FIGURE 4.5 Chief Black Dog. Courtesy Gilcrease Museum.

FIGURE 4.6 Black Dog West Moon altar. Courtesy Daniel C. Swan.

The sun was a major symbol in the cosmology of the Osage people. The endless cycle of the sun came to represent the never-ending life of the Osage people. The association of the setting sun with death and as a symbol of the journey of the spirit to the Creator's realm was at the heart of the funeral ceremony of the Osage Tribal Religion.[11] If, however, the Osage were to follow the Peyote Road to heaven, it would have to be a westward journey. In addition, a case can be made that the traditional pattern of ceremonial settings in the Osage Tribal Religion was for the door of the ceremonial lodge to face west, with the position of honor being in the back of the lodge, to the east. The West Moon altar represents continuity between traditional Osage ceremonial practice and Big Moon Peyotism.

Following the establishment of the West Moon in Black Dog's camp south of the current town of Hominy, Oklahoma, the people of Claremore's band determined that they also would like to adopt the Wilson Big Moon. The altar that Wilson built for Claremore was a West Big Moon of the same design as that of Black Dog, to symbolize the equal status of the two chiefs. John Wilson established an additional Big Moon for Brave at his camp near the modern community of Barnsdall, Oklahoma. This church was located on Bird Creek, fifteen miles below the Osage Agency in Pawhuska. The Osage living in this camp represented the remnants of the Heart-Stays Osage, one of the original five villages of the tribe, which was later incorporated with the Thorny Thicket people to form the Pawhuska District. The scant oral tradition available on Brave's altar states that it was an East Moon altar of the standard Wilson design. Thus, John Wilson's mission among the Osage involved the establishment of East Big Moons for Francis Claremore and Brave and West Big Moons for Chiefs Black Dog and Claremore.

Wilson is reported to have stayed among the Osage for a considerable time and to have returned later to attend and conduct additional religious services. He was killed in April 1901, when a train hit his wagon as he was returning to the Caddo Reservation after conducting religious services among the Quapaw. While Wilson suffered considerable criticism and questions about his character in many Oklahoma tribal communities, he continues to receive great respect among Osage Peyotists. Among the Osage, it was customary to hang a portrait of Wilson

FIGURE 4.7 Moon Head pin. Courtesy E. Sean StandingBear.

FIGURE 4.8 Victor Griffin. Courtesy Smithsonian Institution, National Anthropological Archives.

in their church houses, and many had portrait pins produced with his image that today are cherished heirlooms. The Lookout Church east of Pawhuska continues a long-standing tradition of holding a memorial meeting for Moon Head on April 15 each year.

As the Osage prepared for the allotment of their reservation in 1907 (see Chapter 5, The Richest People in the World), there were fourteen active Big Moon altars among the remaining divisions of the tribe. Virtually all the Osage people from the Hominy District were active Peyotists by that time, as were the residents of the "Peyote camps" scattered throughout the reservation. The number of Osage people who continued to follow the traditional Tribal Religion was waning, even in the stronghold of the Gray Horse Village, where traditional mourning dances continued as late as 1919. In the following decade, the Osage Peyote Religion flourished, additional altars were established, and the majority of tribal members were congregants.

The most important figure in the continued growth of Osage Peyotism was Victor Griffin, one of the first converts among the Quapaw to Big Moon Peyotism when John Wilson visited their reservation near Miami, Oklahoma, in 1894. Griffin was sixteen years old when Wilson visited the Quapaw in 1894, and he was only twenty-nine when he emerged in 1906–7 with a Big Moon variant of his own design and a dedicated following among the Quapaw, Delaware, and Seneca tribes. Nowhere else did he receive the respect and adulation that he experienced among Osage people, with whom he developed a close and enduring relationship that spanned fifty years. Griffin's impact as a Peyote missionary among the Osage is significant, evident in the fact that he established more Big Moon Peyote altars among the Osage than did any other individual.[12]

Osage church houses constructed in the 1920s tended to reflect the relative wealth of the Osage during this period, when they leased the mineral rights of the tribe. Churches constructed during this period were generally larger, and a framed vestibule extending from the front of the basic octagonal structure was a common architectural feature. Osage Peyotists focused their wealth on expressions of religious devotion, including stained-glass windows, cut-glass chandeliers, and marble statuary that can been seen in their churches and associated cemeteries.

FIGURE 4.9 Morrell church house, Hominy, Oklahoma. Courtesy Daniel C. Swan.

After World War II, the elders of the Osage Peyote Religion relaxed some of the strict rules associated with the religious ceremonies in order to encourage survival of the church in the "modern age." The declining number of active churches and worshipers raised concern that the religion might not continue to be available for the benefit of the Osage people. Younger members and future leaders were encouraged to cling to the church by holding at least two meetings per year, one in the spring and the other in the fall. This pattern is in contrast to the previous system of sponsoring a meeting for each significant event in the lives of the congregation. In the last half of the twentieth century, numerous pieces of "church business" were addressed at these meetings, including sympathizing with mourners, naming of children, and praying for spiritual guidance and direction. By the 1950s, the first generation of Osage Peyotists was almost completely gone and leadership of the church had been almost completely transferred to their children and grandchildren.[13]

The final quarter of the twentieth century saw a revitalization of Osage Peyotism, marked by the rededication of inactive churches and the establishment of new Big Moon altars, events that had not taken place since the 1940s. As they have in the past, elder males, with the consult and support of their female relatives, took it upon themselves to adapt Osage philosophy and ritual practice to the physical realities of modern life. By the late 1970s and '80s, there was an increase in the number of younger Osage men and women interested in the Peyote Religion, and active participation in the Osage churches expanded significantly.

Osage Peyote Ceremonies

The basic ceremony of Big Moon Peyotism shares many elements and features with those found in the more widespread Little Moon ceremony. Their common foundation includes an all-night ceremony largely composed of rounds of individual singing, a fire that is maintained according to ritual procedures, the central authority of the Roadman, and, most important, the consumption of peyote as a holy sacrament. The ceremonies of the Osage Peyote Religion conform to the general pattern found in Big Moon Peyotism. The service is led by the Roadman, whose title refers to his seat at the west terminus of the Peyote Road, rendered as a line on the altar. Among the Osage, Roadmen are generally identified with specific churches, at which they are the current leaders. If a Roadman conducts a religious service at an altar that does not currently have its own Roadman, the ritual instruments and ceremonial pattern belonging to the altar are used, rather than those of the visiting Roadman.

The Roadman is assisted by a Drum Chief and a Tobacco Man (also called a Tea Boss), who sit at the head of the altar on his right and left, respectively. Other ceremonial officers include the two Cross Roads Men, who sit at the north and the south terminus of a line that runs perpendicular to the altar's Peyote Road. The Cross Roads Men are usually elders, often visiting Roadmen, who assist in keeping order during the ceremony. Among the Osage there are three Firemen, whose ranked positions are referred to in descending numbers, with the

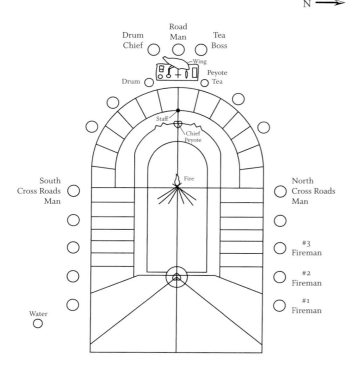

FIGURE 4.10 Ceremonial arrangement for the Victor Griffin altar. Illustrated by Bobby C. Martin and Gregory D. Carmack. Courtesy of Daniel C. Swan.

First Fireman possessing considerable authority in Osage Peyote ceremonies. The Firemen are responsible for the ritual maintenance of the fire and engage in a wide range of activities that include fanning participants as they enter the church house, drumming for an entire round of singing, distributing drinking water, and seeing to other needs of the congregation.

Under the Roadman's guidance, the members of a congregation undertake a series of practical and ritual preparations in the days preceding a religious service: they prepare sufficient supplies of seasoned firewood; they clean the church house and grounds; they make repairs to the altar; and they carry out other regular maintenance tasks before the meeting. The Roadman and the sponsors of the meeting expend considerable effort to secure the groceries, cooking equipment, and table service for the meals that will be prepared, consumed, and cleaned up after during the course of the service.

On the day before the service, the congregation assembles at dawn to participate in a ritual sweat-lodge ceremony to purify them before consuming the holy sacrament, peyote. The sweat is conducted in a domed structure constructed of a frame of saplings over which a canvas cover is placed. Heated rocks are placed in a pit in the center of the lodge and a small amount of water is poured over them to produce steam. Teas brewed from a variety of plants are drunk during the ceremony as emetic and diuretic agents. The ceremony concludes with a breakfast meal.

The Roadman and his assistants gather at dawn on the day of the service to assemble the ritual instruments and to participate in ceremonial singing and prayer. Before noon they retire to the church house to light the fire and place the ritual objects in their prescribed locations. In Big Moon Peyotism, the staff is placed in a hole in the altar immediately behind the Chief Peyote, which is a large, dried peyote plant placed on a beaded platform. The participants from the morning service gather for a noon meal, and the Firemen and other younger males maintain the fire throughout the afternoon.

Following an evening meal for participants, relatives, and invited friends, the religious service begins shortly after sunset. The participants enter the church and are assigned a seat by the Roadman, who begins the service by offering to all in attendance a welcome in which he states the purpose of the meeting. The Roadman initiates the ceremony itself with a prayer as he smokes a ritual cigarette of tobacco rolled in a cornhusk wrapper. After the prayer is offered, a bunch of fresh sage and the sacramental peyote are passed to the participants. The Roadman sings a set of four prescribed "starting songs" attributed to John Wilson's divine revelation. Next the Drum Chief sings, followed by the Tea Boss.

As the ceremony progresses, each Fireman takes a turn drumming a complete round, while another tends the fire and keeps the altar swept clean. At the end of each round of drumming, the Roadman prays for the Fireman and fans him with his eagle-wing fan. The staff is placed in its standing position, and the Fireman moves to the center of the altar, between the fire and the small raised mound, facing the staff. The participants then "fan him off," each offering words of respect and encouragement.

At midnight, the Roadman offers a prayer for the participants with another ritual cigarette. The ceremony continues in this manner throughout the night, with the Roadman offering inspirational talks, additional prayers, and explanations of the history and meaning of the religion between rounds of singing.

If the all-night service ends with a perfectly clear and cloudless morning, a ceremony called "greeting the sun" is observed. This consists of the Roadman, the Drum Chief, and the Tobacco Boss taking the ritual objects outside, where they form a north-south line, facing east. With the other participants gathered in a line behind him, the Roadman offers a prayer that concludes with the ritual objects being raised to the rising sun, as all the other participants raise their arms and open their hands to the east. This ceremony is a direct link to a more ancient practice that was a part of daily life for the Osage people. Accounts from the early nineteenth century recount the prayers offered at dawn each morning as the people gathered to greet the rising sun and to thank *Wakonta* for another day of life.[14]

The ritual singing and drumming resume, continuing until shortly before noon, when the participants file outside to wash, assisted by the Firemen. In some congregations, the Roadman sings the "Dinner Songs" that serve as the formal closing, or "quitting," of the ceremony. The fire is smothered, the altar is swept clean, and dried cedar needles are placed on the hearth at the center of the altar and in the coal mounds. The participants then cleanse themselves in the cedar smoke.

The occasion of a Peyote meeting is a community event that extends beyond the ritual and its participants. This is achieved largely through the noon meal at the conclusion of the services, when the participants are joined by their relatives, the extended families of the sponsors of the meeting, and members of the greater community who have been invited to the dinner. The status of those who participated in the religious service is recognized by their seating at a separate table. The purpose of the meeting is explained and a prayer is

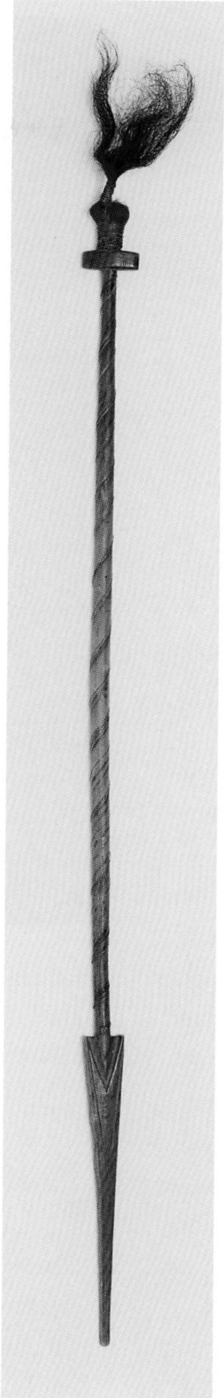

FIGURE 4.11 Big Moon peyote staff of Chief Black Dog, ca. 1898. Osage County, Oklahoma. Photo by Shane Culpepper; courtesy William Fletcher.

offered. These "Peyote Dinners," as they are referred to in the Osage community, feature both traditional and non-traditional foods, including corn soup, hominy, meat gravy, fry bread, meat pies, pork steam-fry, squash, chicken and dumplings, turkey and dressing, salads, fresh fruit, pies, and cakes.

Ritual Instruments

Ritual instruments used in Osage Peyote services are sacred objects. They are associated with a particular altar and ideally are passed down through successive Roadmen. Osage Peyotism utilizes more numerous and complex ritual instruments than those associated with Little Moon Peyotism. Roadmen of Big Moon Peyote often require several suitcases, sometimes even a large footlocker, to store the materials associated with their respective churches.

The core inventory of the ritual instruments used in the Osage Peyote Religion include a Chief Peyote, the staff, a gourd rattle, an eagle-wing fan, several single eagle feathers, an altar cloth, a crucifix, a drum, and drumsticks. The religious service also incorporates a number of plants: dried and cleaned cedar leaves (*Juniperus virginiana*), cornhusk cigarette wrappers (*Zea mays*), tobacco (*Nicotiana tabacum*), and sage (*Artemisia vulgaris*).[15] Cedar is stored in a variety of bags and containers, but the most preferable are finger-woven bags that incorporate traditional Osage patterns and designs (cat. 75).

Osage staffs are approximately forty-eight inches long and have a four-sided arrow point carved at the base (see figure 4.11). An incised line extends from the base of the arrow point to the top of the staff. The staff is called "arrow" in the Osage language, a gesture of respect for its importance in hunting and warfare.

The staff represents the power and will of God as a weapon against sin and evil, and the custom of placing the staff in the hole in the altar symbolizes the way in which Moon Head "made God's word stand up on this earth."[16]

Osage staffs incorporate a headdress of dyed hawk and eagle feathers that is attached to the top of the staff. Additional decorations include an opossum hide that is backed with cloth and edged with small brass bells, strips of otter fur, wide ribbons, feather ornaments, buttons from religious and fraternal organizations, crucifixes, photographs placed in lockets and pins, and other jewelry. The staff is said to represent Christ dressed as an Indian with the feathered headdress, otter-wrapped braids, and distinctive "scalp feather" ornament similar to those worn in the E-Lon-schka dance (see Chapter 6, Osage Dancing Societies and Organizations). Several elders of the religion make reference to the fact that the movement of the staff around the ritual circle represents the word and power of Christ as he traveled over the land.[17]

Many believe that the staff itself should be made from the wood of a fruit-bearing tree to symbolize regeneration, rebirth, and prosperity. The otter and opossum hides also have interpretive meaning for the Osage. Long respected for its industry, swiftness in movement, and dedication to its family, the otter has held a prominent position in Osage folklore, religion, and material culture. Otter hides are associated with healing and protection and have been used in Osage society to distinguish leaders and religious specialists. John Wilson is credited with adding the opossum hide on the Big Moon staff. The opossum is even more respected by the Osage people for its ability to feign death and, as the only North American marsupial, for the manner in which it gives birth. These behaviors of the opossum have symbolic reference to the numerous stories in Big Moon Peyotism that relate episodes of dying and coming back to life through spiritual rebirth. There are obvious correlations in Christian theology and the life of Christ that are incorporated into discussions of the symbolic meaning of the staff and its "dress." The Osage Peyote Religion's staff can be viewed as representing all of the ancestral clans of the tribe, organized into three groups that represent the natural realms of sky, land, and water.

FIGURE 4.12 Preston Morrell holding Big Moon peyote staff, Tulsa, Oklahoma, 1998. Photo by Shane Culpepper; courtesy Daniel C. Swan.

Fans and Feathers

The Roadman's kit includes a variety of feathers and fans that are used during religious services. The eagle-wing fan, from the primary wing section of a mature golden eagle, is used by the Roadman in both the sweat lodge and the actual Peyote ceremony when he fans the participants at different points in the service; in some Osage churches, the fan is passed around for each participant to use after the initial round of singing. As a clear reference to the pre-Peyote religious observances of the Osage people, the eagle-wing fan may represent one of the strongest material connections between the ceremonial equipment of the Osage Tribal Religion and the ritual objects used in the modern practice of the Peyote Religion.

While the staff is representative of a specific church, the eagle-wing fan is emblematic of the Roadman's status within both ceremonial and secular contexts. This is the feather fan that the Roadman uses throughout the ceremony; it sits on the altar cloth when not in use. It is also used by the Roadman when he represents the Peyote Church at funeral services, naming ceremonies, feasts, and other community gatherings of significance, as well as when he prays for the needs of his congregation in their homes, in hospitals, and in situations outside the ceremonial setting of the religion.

Single tail feathers, most commonly from a golden eagle, are referred to as "prayer feathers," and they are held by worshipers throughout the service. In Osage Peyotism, it is customary for each participant to have his or her own single feather, necessary to protect participants as they leave and reenter the church during the service. The shafts of prayer feathers are often beaded and have twisted fringes attached to the end.

Osage Peyotists often have individual feather fans (see cat. 69) that they are free to use after midnight during the ceremony. These fans are either loose, in that the feathers are free flowing and attached to the handle with strips of leather, or they are flat, with the feathers set in a rigid fashion to the handle. Flat fans often incorporate an entire bird tail that is fixed in its natural configuration. The handles of fans are generally covered with beadwork, and the shafts of feathers in a loose fan are sometimes decorated with similar beadwork or with wrapped thread work. Feathers are often trimmed to uniform shape and decorated with brightly colored trim feathers, bits of animal fur, and metal bands. Virtually all Peyote fans incorporate twisted buckskin fringes at the bottom of the handle, and religious medallions, crosses, and other decorative elements are often attached to the ends of the fringes.

Osage Peyote fans conform to general patterns found in virtually all communities in which the religion is practiced. There is a preference for the feathers of eagles, hawks, woodpeckers, cormorants, and flycatchers. The association of the waterbird, a species of cormorant, with the Peyote Religion is so strong that it is generally referred to as the "Peyote bird" (see cat. 72). Scissortail flycatcher fans, highly valued both for the number of feathers needed to create a fan and for the pink tint of the feathers that suggests the colors of dawn and a new day, are considered morning fans, often not brought out

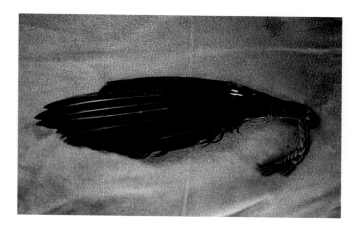

FIGURE 4.13 Eagle-wing fan from Hominy, Oklahoma. Preston Morrell Collection; courtesy Daniel C. Swan.

FIGURE 4.14 Prayer feather from Osage County, Oklahoma, ca. 1920. Mary Whitesell Collection; courtesy Gilcrease Museum.

until after sunrise. Other species of birds whose feathers are used in Peyote fans include macaw, pheasant, road-runner, and magpie (see cat. 74). Bird symbolism in the Peyote Religion focuses on each bird's role as a messenger or a conveyor of prayers to the Creator. Feathers and fans perform a similar role by physically transferring the blessings of cedar smoke, the sacred fire, and the Chief Peyote to participants when the feathers are held toward these elements and then touched to their bodies.

Musical Instruments

The instruments that accompany the singing of Peyote songs are important elements in the material culture of the religion. The songs sung in Osage Peyote meetings are generally adapted from the Caddo Big Moon Peyote tradition and contain many words from the Caddo language. Early Osage Peyotists did create a small repertoire of original Peyote Religion songs that have survived along sectarian and familial lines.

The drum is an integral part of the ritual equipment associated with the Peyote Religion. It is a water drum that uses an iron or brass three-legged kettle as a vessel for three or four inches of water. A circular piece of native tanned and smoked deer, elk, or moose hide is stretched over the opening and attached through seven rocks or marbles that function as bosses for a length of rope that secures the head to the kettle. Assembling the drum before the service is called "tying a drum."

Considerable skill and experience are required to tie the drum so that it will remain intact throughout the service and produce the desired sound. When a drum is properly tied, the rope forms a seven-pointed star on the bottom of the drum. The First Fireman is generally responsible for the church's drum kit and for its assembly for religious services.

The Osage have a specialized technique to tie the drum hide tighter than can be achieved by the standard methods of other Peyotists in North America. The additional tightness causes the drums played in an Osage Peyote meeting to have a higher pitch and sharper tone than those found in Little Moon meetings. Since a single drummer hits the drum for an entire round of the Osage Peyote singing service, a tighter drum requires less energy to produce the desired sound and beat—an important advantage for a drummer who might hit the drum for fifty to sixty different songs during a Big Moon meeting.

FIGURE 4.16 Peyote drumsticks, early 20th century. Mary Whitesell Collection; courtesy Gilcrease Museum.

FIGURE 4.15 Peyote drum, 1988. Courtesy Daniel C. Swan.

The drumsticks used in the Osage Peyote ceremony are carved from a variety of hardwoods and are commonly decorated with bas-relief carving and inscribed designs. Osage drumsticks generally have a barrel-shaped head at each end. Although a Roadman will have a number of sticks in his kit, most Osage men have personal sticks that have the right weight and balance for their drumming style. As with other personal objects, the tacit rule for drumsticks is that they are not used until after midnight.

The rattles used in connection with the Native American Church are always made from a certain species of gourd (*Lagenaria* spp.). Pebbles, beads, and other objects are placed inside the gourd to produce the sound when the rattle is shaken. From the early development of the religion, Osage Peyote rattles have used a "choke-neck" gourd that causes the handle of the rattle to fit tightly into the opening at the bottom of the gourd, softening the sound produced (see cats. 70 and 71). The handle protrudes through the top of the gourd, and a tassel of dyed deer tail is often attached to the tip. This section is usually beaded in a pattern complementary to that displayed on the remainder of the handle. Big Moon gourds have been referred to as "whispering gourds" because of their subdued tone and lower pitch.[18] Gourd rattles of a slightly different configuration were prominent in the ceremonies of the Osage Tribal Religion.

The handles of Osage rattles are commonly fully beaded in a technique of interlocked net beading referred to as "gourd" or "peyote" stitch (see cat. 73). Color selection and juxtaposition are the hallmarks of "good beadwork." Pale blue is a common background color for Osage beadwork. The designs are related to the religious service, with the fire providing the greatest source of inspiration. Osage gourd handles show a range of beadwork designs, the most common being a scheme of zigzag and spiral lines, separated by blocks of solid color. As with personal fans and drumsticks, singers often have a rattle that has been tuned to their voice and singing style by varying the amount and weight of the load placed inside the gourd.

Peyote Attire and Accessories

Most male members of the Osage Peyote Religion have a box in which to store and transport the personal objects they use in the ceremonies. A wide range of types of Peyote Religion boxes exists, from commercially made containers adapted for this use to custom-made Peyote boxes constructed of wood and leather (see cat. 68). Peyote boxes are generally made of red cedar. Commercial metal hardware is used for the hinges that attach the lid and carrying handle. They are often decorated with carved, incised, stamped, and painted designs and scenes associated with the ceremony and theology of the Native American Church. The interior surfaces of the boxes are sometimes painted or lined with felt, with the red and blue symbolism of the Native American Church a common motif.

The primary contents of Peyote boxes are the personal items used during religious services, including feather fans, gourd rattles, and drumsticks (see cat. 67). They also contain practical items that may be required during the nightlong service, such as handkerchiefs and hair combs. The inside of the lid provides a place for mementos, membership cards from the Native American Church chapters, and photographs of relatives and friends. Baby moccasins, sage bundles from previous meetings, jewelry, drumsticks, drum tools, dried peyote plants from previous events, crosses, crucifixes, religious medals, and other items of meaning and significance are also placed in Peyote boxes.

The attire for attendance at religious services was summed up by an elder who stated, "Just wear the best you got." Among his generation of Peyotists, this meant, ideally, a suit and tie. For the first generation of Osage Peyotists, however, this would have included leggings, moccasins, and the traditional dress of the day. In the early twentieth century, younger members of the religion began to wear their hair long and braided, an early hallmark of Peyotists in Oklahoma, which stands in stark contrast to the traditional roached haircuts of earlier generations.

The Osage Peyote Religion originally employed a series of face paint designs to denote the ceremonial positions of the various officials; there was a separate paint for the Roadman, the Cross Roads Men, and the Firemen. Face painting in Peyotism declined in the 1920s and 1930s, when it was only older members and Roadmen who used it. It is almost unknown today, although the Black Dog ceremony continues to use face paint as an important element in its funeral rites, with separate paints designated for members, infants, and nonmembers.[19]

Another item that has fallen into limited use among Osage Peyotists is the otter-fur turban, a style of headdress with a long history in their community. Osage turbans are made of a strip of otter fur approximately five or six inches wide that is joined in an open-top headdress decorated with ribbon work and beadwork along the top edge.

Today, Peyotists dress in Western clothing, with little to distinguish them from any other member of modern society. There is some reflection of regional style and a preference for what Anglos might refer to as "fancy Western wear." Dress slacks and long-sleeve shirts are common among older members, but younger members do attend services wearing blue jeans, T-shirts, and sneakers. In general, attire is supposed to be neat and clean, yet understated.

The basic attire is augmented with accessories that often incorporate designs and symbols drawn from the theology and ceremony of Peyotism. Men wear bola ties, belt buckles, and other accessories rendered in beadwork, Southwest-style turquoise and silverwork, and southern Plains metalwork. Men and women wear jewelry that includes pins, earrings, bracelets, and scarf slides constructed from German silver and decorated with stamped and incised designs.

Each adult male is expected to have a blanket and to be versed in its use as a basic garment in Osage Peyotism. Men can wear a commercially made wool blanket or a special "Peyote blanket" constructed from wool cloth and trimmed with ribbon work. Most Peyote blankets incorporate equal amounts of red and dark blue cloth that are sewn together at the selvage. The prescribed manner of wearing the blanket is with the red on the left, over the heart, and the blue on the right side. The most common type of blanket used is a commercial, summer-weight serape worn with the striped design elements in a vertical position. As a sign of respect, men often wear a blanket wrapped high on the waist around the lower body, in the style of a kilt. The blanket is held in place by wrapping the upper edge downward over itself. When properly folded and wrapped, the blanket is extremely functional. Women at Peyote services almost always wear a fringed cloth shawl that incorporates tepees, waterbirds, fans, rattles, and other design elements associated with the Native American Church. Worn over the shoulders when a person is seated or standing, the shawls can also be wrapped around the waist to form a skirt, particularly when the person is exiting or entering the church house.

Osage Peyotism Today

The Osage Peyote Religion not only provided spiritual comfort and guidance for thousands of community members when it was introduced in 1898, it also is seen by

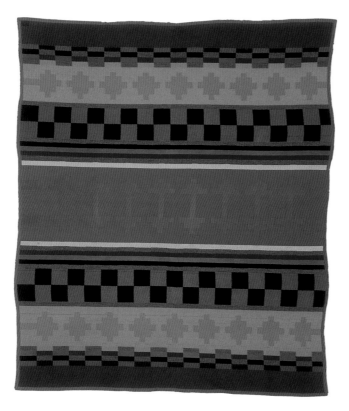

FIGURE 4.17 Shoshone pattern blanket, ca. 1912, J. Cupps and Sons. Courtesy John Nunley; © David Ulmer, photographer.

FIGURE 4.18 Drumstick with lightning design. Preston Morrell Collection; courtesy Daniel C. Swan.

the Osage to have "saved us as a people."[20] Over the past century, Osage elders have continued the tradition of philosophical reflection and practical action with regard to the religious system of their people. As with all true religions, Osage Peyotism is continuously dynamic in its response to the social, economic, and political milieus in which it functions.

The deliberation that characterized the adoption and initial development of Peyotism among the Osage people involved a period of judicious thought and study among the religious leaders as they attempted to guide their people in a time of rapid and often cataclysmic change. The form and content of the Osage Peyote Religion were arrived at through a gradual process of trial and revision in which a new sense of social order and spiritual harmony was achieved. The decision to adopt Peyotism was made at the community level, with the majority of the members of the tribe converting to Peyotism within a relatively short time.

The ceremony and ritual instruments of Osage Peyotism provide numerous examples of the manner in which elements and concepts from traditional Osage ideology were transferred to Big Moon Peyotism. One of the great strengths of Peyotism is its ability to incorporate local customs and traditions while maintaining its ceremonial and theological integrity. It is important to remember that at the theological foundation of the Osage Peyote Religion is the acceptance of certain Christian tenets, beginning with the belief in Christ as the Son of God.

The ritual instruments and their associated components provide material expression of the negotiation between the Osage tribal priests and John Wilson. The "Peyote Road" that is symbolized by the east-west line in Big Moon Peyote altars coincides with the path of the sun as it arrives each morning and sets each evening, a

fundamental principle in the Osage Tribal Religion, as both a testament of God's power and a guide for long life and happiness. The elaborate "dress" of the ritual staff provides a multifaceted expression of the convergence and continuity of ancient symbols that were imbued with new interpretations and meanings within the religious idiom of the day.

The seven-peaked, zigzag, or lightning design that is found marked on altars, incised on staffs, drumsticks, and drum tools, and worked into beadwork patterns on fans and gourds is an ancient symbol among the Osage people. Its interpretation as a representation of the power of God and the speed of His actions is an example of concepts that did not require modification or alteration in the transition between the Osage Tribal Religion and Peyotism, for at the core of both is the belief in a supreme power that guides people's lives. God is God, regardless of the manner in which the Osage invoke His divine intervention.

The Osage Peyote Religion provides the means to restore order—a holy concept for the Osage people—in times of spiritual crisis and social chaos. The ceremony and its underlying ideology affected a series of movements, both spiritual and practical, that have guided the lives of several generations of Osage people over the past century. Elders and leaders in contemporary Osage Peyotism tacitly accept as an act of faith the decisions of their ancestors as divinely inspired. The power of the Osage Peyote Religion to provide spiritual comfort and moral direction would again be tested as the Osage people entered a period of dramatic affluence in the early decades of the twentieth century. The renewed vitality of the religion in the early years of the twenty-first century is testament to the wisdom of those elders who formulated a new religious system for their Osage people in the late 1890s.

CAT. 65

PEYOTE MOCCASINS

hide, glass beads, copper, brass, and bronze
14 × 4½ × 3½ inches each
Department of Anthropology, Smithsonian Institution

These early twentieth-century moccasins were worn by participants in the Native American Church. The beaded medallions at the base of the upper flaps represent peyote buttons, symbols of religious ritual. As the wearer moves about, the rows of tin cones attached along the outside of each moccasin create the sound of rain. The yellow and green ocher colors symbolize life and rebirth, and the green represents the new grasses of spring. Lightning patterns and stylized dragonflies adorn the beaded strips on top of the moccasins. Dragonflies are associated with protection.

CAT. 66

BIG MOON STAFF

mid- to late 20th century
wood, glass beads, horsehair, leather, opossum hide,
commercial cloth, ribbon and fringe, otter hide, metals,
feathers, pigment, and plastic
50 × 1⅛ inches
Gilcrease Museum, Tulsa, Oklahoma

A peyote staff is one of the most important objects of the Native American Church. The Osage call the peyote staff a *mon*, which means "arrow." The staff is also likened to a man, with the main shaft symbolizing the body and the feathers on top representing a headdress. The music, song, and motion associated with this ritual object are meant to deliver the worshipers to heaven for eternal life. The white pelt of the cinnamon opossum with its guard hairs removed was attached to the upper part of the staff, a reference to purity. This quality is paired with two other attributes of the animal: its extreme cleanliness and its peaceful character. The otter hide suspended from the staff represents purity because it is believed that otters are so quick that evil cannot touch them.

CAT. 67
PEYOTE KIT

mid-20th century
wood, brass locks and handle, cloth lining, and assorted objects inside
8⅞ × 21⅛ × 7¾ inches
Gilcrease Museum, Tulsa, Oklahoma

The Peyote kit is a portable shrine that contains ritual and liturgical implements. Peyote kits have been referred to as "grips," a term also used for the equipment and supplies a man carries on the back of his horse to get him through the journey. Like the grip, the Peyote kit contains the liturgical equipment that will assist worshipers on the road of life. Every male member of the Osage Peyote Church ideally owns such a kit, which he uses when he attends services. Some of the articles in the kit include rattles, fans, personal pictures, and belongings as well as official papers authorizing him to use peyote as a holy sacrament.

CAT. 68

PEYOTE BOX

ca. 1920
wood, beads, and leather
4 × 4½ × 19 inches
Loaned by the University of Pennsylvania Museum of Archaeology and Anthropology

This intricately carved, painted, and lacquered box held ritual objects that were used in the ceremonies of the Native American Church. A dazzling pattern of beaded lightning bolts covers the handle's leather strap. Symmetrical patterns consisting of lozenges, triangles, and comblike forms are carved all over the box. The eroded plating of the metal clasp and the shiny patina on the front edge of the lid suggest much usage.

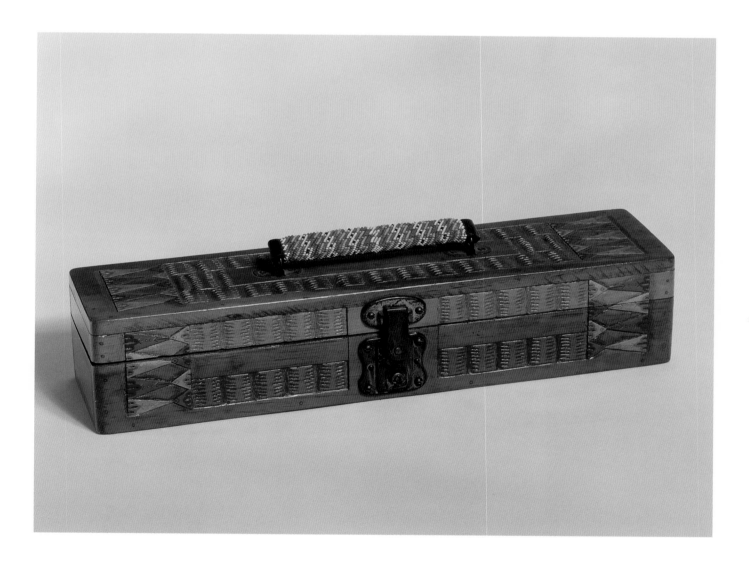

CAT. 69

PEYOTE FAN

early 20th century
feathers, glass beads, pigment, and hide
27 × 12 inches
Nancy Pillsbury Shirley, O-TAH-ZHA NA^N-ZHE
Collection

Used during religious services, this fan is
made of macaw and eagle feathers. The
cylindrical, beaded feather shafts depict-
ing the zigzag lightning design are worked
over hide strips that have been painted
yellow to represent the sun. Interestingly,
the beaded shafts are in matched pairs,
with the exception of two unique shafts.
Contemplation of the beautifully intricate
design of this fan served to steady and bring
focus to many participants during the long
and often arduous church service. The "M"
or "W" motifs on the handle have several
meanings: they may refer to John Wilson,
also known as Moon Head, the founder of
the Peyote Church among the Osage; they
may also be personal paint designs reserved
for special occasions; or they may suggest
the last earthly footprints of Christ before
his ascension into heaven.

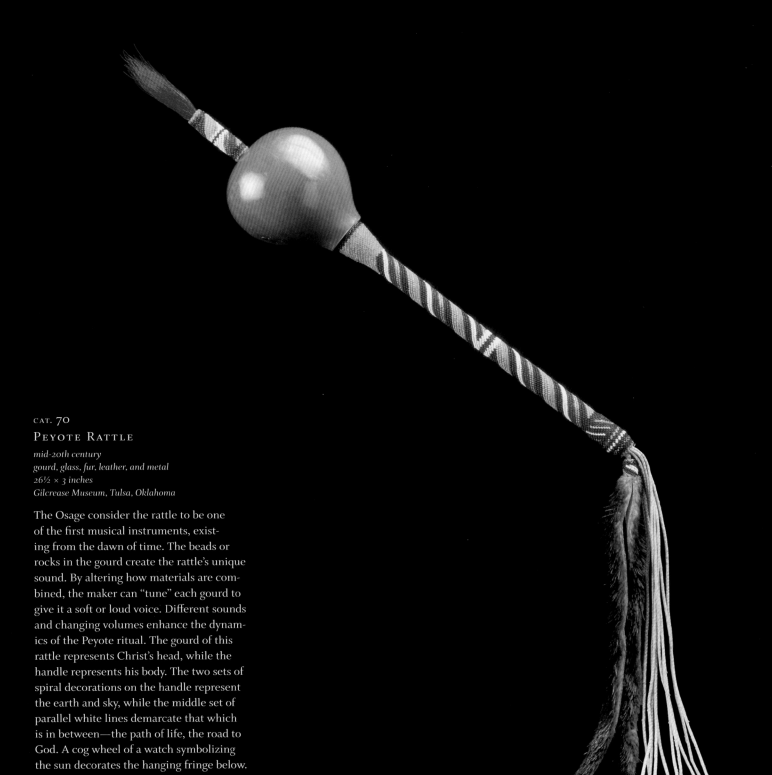

CAT. 70

PEYOTE RATTLE

mid-20th century
gourd, glass, fur, leather, and metal
26½ × 3 inches
Gilcrease Museum, Tulsa, Oklahoma

The Osage consider the rattle to be one
of the first musical instruments, existing from the dawn of time. The beads or
rocks in the gourd create the rattle's
unique sound. By altering how materials are combined, the maker can "tune" each gourd to
give it a soft or loud voice. Different sounds
and changing volumes enhance the dynam-
ics of the Peyote ritual. The gourd of this
rattle represents Christ's head, while the
handle represents his body. The two sets of
spiral decorations on the handle represent
the earth and sky, while the middle set of
parallel white lines demarcate that which
is in between—the path of life, the road to
God. A cog wheel of a watch symbolizing
the sun decorates the hanging fringe below.

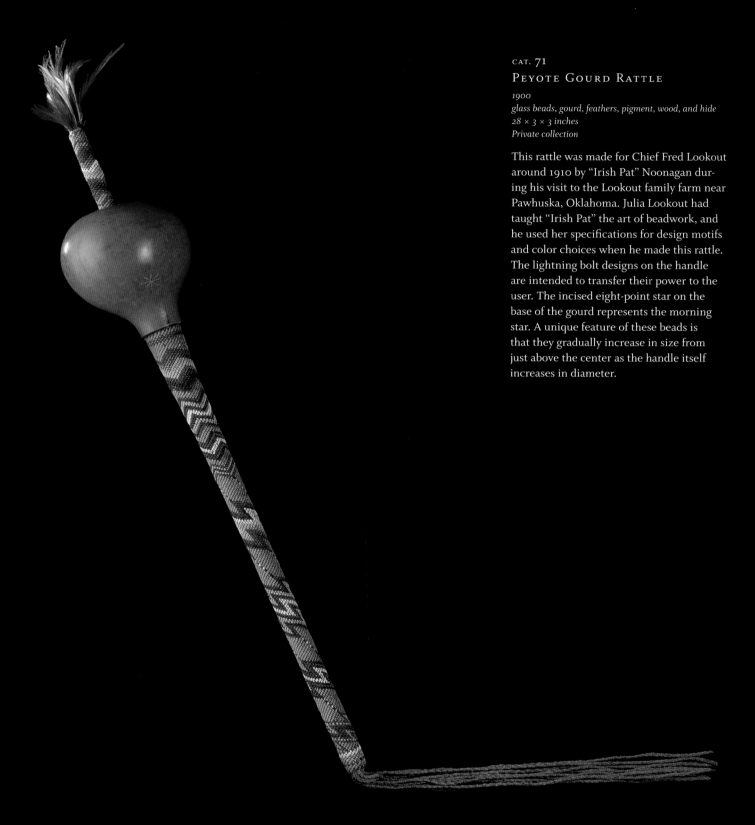

PEYOTE GOURD RATTLE

1900
glass beads, gourd, feathers, pigment, wood, and hide
28 × 3 × 3 inches
Private collection

This rattle was made for Chief Fred Lookout around 1910 by "Irish Pat" Noonagan during his visit to the Lookout family farm near Pawhuska, Oklahoma. Julia Lookout had taught "Irish Pat" the art of beadwork, and he used her specifications for design motifs and color choices when he made this rattle. The lightning bolt designs on the handle are intended to transfer their power to the user. The incised eight-point star on the base of the gourd represents the morning star. A unique feature of these beads is that they gradually increase in size from just above the center as the handle itself increases in diameter.

WATERBIRD FAN

leather, glass, feathers, and pigment
15 × 3 inches
Private collection

The feathers of this brilliantly colored fan
come primarily from the tail of the cormorant, which is also known as the *anhinga
anhinga*, "snake bird or water turkey." Lack-
ing oil glands, the cormorant feathers are
not water-resistant and must be dried in the
sun and wind. The male bird is primarily
black and white, and from a distance the
underside of the body with its outstretched
wings resembles a Christian cross. Around
the top of the handle grip are plumes from
the underside of a golden eagle that have
been dyed red. They contrast with the green
and black feathers that come from the throat
of the male mallard duck. The intricate and
colorful zigzag patterns on the handle are
symbolic representations of lightning and
rain. Waterbird fans are used exclusively
by women in the Native American Church
of the Osage.

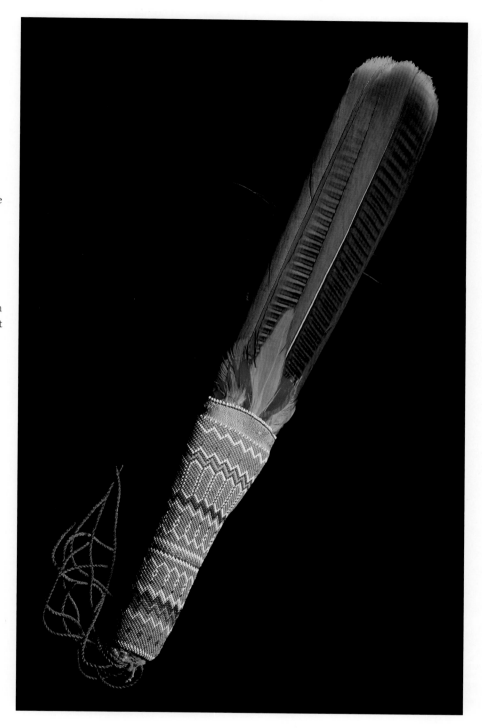

CAT. 73

LITTLE GOURD RATTLE

early 20th century
gourd, glass beads, wood, cloth, and hair
length: 34¾ inches
Private collection

This rattle belonged to George E. Standing Bear, who used it when he attended Native American Church services as a child. The four small holes drilled near the base of the gourd amplify the sound of the rattle. The variety of zigzag lightning patterns is unusual, and each motif has a unique combination of color and design.

CAT. 74

PHEASANT FEATHER FAN

ca. 1870
feathers and hide
18 × 10 × ½ inches
Private collection

Made specifically for religious purposes, this fan was used during services to fan individuals who were dealing with personal crises. The fan served to bring relief and comfort. These tail feathers are considered suitable for that purpose because they came from nonaggressive birds such as the magpie, pheasant, and prairie chicken. A special feature of this fan is the black and white horsehair braid secured at the bottom by a sterling silver ring.

CEDAR BAG

yarn with glass beads
12 × 6 × 2 inches
Osage Tribal Museum

Henry Lookout, a Roadman schooled in sacred practices, once said, "Cedar takes care of the unseen elements of our being." The smoke from the juniper cedar is used to purify and consecrate sacred objects as well as personal items owned by individuals. Cedar smoke also gives comfort and relief to those in mourning. This finger-woven bag, which once contained cedar, was constructed by splicing together chevron-patterned sections with sections of red lightning appliqués. The red lightning strips are stitched with white, adding to the vibrant design. The tassels are made from the ends of the four-strand braided cords, which were first steamed and combed, then trimmed. The faded velvet at the top is edged with delicate Czech porcelain beads.

Tomorrow we will bury this one. This Pipe Person. When we needed courage this one gave us courage.
Courage to face our enemies and courage to face the challenges of nature. This Pipe spoke for us.
This one has been our messenger to Wah-kon-tah.

This world has changed. It is time for us to bury this Pipe with dignity and put away its teachings. . . .
The children who are outside listening, they will learn another language. They will be taught by
white people. They will learn new ways and will not know our ways. —Charles Red Corn
(Osage writer, speaking of the changes in the early twentieth century), 2002

In 1903 a story appeared in the magazine *The World Today* proclaiming the Osages to be the "richest people in the world."[1] In the decades that followed, other similar articles appeared in popular magazines and newspapers throughout the United States describing the exorbitant wealth of the Osages and their increasingly extravagant lifestyles.

Between 1900 and the Great Depression of the 1930s, an extraordinary series of events profoundly changed Osage life. Their relations with the white world were dramatically altered as their reservation was allotted (see "Allotment of the Osage Reservation" later in this chapter). Tens of thousands of whites invaded their reservation, reducing the Osage to a small minority population. At the same time, royalty income from oil and natural gas reserves on their land made them wealthy beyond belief. Against this background of change, the Osage were able to transform and adapt their cultural institutions and lifestyles to their dramatically changed circumstances.

In the early twentieth century, full-blood Osages were already wealthy, but they had continued as one of the most traditional Indian communities in Oklahoma. Traditional mat- or canvas-covered longhouses were still common, although most families also had small wood-frame houses. The vast majority of full-bloods still dressed in "Osage clothes," still rode horses or in wagons, still practiced either their traditional Osage Tribal Religion or the newly introduced Peyote Religion, and still spoke

Osage as their first or only language.[2] Within a generation, this picture of Osage life changed drastically. Longhouses vanished, and families now lived in spacious modern homes, many of which could be classified as mansions. Younger Osages drove automobiles, while older members of the family could be seen traveling in chauffeur-driven limousines or touring cars. While older Osages still usually dressed in Osage clothes, younger men and women were choosing to wear their Osage clothes only for special community events, preferring the more stylish clothes they bought in Tulsa or Kansas City. Traditional religious ceremonies were virtually gone, and the Peyote Church had already peaked. Most younger

FIGURE 5.1 Osage family with touring car. Courtesy Osage Tribal Museum.

people were becoming active in Catholic, Quaker, or Baptist churches. Finally, children were no longer learning Osage as their first language, although most still understood Osage. However, the changes in Osage life, though seemingly dramatic, were in many ways superficial. Their wealth allowed the Osage to live within the white world without becoming a part of it. Osage family and community life were still vibrant and dynamic, and the Osage maintained a social unity separate and distinct from their neighbors—whether white or Indian.

Osage Wealth

In 1893 Eugene White, a former special agent to the Osage, noted in his memoirs that more than $8 million was held in trust for the tribe by the U.S. government from the sale of their Kansas Reservation and that the tribe held title to almost 1.5 million acres of land. White declared that the Osage would be the richest people per capita in the world if these resources were equally divided among tribal members.[3] A decade later, in 1903, the journalist Evander Sweet determined that Osage wealth (the total value of their trust funds and lands) amounted to $11,500 per capita. In contrast, a similar division of wealth in the United States at that time amounted to only $1,236 per capita. The Osages thus were truly, as Sweet titled his article, the "Richest People in the World."[4]

Interestingly, neither White nor Sweet mentioned oil or the value of mineral rights. Oil was not discovered on the Osage Reservation until 1897, four years after White published his memoirs. Even in 1903, oil royalties were an insignificant part of Osage incomes. However, in the two decades that followed Sweet's article, the richest people in the world became far richer.

Allotment of the Osage Reservation

Indian Territory (present-day Oklahoma) had been created to be a permanent home for all the Indian peoples of the United States—where the tribes could live unmolested by white settlers. Osage people had hardly arrived on their new reservation in Indian Territory when the flood of white settlement began lapping at the boundaries of the territory. Political groups representing farm, railroad, and other interests soon began calling for the opening of still more Indian land for white settlement.[5] In 1887 the General Indian Allotment Act was passed by Congress. Under the terms of this act, reservations were to be divided up and land was to be allotted to individual Indians with title in fee simple. The "surplus" land, meaning land not allotted to Indians, was to be opened for non-Indian settlement. The tribal governments would be dissolved, and instead of being socially isolated and segregated on reservations, Indian peoples would be assimilated into the larger society.[6]

The Osage were the last tribe in Indian Territory to have their reservation allotted. In fact, it was not until 1906, the year before Oklahoma was admitted to the Union, that the Osage Allotment Act was passed by Congress. There were two unique issues that confronted government officials and hindered their attempts to allot the Osage's land. First, unlike other tribes who had received their reservations in exchange for land, the Osages had actually purchased their reservation with money from the sale of their reservation in Kansas and already held title in fee simple to the land. Second, in 1896 the Osages had leased the mineral rights on their reservation to Edwin Foster. Just a year later, oil had been discovered there, and by 1906 oil production was under way in a number of areas on the reservation.[7] If mineral rights were linked to surface land allotments, as in the case of other tribes, a few Osages could end up wealthy from royalties, while the vast majority would receive little or nothing. The Osage made sure that allotment of the Osage Reservation did not follow that pattern.

Osage allotment was unlike that of any other tribe. With the exception of a few small tracts, all reservation land was to be equally divided among tribal members. Mineral rights were to remain collectively owned by the tribe, and income was to be equally shared by allottees on the basis of head-right shares—a unique system. A new Osage Tribal Council would be established with limited authority to manage the mineral properties of the tribe. Because of the tribal ownership of mineral rights, the Osage Reservation would retain limited reservation status. Congress did not consider this to be a permanent solution. In fact, trust status for individual and tribal properties was to last for only twenty-five years and was scheduled to end on January 1, 1932. At that time, the Osage Agency would be closed, the tribal council dissolved, and mineral rights would revert to the surface owners of the land, Osage or non-Osage.[8]

When Oklahoma became a state the following year, Osage County was established, with the same boundaries as the reservation. As a result, the Osage Reservation became somewhat of an "underground reservation." The Osage County government held authority over only the "surface" of the land. Because for some purposes this region was a county and for others a reservation, local people quickly came to refer to the area as simply "the Osage."

Under the provision of the 1906 Osage Allotment Act, an allotment roll of all the eligible tribe members was drawn up. This roll included any Osage living between January 1, 1906, and July 1, 1907. The 2,229 individuals listed on this final roll would be the allottees, and each allottee would receive an equal share of tribal properties. Individuals born after July 1, 1907, could receive tribal properties only through inheritance.

Certain limited areas of the reservation were not allotted. Townships had already been surveyed at Pawhuska, Hominy, Fairfax, and other areas of the reservation. The proceeds from lots sold to non-Osages went to the tribe. However, in addition, three 160-acre tracts were set aside for tribal villages at Hominy, Pawhuska, and Gray Horse. These areas were to remain tribal property, and any Osage could claim a lot and build a house in these villages. Other land was set aside for government and tribal offices and for mission schools. The remaining 1,465,380 acres were divided equally among the 2,229 allottees, with each allottee receiving approximately 657 acres of land.[9]

All mineral rights on the reservation were to remain the collective trust property of the tribe, to be administered by the tribal council and the Indian Service. Every allottee received a head right entitling its owner to 1/2,229th of tribal mineral income, less the administrative expenses of the tribal and federal governments. A head right was the private property of the allottee, much like a share of stock in a corporation. Head rights could be inherited and, at one time, they could even be sold. They also could be divided or fragmented. An individual Osage could own, through inheritance, multiple head rights.

To manage the leasing of tribal mineral rights and other tribal and individual trust properties, the Osage

Agency remained and a new Osage Tribal Council with limited powers was established. The new tribal council consisted of a chief, an assistant chief, and eight council members. Service on the council was limited to adult male allottees, as was voting. Since the Osage were wealthy, all government expenses for the management of Osage affairs had to be paid from tribal income. All agency workers were paid from tribal, not U.S. government, funds.[10] The same was true for the Osage Boarding School and the two Catholic schools on the reservation. Individual Osages were not entitled to participate in any federal Indian Service programs that were not paid for from tribal funds approved by the tribal council.

World War I and Its Consequences

When oil was first discovered on the Osage Reservation in 1897, the market for petroleum-based products was limited. The main product was kerosene, used in oil lamps for a source of lighting.[11] In was not until 1899 that the internal combustion engine was perfected and the manufacturing of gasoline-powered automobiles and trucks began. By 1910 there were more than 450,000 gas-powered automobiles and 10,000 trucks in use.[12] The increasing market for gasoline quickly resulted in a demand for increased oil production and a boom in the Osage oil industry. As late as 1903, there were only nineteen producing wells on the reservation.[13] Seven years later, by 1910, there were more than a thousand wells, with an annual production of more than 5 million barrels of oil.[14]

As the Osage oil industry expanded, the non-Indian population on the reservation grew rapidly as new workers poured into the area. Between 1907 and 1910, the population jumped from 15,000 to more than 20,000.[15] The oil rush was on, and the relative social isolation of the Osage ended. They had become a minority within the boundaries of their own reservation.

In August 1914, World War I started in Europe, and the economic effects of the war were quickly felt. As the war progressed, American industry increasingly shifted from the production of domestic goods to military goods to supply European countries involved in the war. After America entered the war in 1917, this process accelerated.

While automobile production declined, the effect of this on the Osage oil industry was more than offset by the increasing demand by the military.

George Wright, the Osage Agent during the war, actively discouraged Osages from joining the military, saying that the full-bloods were not citizens and thus not subject to the draft. In spite of their agent, at least 153 Osage men served in the military; almost all of the younger full-blood men joined.[16] Many were members of the Thirty-sixth Division, the division formed out of the combined Oklahoma and Texas National Guards.[17] While the largest number saw service as enlisted men in the infantry, Osages served in every branch of the military. At least five, including John Joseph Mathews[18] and Clarence Tinker,[19] served as officers and pilots in the Army Air Corps. Only one Osage, Charles Donovan, was killed in action.[20]

The Osage who remained at home were also quick to support the national war effort. In 1917 the Osage Tribal Council created the Naval Reserve, a 5,120-acre tract of valuable oil land that could be used by the Navy Department for emergency wartime oil production.[21] Meanwhile, individual Osages demonstrated their support for the war effort by buying liberty bonds. Agency records show that Osages purchased more than $2,240,000 in liberty bonds and war saving stamps.[22] In addition, a group of Osage women, led by Mrs. Charles Wah-hre-she, actively collected supplies, made bandages, and raised money for the American Red Cross.[23] In one way or another, almost every member of the Osage community did something to support the war effort.

World War I changed the lives and lifestyles of not only the Osages but Americans in general. American entry into the war in 1917 increased the need for oil. At the same time, the Osage tribe changed the manner in which mineral leases were handled. In place of the earlier practice of negotiated leases with set royalties, the tribe instituted a new policy of leasing tracts of land on the basis of competitive bidding. These bids, or lease bonuses, as they were called, were paid immediately and were paid in addition to the royalties on production. The effects of lease auctions on mineral income were dramatic and immediate: in 1916 a single head right earned its owner $384; the following year, that same head right earned $2,719.[24]

However, the real boom came in the years just following the war. With consumer goods in short supply and high

FIGURE 5.2 Dance held in honor of Mrs. Wah-hre-she for her work with the American Red Cross during World War I. Photograph by Grigg Studio on October 24, 1924, in Pawhuska, Oklahoma. Courtesy Osage Tribal Museum.

wartime wages, American workers, just like the Osage, invested their surplus dollars in savings bonds. The end of the war in 1918 found Americans with money in their pockets and a strong desire to buy. As the horse-and-buggy days were coming to an end, automobiles became the primary interest of the American consumer, and the demand for gasoline rocketed. Oil production increased 114 percent between 1919 and 1926.[25] The effects on the Osage were sudden and dramatic. The Osage oil fields were some of the largest in the world, and the term "the Osage" became used in the oil world in the same manner that "the Comstock" and "the Klondike" had been used earlier in the gold fields. In 1917 there were 3,755 producing oil wells in the Osage, with annual production of 11 million barrels.[26] By 1920 there were 5,849 oil wells with an annual production of more than 17 million barrels. In 1910 the average price of a barrel of oil was only $0.35. By 1916 the average price per barrel had jumped to $1.20. In the next four years, it almost tripled, reaching $3.35 in 1920.[27]

In May 1920, when it seemed that things could not get much better, the Marland Oil Company struck a new oil field. The Burbank field, as this region became known, soon proved to be the largest oil field in the history of the world up to that time. In 1921 the Burbank field alone produced almost 5 million barrels, and the following year production in the Burbank field exceeded 24 million

barrels. Production in the Burbank field peaked in 1923, when it produced more than 26 million barrels. Meanwhile, other, smaller fields were being developed in the Osage. In 1923 these other fields produced an additional 42 million barrels,[28] for a total of 68 million barrels for the year.

With oil exploration in the Osage in full swing, thousands of new workers poured into the region. In the decade of the teens, the population almost doubled, numbering more than 36,000 by 1920. Oil production and exploration in the Osage peaked in the mid-1920s, by which time the population on the reservation had swollen to more than 50,000.[29]

Individual and Family Incomes

To understand the Osage lifestyle during the late teens and 1920s, one has to first understand the amount and sources of income for individuals and families. Prior to July 1928, every Osage twenty-one years of age and older was an allottee, meaning that he or she had at the minimum a trust fund account of more than $3,000, one head right, and more than 640 acres of land. An Osage family of the late teens or early 1920s consisting of two parents and three minor children who had all been born before July 1, 1907, had a total of $15,000 in trust funds, five head-right incomes, and more than 3,200 acres of

land. Income from head rights varied significantly from year to year. In 1917 those five head rights would have yielded more than $13,500; in 1919, almost $20,000; in 1920, $40,000; and in 1923, more than $60,000 in total income. At their peak in 1926, these five head rights would have produced an income of close to $80,000.[30] While some Osages involved themselves in farming and ranching, most leased part, if not all, of their allotments for grazing or farming, generating an additional $1,000 or more in income every year. The trust funds, which earned 5 percent interest from the federal government, would have yielded the family an additional $750 a year.

By 1920 significant differences were already apparent in both individual and family incomes. Several hundred of the original allottees had died prior to 1920, so that many individuals had inherited additional trust funds, head rights, and land from their deceased relatives. As a result, many individuals, particularly full-bloods, now owned multiple head rights and a thousand or more acres of land. In 1922 the wealthiest Osage was a twenty-year-old full-blood girl, Mary Elkins, who owned eight and a half head rights.[31] In the early 1920s, all Osage adults and families were wealthy by white standards, but some individuals and families were far richer than others.

Under the original provisions of the Osage Allotment Act, all individual income from the trust fund, head rights, and land leasing had to be distributed on a quarterly basis. As a result, in 1920 every allottee received more than $8,000 cash for the year (more if they had inherited additional head rights and property). Parents also received the same amount for each of their minor children who had been allotted. In response to local agency officials, Congress changed this policy. Starting in 1921, payments to individual adult Osages were limited to $1,000 per quarter, and minors could receive no more than $500 per quarter.[32] Although head-right income might far exceed these payments, a family of five could still receive no more than $14,000 per year in cash. Income that exceeded these limits was placed in individual surplus funds accounts managed by the agency and invested in government bonds. With the permission of the agency, money from the surplus funds could be withdrawn from these accounts for special purposes, such as the building of a house, improvements to the land, or education. By 1929 the agency

held more than $27 million in 883 individual surplus funds accounts. The vast majority of these accounts belonged to full-bloods.[33]

It is difficult to equate Osage income during this period with incomes today, but if one merely makes adjustments on the basis of the increase in the consumer price index (CPI), $1 in 1920 was worth about $8 in 2000. The $8,000 paid per head right in 1920 would be the equivalent of $64,000, while the peak income per head right of $13,400 earned in 1926 would be the equivalent of about $107,000 today.

Like the gold fields of the nineteenth century, the oil fields of the early twentieth century became centers of lawlessness. This was particularly true of the area known as the Osage. With the oil-field workers came criminals of all types. Armed robberies, burglaries, and even murders became common. Many Osages fled the crime on the reservation and moved to Tulsa, Oklahoma City, and Wichita. Southern California became the new home to the largest number of nonresidence Osage. While most of these families were acculturated mixed-bloods, many full-bloods from traditional families also joined them. Charles Wah-hre-she, a Peyote Church leader in Hominy, Oklahoma, came up with the idea that the Osages should move to Mexico and buy land there. In 1919 or 1920, Wah-hre-she and some families from Hominy traveled to western Chihuahua and looked at land near the Mormon settlements. Later, accompanied by several other Osages, he actually traveled to Mexico City to discuss such a move with the president of Mexico. Although the Mexican government was agreeable, Wah-hre-she could not recruit many Osages to follow, and the plan was abandoned. In the mid-1920s, the idea developed to purchase Vermijo Park, a large ranch at the edge of the mountains in northeastern New Mexico. One summer, several families traveled to the ranch to look at the property. Once again the plan failed due to a lack of support.[34]

Osage Family Life

By the 1920s, important changes were appearing in Osage family life, and the most significant were generational. Many of the ideas, tastes, and aspirations of younger adult Osages differed from those of their parents and grandparents. The reasons for these differences were complex.

The older generation of Osage, even the traditional full-bloods, were far from ignorant of the white world. In 1847 the Jesuits had opened Osage Manual Labor School, or Osage Mission, on the Osage reservation in Kansas to educate Osage boys. Later that same year, the Sisters of Loretto established a school for Osage girls. Prior to the removal of the Osages to Indian Territory in 1872, several hundred Osages had attended these schools.[35] Schools were quickly established for Osages on their new reservation. An Osage boarding school, staffed by Quakers, for both girls and boys was established in Pawhuska. Later a Catholic boys' school, St. John, and a girls' school, St. Louis, were opened on the reservation. After the mid-1880s, virtually all school-age Osage children were attending one of these reservation boarding schools or an off-reservation school, usually Chilocco, Haskell, or Carlisle.[36] By the first years of the twentieth century, almost all older Osages could speak English and most were literate. Thanks to the Jesuits, there was at least one full-blood who could read and write Latin.[37] However, exposure to white culture through these schools had little overt effect on individual Osages or Osage lifestyle during the late nineteenth century. There is a widely known story concerning Pawnee-no-pashe, who was also known as Governor Joe. In the 1860s, he returned home from the Osage Mission school, with his hair short and neatly combed and dressed in his school clothes and shoes. To the assembled group that came to welcome him, he proclaimed, "It took Father Schoenmaker fifteen years to make a white man out of me, and it will take just fifteen minutes to make an Osage out of myself."[38] He emerged from his parents' longhouse soon after with his hair shaved into a roach and wearing a breechcloth, leggings, and moccasins. Until the early years of the twentieth century, the majority of returning full-blood students followed Governor Joe's example. Officials at the Osage Agency regularly complained about former students "putting on the blanket" when they came home.

This pattern of overt conservatism changed for Osages coming of age during the late teens and 1920s. Younger Osages quickly adopted the material trappings of middle-class and even upper-middle-class white Americans. The change was most apparent in their daily physical appearance. Unlike their fathers and grandfathers, who still wore their hair either in roaches, indicating their adherence to the traditional Osage Tribal Religion, or in braids, indicating that they were members of the new Peyote Church, the young men of those years wore their hair cut short and parted. Their fathers and grandfathers still commonly wore either their Indian clothes or the regional Western-style clothes with blankets, but the younger men usually dressed in a more urban style, with ties, suits, jackets, sweaters, and low-cut shoes. Older women almost always kept their hair long and parted in the middle and wore homemade Osage-style skirts, blouses, blankets, and moccasins. In contrast, their daughters and granddaughters chose to wear their hair in the latest styles, painted their nails, and wore makeup. They shopped for their clothes in Tulsa, Kansas City, and other cities and wore the latest fashions in dresses, coats, and shoes.[39]

This is not to say that the younger Osages no longer owned traditional Osage clothes. Most still had trunks full of blankets, moccasins, yarn belts, and broadcloth clothes decorated in ribbon work and beadwork. Freed by their wealth from most of the more mundane household tasks, many of the older Osage women spent their time in the more pleasurable tasks of making ribbon work, beadwork, and other items of clothing for themselves, their children, and grandchildren. Younger Osages were more likely to wear their Osage clothes only for traditional "Osage events," dances, or other special occasions.[40]

During this period, younger Osages began to compartmentalize their behavior and dress. Because Osage clothes were considered appropriate only for Osage events, an individual wearing "white" clothes at an Osage event would put on a blanket to cover the white-style clothes. Rarely would an Osage mix the two styles. Young people began to differentiate between Osage clothes and more generic "Indian" clothes. Young boys were frequently attracted to the flamboyant "fancy dance" clothes worn by powwow dancers. During the 1920s, when boys appeared at the E-Lon-schka at Pawhuska wearing such fancy clothes, officials told them to go home and change. They might be allowed to wear them at powwows, but they were not acceptable at an Osage dance.[41]

There were a number of reasons why the styles and behavior of younger Osage people changed so dramatically

FIGURE 5.3 Osage tribe received by President Coolidge. Photograph taken in Washington, D.C., on January 12, 1928. Courtesy Osage Tribal Museum.

during the years between 1910 and 1930. One reason was simply their greatly increased exposure to white culture. Unlike their parents, they had not grown up socially isolated from non-Indian peoples. In their daily lives, they were constantly interacting with people of other cultures. Outside their homes, on the streets, and in the stores in Pawhuska, Hominy, Fairfax, and other local towns, they saw many more whites than Osages. In 1915 St. John, the Osage Catholic boys' school, was closed, and in 1921 the government-operated Osage Boarding School followed suit. While some girls continued to attend St. Louis until it closed in 1948, most families had to find other schools for their children. Many attended local public schools, in which the vast majority of their classmates were white. In 1924, 154 full-blood Osages, or almost half of the total school-age full-blood population, were enrolled in private off-reservation boarding schools.[42] These were not "Indian" schools but, in most cases, military schools. Missouri Military Academy had the largest Osage enrollment.[43] As with the local public schools, the majority of students in these schools were whites.

Service in the military during World War I also greatly increased their exposure to the white world. When an Osage served in a white military unit, he was usually the only Osage, if not the only Indian, in the barracks.

While only a few saw service in European cities, all of them were trained and stationed at bases far from home.

Contact with non-Indians wasn't limited to school or the local community. Families regularly shopped in nearby cities. Virtually all of them spent part of every summer in Colorado or New Mexico. Others accompanied their parents on official trips of the Osage Tribal Council to Washington, D.C., and other eastern cities.[44] Younger Osages of the 1920s traveled farther and saw more of the United States than did their white peers in Osage County.

The single most important factor, however, was the general attitude of their parents and grandparents. Most older Osages encouraged their children and grandchildren to adapt to the white world. About the time of World War I, many bilingual couples simply stopped speaking Osage to their children and even actively discouraged their children's attempts to learn the language. Some Peyote Church families discouraged participation in Peyote Church meetings and encouraged their children to participate in the Catholic, Baptist, or Quaker churches. Interestingly, Osage Peyotists contributed to the purchase of the large stained-glass windows in the Catholic church in Pawhuska, while the Quaker church in Hominy was paid for primarily by local leaders in the Peyote Church.[45]

Osage families frequently had two homes: one on their allotment and one in town. The Osage Allotment Act set aside three 160-acre tracts as "Indian villages." The Pawhuska and Hominy villages were located on the edges of the towns of the same name. A third village was established at Gray Horse, five miles east of Fairfax. These three villages constituted the centers of Osage community life. The Pawhuska village was the center for the Thorny Thicket band, which by this time had incorporated the surviving families of the Little Osage and Heart-Stays bands. Hominy was the center for the Upland Forest band, while Gray Horse was the center for the Big Hills band.

The main structure and focal point for each of these three villages was the round house, a large circular structure with closed sides and doorways. The earliest structures had roofs covered with tree branches to provide shade. In 1917 and 1918, the round houses were rebuilt in all three villages. These new structures were much larger and had pitched wood-shingled roofs. There were usually two doors, one on the east side and one on the west. The new structures had tiered benches around the inside walls. The round houses were used for a wide range of community events. Political meetings would be held there, and the winter dances and other social events would take place in them. A large open area was adjacent to the round house. During the summer, large dances or celebrations would be held outside in this space. Surrounding this open area were cooking pits, fireplaces, and arbor frames. During dances and celebrations, these areas would be used for cooking feasts and serving guests. Visiting members of other tribes, as well as Osages from other communities, would also frequently camp in this open area using tents or arbors.[46]

Osage families were free to claim unused lots in these villages to build houses. In fact, the round houses at these three sites predated allotment, and many Osages owned homes there in 1906. During the teens and 1920s, still other Osage homes were built in the villages, although for the most part these were small wood-frame houses used as secondary homes when families came to town during the dances and other celebrations.

The primary home for most families was usually on the homestead allotment of one of the senior members of the family. Although the Osage themselves usually referred to these homes as "camps" or "farms," they were really more like country residences that frequently took the form of a complex of structures. The main structure was the family home. These houses varied greatly in both size and architecture. Although all were spacious by the standards of the day, the smallest usually took the form of a wood-frame bungalow with a large front porch. The largest and most expensive were two-story brick structures whose designs were derived from English country houses.[47]

The furnishings in these houses varied with the age and taste of the family members. The homes of older, traditional couples were sometimes sparsely furnished with only a few rugs, chairs, tables, beds, framed photographs, and trunks for the storage of personal items. However, the homes of many younger families were luxuriously furnished with Oriental or Navajo rugs, curtains and drapes, heavily stuffed chairs and sofas, end tables, dining room tables and chairs, china cabinets, beds, chests of drawers, and sewing machines. Many also had pianos, and those with electricity usually had radios and phonographs as well. Some homes even had crystal chandeliers.[48]

There was often a unique Osage structure called a "summer house." This was a long rectangular building with screened windows along its sides. These were multipurpose structures. They were used to store extra tables, chairs, beds, bedding, and dishes and usually housed cookstoves for cooking in the summer. Many families used their summer houses for special family feasts and dinners, and some families held hand games and other social events there. Meals were served in them during Peyote meetings, and they were sometimes used as guest quarters. Osages were great hosts, and visiting family friends, particularly from other tribes, frequently stayed for weeks at a time. One woman recalled that while growing up, she could not remember a single meal at her family's home at which there was not a guest.

Many, about thirty, of these country residences also had their own Peyote Church house. These eight-sided wood-frame structures were usually located not far from the main house and the summer house.

The country residences could have a number of other special structures that varied from family to family. Some had garages for cars, barns and corrals for horses or cattle, hog pens, chicken coops, and smokehouses. Other families had benches under trees scattered around their yards. As a result, many of these country residences were relatively large complexes of structures.[49]

A government survey in 1924 noted that "owing to the constant traveling and absence of many Osage families . . . it [is] very difficult to obtain data." The surveyor estimated that they were gone 50 percent of the time.[50] Lots of free time, high incomes, and automobiles gave Osage families the freedom to do what they wished.

In early July, with their children home from boarding school, almost every family moved to Colorado Springs with their chauffeurs and other servants. One woman was said to have even taken one of the local priests with her family. Some people traveled by train, but most families traveled by car. To withstand the July heat during the drive from Oklahoma to Colorado, Osage families would tie new mattresses onto the tops of the cars and wet them down, an early form of automobile air conditioning. Several families would usually travel together as a caravan of three or four cars and frequently a truck to carry their luggage. One Osage recalled stopping at a small town in western Kansas that had one service station. The townspeople did not know what to think when they saw the big cars, the older men with long braids, and the older women in Indian clothes and blankets. Filling their cars with gasoline, the travelers emptied the pumps at the station and drove on.[51]

The two months that most families spent in Colorado Springs were a way to escape the summer heat of Oklahoma and enjoy the recreational attractions in the area. Some families stayed at the main hotels in Colorado Springs, the Broadmoor or the Antlers. Other families rented summer houses or camped in Stonewall Park. They rode the cog railroad to the top of Pikes Peak, took the incline ride to the top of the mountain at Mount Manitou Park, or rode donkeys or horses on the trails. Cheyenne Canyon with its waterfalls and riding trails was also popular, as was the Garden of the Gods. Sometimes a rodeo with Sioux Indian dancers would come to town, and there were Pueblos who worked at some of the tourist spots in town. However, for the most part the Osages socialized with one another. The older people frequently just visited and talked. Sometimes there were card games, Indian dice games, or hand games (see cat. 90). On at least one occasion, someone brought an E-Lon-schka drum and there was a dance at Stonewall Creek.[52]

Toward the end of August, families began to leave Colorado Springs. Some drove straight back to Osage country, and some returned the long way, visiting friends and family on various reservations in Montana or the Dakotas before returning home. Still others headed south to New Mexico and the Pueblos, where several families had relatives.[53]

During the winter, usually in February, many families would travel to San Antonio, Texas. Once again, they stayed in hotels or rented apartments. Not as many families went to San Antonio as to Colorado Springs, and they usually stayed only a few weeks, since children were in school and most of them could not accompany their parents or grandparents on this trip. It was primarily a social trip, with the Osage socializing among themselves. From San Antonio, some individuals would go on to Mexico to watch the bullfights, walk the beach, or go fishing. Many of the Peyotists used this time to visit the "peyote garden," the source of the peyote cactus used in their rituals.[54]

Whether traveling or staying home, Osage people followed a lifestyle in the 1920s that took the form of one almost continuous social activity. Some were strictly Osage events, such as the Peyote Church meetings, the E-Lon-schka dances, and the Soldier dances, but individuals and communities came to adopt a wide range of more generic forms of American and Indian activities.

The Osage adopted Christmas, and the holiday became a major celebration. Even traditional Osage families became involved in giving gifts and sending Christmas cards. Christmas pageants were also popular. Most of these took place in the local churches, but in Hominy they had a Christmas pageant and feast at the round house. Big birthday parties for children came into vogue. Families would send out formal, engraved invitations to children's parties that included the feasting of guests, giving of gifts, and, frequently, games.[55]

Circuses, rodeos, and powwows were also popular. Sometimes a family would sponsor and pay for such events, and at other times the local Osage community would sponsor them. In Hominy there were sometimes combinations of these events in which a rodeo, a small carnival with rides, and hired Indian dancers from other tribes would come together. The rides would be free, guests would be feasted, and foot races and other games between children would be held, at which the winners would receive prizes.[56]

Competitive sports had always been a popular activity among the Osages, and during the early twentieth century, younger Osages participated in a wide range of American sports. Most of the Osage boys played football, basketball, and baseball in high school, and their parents became avid fans. Older boys and men competed in horse racing and rodeos. In 1924 a group of Osages in Hominy organized a professional football team. Called the Hominy Indians and composed of only Indian players, they played other professional teams throughout the Midwest and as far east as New Jersey.[57] By the late 1920s, many of the younger men had even taken up golf.[58]

During the late 1920s, oil production in the Osage territory began to decline along with oil exploration activity. Oil companies shifted much of their attention to other newly discovered fields in Oklahoma, Texas, and California. As increased production from these new fields flooded the market, the price of oil dropped. The start of the Great Depression in 1929 further collapsed the price of oil until at one point in 1930, it fell to only $0.25 a barrel. The major oil boom for the Osage lasted from only 1917 to 1929. During this short period, mineral royalties and lease bonuses earned the Osage people more than $230 million, or about $110,000 per head right.[59]

Continuity in Osage Art and Culture

The removal of the Osages to Indian Territory had signaled the beginning of a major period of change in Osage art and culture. The extinction of the buffalo herd on the southern plains in 1875 and the increased crowding of both whites and Indians in the areas just outside the boundaries of the new reservation not only destroyed the self-sufficient subsistence economy of the Osages, but it resulted in an increasingly scarce supply of the raw materials used to make domestic goods. In 1878 the Osage Agency, using the interest from the tribal trust fund, began making quarterly per-capita cash payments to the Osage. Later, mineral royalty income became part of these quarterly payments. With this transition to a cash economy, the old trade posts vanished, replaced first by general stores and later by department stores. Starting in the 1880s, but rapidly increasing after the turn of the twentieth century, Osage material culture changed dramatically.

The traditional longhouses were slowly replaced by American-style houses, and traditional Osage architecture disappeared. With these new houses came wood-burning stoves, and open-pit fires were seldom used for preparing food, except for special "Osage" occasions. Just as brass buckets and iron kettles had replaced domestically made pottery during the eighteenth century, now metal skillets, pots, and pans began displacing the older buckets and kettles.

The Osage stopped making traditional wooden bowls, ladles, and horn spoons. It was easier to purchase china bowls, metal ladles, and metal spoons from local stores. The artistic traditions associated with the forms and decoration of these items vanished.

Hide bags, or parfleches, and woven bags made of yarn had been used to store food, clothing, and other personal items, but now families didn't store large quantities of food because they could purchase it at local stores or butcher their animals as needed. Flour, coffee, beans, sugar, salt, and other foods came in store containers that could be shelved in kitchens or pantries. For the storage of clothes and other small items, metal trunks, cedar chests, and chests of drawers were readily available. Since Osages no longer traveled to the buffalo hunt several times a year, the size and weight of storage containers were no longer the considerations they once were. Hide storage bags disappeared. The production of yarn bags persisted slightly longer, since they were used at feasts in addition to their function of storage. With the demise of these bags, the artistic traditions associated with the decoration of these items also disappeared.

Since there was no more intertribal warfare and since hunting was now done with rifles, the Osage no longer needed to make bows, arrows, quivers, shields, clubs, or spears. Once again, the decorative motifs associated with these items were extinguished.

Some families continued to make and use cradleboards for their children, and other individuals still produced dolls, toy cradleboards, and other traditional toys for children (see cats. 61, 62, 63, 64). However, other than these items and clothing, by 1930 the making of traditional domestic goods had stopped, and the artistic traditions associated with the making of them had vanished.

In 1911 a Mourning Dance was held at Gray Horse. It was to be the last public performance of a major traditional religious ceremony among the Osages.[60] Although a few men would be initiated into the clan priesthoods as late as the 1930s, the traditional Osage Tribal Religion was gone. The clan and tribal sacred bundles were sold, buried, or otherwise disposed of. With the passing of the traditional religion, all the ceremonies, rituals, and other activities that had been associated with it were also gone. The most significant loss was the pipe, which had been the primary symbol of the traditional religion and was rejected by the Peyotists. The production and use of other traditional ritual items—war standards, rattles, sacred mat cases, and buffalo-hair bags—disappeared as well. Ritual face and body painting and tattooing also stopped.

There was a general erosion of the Osage artistic tradition during the late nineteenth and early twentieth centuries. Whole categories of material items disappeared, along with the techniques to make them and motifs to decorate them. Yet by the 1920s, the decline in Osage artistic tradition was slowing down. There were items the Osages considered to be necessities that were neither produced commercially nor had any acceptable commercial equivalent. These items fell into two main categories: ritual objects for the new Peyote Church (see Chapter 4, Osage Peyote Religion) and Osage clothing that could be worn at Osage dances and other special events (see "Osage Family Life" earlier in this chapter). These were items that had to be specially made and properly decorated by the Osages themselves or by knowledgeable craftspeople from other tribes.

The Peyote Religion introduced new architectural structures, new symbolic design elements, and new forms of ritual objects that still incorporated many traditional ideas. The most apparent and impressive were the Peyote churches themselves, eight-sided structures with high, pointed roofs. Inside the churches were permanent decorated concrete altars, or "Moons." Peyotists introduced new forms of rattles, fans, carved drumsticks, and carved wooden staffs or "arrows" that came to replace the pipe in its symbolism. A range of new items produced for use by the church members in their services include cedar boxes with carved or painted designs, yarn finger-woven tobacco or cedar bags, and beaded peyote bags. With the flourishing of the Peyote Religion came new symbolic design elements: peyote buttons, waterbirds, tepees, and water drums.

The E-Lon-schka dance, the Soldier dance, and many other "Osage events" still required participants to dress in traditional Osage clothes, and most Osages continued to make and own traditional Osage clothing. While new and improved materials and techniques were incorporated regularly, the basic styles and decorative motifs remained the same. In the 1870s, cloth became increasingly available as buckskin became scarcer. This affected the making of Osage clothing. Cloth had been replacing hides and leather for robes, breechcloths, skirts, leggings, and other pieces of clothing since the eighteenth century. Robes and leather clothing virtually disappeared in the last decades of the nineteenth century, yet this had only minimal effect on the associated artistic tradition. As painted designs on robes and leather clothing disappeared, the more important traditions of ribbon work and beadwork decorations continued virtually unchanged. Loom beadwork and yarn work in the form of belts and garters survived this period with minimal change.

The Great Depression of the 1930s brought to a close the period of great Osage wealth. However, income from mineral rights did not end in 1932, as had been called for in the provisions of the Osage Allotment Act. In 1921, 1929, and 1938, the trust status of the Osage was granted an extension by Congress, and the Osage Agency and the Tribal Council continued to function with some modifications.[61] In 1942 the right to vote and hold tribal office was extended to all head-right owners, male or female, allotted or unallotted.[62] The tribal election laws were again changed in 1958 so that voters would vote their head-right shares and not their "persons." Thus an individual with two head rights had two votes, while an individual with one-quarter head right had only one-quarter vote.[63] In 1964 Congress extended the trust period "indefinitely" and finally in 1978 "in perpetuity."[64]

While mineral royalties still earn some income for individuals who own head rights, the Osages are no longer the wealthiest people per capita in the world. Today most individuals earn their living as businesspeople, lawyers, doctors, engineers, schoolteachers, college professors, government employees, or wage laborers. The majority do not live on the reservation. While many live in Tulsa, Oklahoma City, Wichita, or some smaller town in Osage County, others live on the East Coast, in California, or in Denver, Albuquerque, Phoenix, or some other distant city. Still, most Osages return "home" regularly. The families nearby come to attend Peyote Church meetings, War Mothers Society dances, hand games, and other Osage events, while families at greater distances return at least in June for one or more of the E-Lon-schka dances. Although Peyotists still produce ritual items for their church meetings, they are today a small minority of the Osage population. The dance societies, the E-lon-schka and War Mothers Societies, have become the social and cultural core of the Osage community. It is primarily within the context of these dance societies and the other events they sponsor that the traditional social institutions of the Osage are maintained and traditional cultural knowledge is communicated to the younger generation. In the making and decorating of the clothing and other items needed for these dances, the Osage artistic tradition still thrives.

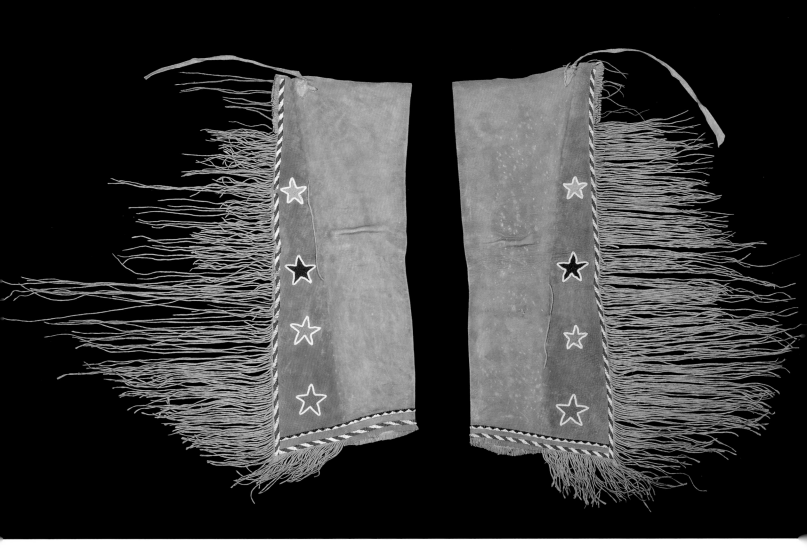

CAT. 76

LEGGINGS

ca. 1900
deer hide, glass beads, and pigment
30 × 15 inches each
U.S. Cavalry Museum, Fort Riley, Kansas

Chief Bacon Rind of the Black Bear clan owned these leggings. The star image refers both to an earthbound comet and to the white starlike shape on a black bear's chest; the bear's fur represents the night sky. The stars on the leggings may represent specific constellations important to the Black Bear clan. The green and yellow colors on the leggings suggest grass and the sun, elements important to Osage survival. Edging the legging flaps are reversed and twisted fringes that imitate the tarsal leg feathers of the eagle, which drag on the ground when the animal walks.

PLAY COAT

ca. 1933
hide, beads, and cloth
24 × 18 inches
Private collection

Made in the 1930s, this double-breasted play coat has a single-wing plane on the back executed from a hawk's-eye view. The interior voids on the airplane are filled with vertical adjacent rows. The repeated motif on the jacket front that combines an eagle and an American shield is unusual because both eagle heads are turned in the same direction. This may denote a clan affiliation or it may simply be the result of an aesthetic decision. The movement of the eagle's wings is illustrated by the rows of beads following the contour of the upper wings. The softest pieces of hide were reserved for the collar, pockets, and sleeve cuffs. This play coat was made by Julia Lookout for her grandson, George E. Standing Bear, whose other grandmother, Laura Cloudshield Standing Bear Soldier, provided and tanned the hide of an unborn bison.

CAT. 78

OWL FAN

ca. 1870
owl feathers, turkey feathers, glass beads, and hide
24½ × 2¼ inches
Private collection

This fan was once used in the ritual ceremonies of the old Osage religion by the clan priest Steven Mongrain of the Black Bear people. It continued to be used in this manner until the old religious order disintegrated in the mid-1870s. Under the Christian-based Native American Church of the Osage, the fan was used in a personal rather than a ritual context. It has been said that the design depicts various regions of the universe. The zigzag pattern at the center of the handle represents lightning, and the randomly placed teal green translucent beads symbolize rain. The full tail of the immature great horned owl and the tip of the male wolverine tail on the other side are symbols associated with the powers of night.

CAT. 79

BELT

ca. 1900
yarn and glass beads
length: 34¾ inches
Private collection

The Osage have always taken great pride
in the art of finger weaving. Early ritual
belts were made from hair taken from the
left side and right side of a bison's hump.
Weaving together the hairs taken from the
left side with those taken from the right
side represents the unity of the cosmos
and the tribal divisions of peace and war.
Made by Julia Lookout for her husband,
this yarn belt would have been worn so
that the fringe hung down his left side, as
is the proper style for males of the Sky clan.
The concentric diamonds in red, yellow,
blue, and purple establish a visual pattern
that suggests the dynamic flow of lightning,
which continues down the chevrons and
onto the lightning-bolt patterns of the bias-
woven fringe.

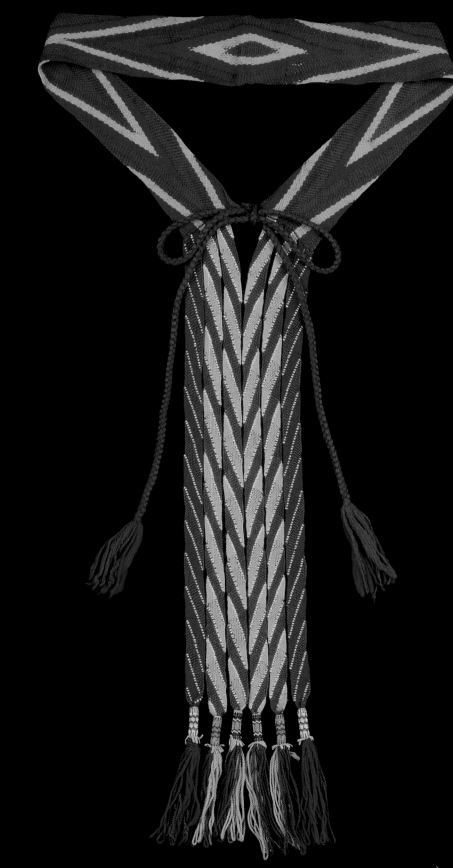

CAT. 80

Feather Bonnet

ca. 1900
feathers, glass, pigment, cloth, horsehair, and fur
18 × 12 × 24 inches
Private collection

Whirlwind Soldier, an Oglala Sioux, created this headdress for Julia Lookout to
wear during the Soldier Dances in 1924
when President Calvin Coolidge formally
recognized the Osage contribution to the
World War I effort with a certificate of
appreciation. Paul Red Eagle, former prin-
cipal chief, placed this headdress on Julia's
head at the beginning of the dances. The
fully flared headdress, with its generously
spreading feathers, required the use of
many golden eagle feathers. The tips of the
feathers are decorated with red-dyed horsehair that is attached with fabric and hoof
glue. The soft white ermine fur strips suspended from the beaded medallions at the
sides of the bonnet would caress the face
when the headdress was worn. Ermine
was reserved for special ceremonial pieces,
similar to its use on the robes of European
monarchs.

When this ceremony was first introduced, we were told that a select group of tribal elders and authoritarians set the standards and created an extraordinary social device that transmitted a powerful spiritual foundation. It encompassed such force that today it is the basis for the perpetuation of all of our cultural values, and subsequently provides the only sense of tribal unity we have . . . it is the strength of the Elonschska, its vitality and flexibility, which has enabled the Osage communities to survive.
—Frederick M. Lookout, 1998

Frederick Morris Lookout is arguably the most significant individual in the development and evolution of Osage music in the last half of the twentieth century, and his comments above allude to the general importance of dancing traditions as expressions of identity for individuals and tribal communities in the twenty-first century. A former Drum Keeper in the Pawhuska District, Lookout became an accomplished singer and at various times assumed the respected position of Head Singer on each of the three Osage E-Lon-schka committees. He also inspired a florescence of interest on the part of younger Osage people in learning the songs used in the ceremonial and secular dances of Osage society. Native Americans continue to observe a diverse range of religious, ceremonial, and social dances and to perform their associated musical repertoires. Most visible in this contemporary performance milieu is the intertribal powwow, the primary cultural activity for the majority of Native Americans in North America.

The Osage people have always used a diverse range of dances and songs in the ceremonies and rituals of the Osage Tribal Religion. Many of the lengthy prayers delivered by the clan and tribal priests were sung as opposed to spoken. European accounts of Osage culture in the eighteenth century are replete with references to dance and music as important aspects of Osage life.[1] Many of these performances were part of the ritual preparations the Osage undertook to invoke supernatural sanction for war and hunting expeditions. In the late nineteenth and early twentieth centuries, the Osage attempted to perpetuate selected aspects of their Tribal Religion through ceremonial and ideological modification, which can be seen in the changing form and content of the Mourning Ceremony, the Tattooing Ceremony, and the Child Naming Ceremony.[2]

As the songs, ceremonies, and dances associated with the Osage Tribal Religion were modified and ultimately abandoned, they were replaced with a number of intertribal revival movements that spread broadly among Indian communities in the American Plains and Prairie regions during the late nineteenth century. The majority of those movements involved the revival of dancing activities to restore health and vitality to native communities and their members. The Osage were exposed to many of these ceremonies and participated in some marginal trials of the widespread Ghost Dance Religion, the Faw Faw Dance, and the Drum Religion.[3]

Osage E-Lon-schka

Several of the social and religious movements introduced to the Osage in the nineteenth century were adopted by them, and a few continue to flourish among the Osage today. The most important of those is the Osage E-Lon-schka. While not a religion and certainly more than a social dance, the E-Lon-schka is a ceremonial society of male members that preserves and perpetuates many traditional Osage values while providing a focal point for the ethnic identity of Osage people. The E-Lon-schka has been an important part of the cultural life of the Osages for more than a century. The dance and its associated organization provide a spiritual charter for the survival of the ancient Osage physical divisions, or "districts," as they are called today. As the Osage people enter the twenty-first century, the E-Lon-schka represents the most significant ceremonial and social activity for most of its tribal members.[4]

The term *E-Lon-schka* is generally translated to mean "playground of the eldest son," which is a reference to the joyous spirit associated with the performance of the dance and the elevated status the oldest male child enjoys in a traditional Osage family. The E-Lon-schka is the Osage version of the Grass Dance, a major American Indian cultural movement adopted by dozens of tribes in the plains and prairie areas in the late nineteenth century.[5] The Grass Dance assumed many forms as it spread, with individual groups adapting the dance to both their historical experience and their contemporary situation. Among the Osage, it was referred to as the Charcoal Dance, referring to the black paint the warriors used in their ritual preparations for warfare. The original version of the dance among the Osage was discontinued, probably after the cessation of intertribal warfare and raiding in the middle of the nineteenth century.

The modern E-Lon-schka was introduced among the Osage in the late nineteenth century and developed

FIGURE 6.1 Osage dancers at Gray Horse dance hall, Fairfax, Oklahoma, before 1914. Photograph by Vince Dillon, Ruth Mohler Collection; courtesy Oklahoma Historical Society.

along district lines: a separate drum and dance organization was established in each physical division of the tribe. It was introduced in the Pawhuska and Hominy Districts in the mid-1880s by their neighbors, the Kansa. In the Gray Horse District, the dance was received from the Ponca people. Osage elders remember that their parents told them about the decision to adopt the dance and how a lengthy process of evaluation and negotiation accompanied it.[6]

From its earliest practice, the E-Lon-schka has been associated with the dance houses in which it was performed in bad weather and at night. Early dance houses consisted of an enclosure created from vertical boards and a brush roof. In 1894 there were four such houses on the reservation: one each in Pawhuska, Hominy, and Gray Horse, and another on Bird Creek, near the modern town of Barnsdall.[7] The fourth dance house represents the continued existence of the Heart-Stays physical division of the tribe. Little history of this E-Lon-schka district survives, primarily because the Heart-Stays division was consolidated into the Pawhuska District in the early twentieth century.[8]

The E-Lon-schka dance assumed many different roles in its early history among the Osage people. It was used to perpetuate elements of the Osage Tribal Religion; it was a replacement for the traditional funeral services; it served as a mechanism to enhance tribal solidarity; and it was a way to promote peaceful relations with neighboring tribal communities. When first adopted, the E-Lon-schka was used by Osage religious leaders to continue certain practices of the Osage Tribal Religion, including the use of sacred medicine bundles and recognition of their associated powers. The spiritual nature of the dance focused on the sacred power of the drum and the strict rules that governed the performance of the dance. When the E-Lon-schka was first introduced, certain elements of the dance, such as the use of tobacco and cedar, followed the ceremonial division of labor found in the Osage Tribal Religion.[9]

When the Peyote Religion was introduced to the Osage people in the late 1890s, it brought newly converted Peyotists into conflict with the E-Lon-schka dance. Many Osage people who were trying to follow the teachings of John Wilson abandoned the E-Lon-schka because it incorporated elements from the earlier Osage Tribal

Religion. As Peyotism grew in popularity and acceptance, the E-Lon-schka suffered a dramatic decline in participation and support. Walter Matin, a former Drum Keeper for the Hominy District and a Roadman in the Peyote Religion, stated that the E-Lon-schka dance in Hominy almost died out when participation declined to only a few families. In 1914 the Drum Keeper left the drum hanging at the dance hall after several years of failed attempts to pass the drum to a new keeper. Matin assumed the position of Drum Keeper in 1916, marking the return of Peyotists to the dance in the Hominy District.[10]

In Pawhuska, the situation became so critical that on one occasion there were only five dancers at the E-Lon-schka, while a large Peyote meeting was in progress at nearby Barnsdall. Chief Bacon Rind, an active Peyotist, is said to have traveled to Barnsdall to induce the Osage there to save the dance from extinction. The impact of Peyotism on the E-Lon-schka dance seems to have been less severe in the Gray Horse District, where the dance continued to retain many of its original traditions and practices.[11]

Pony Smoke

The original Osage version of E-Lon-schka was often referred to as the "Pony Smoke" or "Smoke Pony" dance by non-Indian observers. The Pony Smoke was a common form of intertribal activity in Indian Territory in the late nineteenth century and was used to facilitate social interaction and peaceful relations among geographic neighbors. The Osage maintained a reciprocal pattern of dancing with several tribes, including the Pawnee, Oto, Ponca, Kansa, and Delaware.

Long-stemmed, elbow-shaped stone pipes, different in shape from the disc pipes used in the Osage Tribal Religion, were key objects in early E-Lon-schka dances (see cat. 42). In those early dances, each drum had a pipe that it "owned," and the Pipe Bearer or Pipe Lighter was an important ceremonial officer whose duties included the care of the pipe and its ceremonial lighting during the dance.[12]

Before the performance of the Pony Smoke, the visiting party would stop a short distance from the host community and send a messenger into the village to announce their arrival for a tribal "visit." After waiting

FIGURE 6.2 Postcard of Pony Smoke Dance, Osage Indians, Oklahoma. Cherokee Strip Museum Collection, Perry, Oklahoma; courtesy Oklahoma Historical Society.

an appropriate time, the visitors would parade into the village and arrange themselves in a semicircle in front of their assembled hosts. At this point, a member of the host community would come forward, light the pipe, and, after taking a single puff, offer it to a member of the visiting delegation. The offer of the pipe was a sign that the bearer wished to make a gift, while receiving and smoking the pipe was indication that the gift was accepted. The major ceremonial currency of the day was horses, and the Osage were reported to own in excess of 12,000 head of horses in 1873.[13] After the smoking of the pipe and the bestowing of gifts, both hosts and

FIGURE 6.3 E-Lon-schka dancers, Pawhuska District, ca. 1886. Courtesy Gilcrease Museum.

visitors participated in rounds of dancing. The hosts served the visiting delegation an extensive feast at the close of the ceremony.[14]

That the Osage would decide to expend their relative wealth in the form of blankets, ponies, and food for a Smoke Pony was a constant source of conflict with the Indian Agents, who failed to comprehend a system in which great status was afforded to those who gave away their tangible goods. It became a custom among the Osage to use these acts of gift giving to honor their young children by allowing them to make the actual presentation after the smoking ceremony had been completed.[15]

Among the Osage, the pipe that belonged to the drum was expanded to pipe ownership for each participant. The use of the pipe in conjunction with the dance seems to have waned after 1910, which coincides with the return of the Peyotists to the dance and its reconfiguration into its contemporary structure and content. The spirit of hospitality, seen in the giving of gifts and feasting, remains an important feature of the modern E-Lon-schka.

Contemporary E-Lon-schka Dances

A key tenet of the E-Lon-schka dance is the often repeated phrase "don't add anything; don't take anything away." The faithful adherence of successive generations of Osage to this philosophy has caused the E-Lon-schka to retain many of the older elements abandoned by most of the other communities that adopted the Grass Dance. Today the E-Lon-schka is viewed by other native communities as an inherently Osage ceremonial event, open to the community and invited guests.

As a formal society, the E-Lon-schka is organized around a committee composed of ceremonial officers and a general membership. At the head of the organization is the Drum Keeper, charged with the care and protection of the drum and sponsorship of the annual dance in his district. The position of Drum Keeper is both ceremonial and practical, requiring the support of both an extended family and the community in general. The Drum Keeper and his family name the members of the committee that will serve with them in their tenure as leaders of the dance. The Drum Keeper is also responsible for supplying the groceries and the cooks for the meals that accompany meetings of the committee

throughout the year. The Drum Keeper is expected to dance all four days in each of the three districts each year. Given the scale of participation in the contemporary E-Lon-schka, very few families will enjoy the level of respect and responsibility associated with the office of Drum Keeper.

The size of E-Lon-schka committees has increased over time, a reflection of the level of community participation in the dance. One modern leader in the dance remarked that the trend has continued to the point that many Osage believe every member of the dance should be on the committee.[16] In 1941 Leo Miles received the drum in the Pawhuska District from Paul Red Eagle and named a committee comprised of two advisors, eight committeemen, four Tail Dancers, two Whip Men, two Water Boys, a Drum Taker, and several male singers.[17] Today committees include in excess of seventy members, with considerable increases in the number of officers, including singers, cooks, and water boys.

A Head Committeeman is named by each Drum Keeper as his spokesperson and advisor on issues of protocol and traditional practice. The Head Committeeman functions as the master of ceremonies for the dance in his district. Other important officers include the elders that are designated as advisors to the committee. The Head Singer leads the male and female singers in the performance of the E-Lon-schka songs. There are more than three hundred songs associated with the dance, and to learn them all requires considerable time and effort.

Additional officers include the two Whip Men, who carry out a variety of ceremonial and practical duties during the dance. Their symbolic badge of office is a traditional-style quirt that they receive from the Drum Keeper when they are named to the committee. The Whip Men are responsible for preparing the dance ground, seating the visiting committees as they enter the arbor, and policing the dance arena for lost or dropped objects. Their unique role is further enhanced by their distinction as the only individuals who circle the drum in a clockwise direction, counter to all other dancers.

The Water Boys are also committee officers, who provide drinking water to the singers and dancers during breaks in the dance. The positions of Tail Dancers date to the early history of the dance and are marked by the beaded sticks they alone are authorized to carry (see cats. 97 and 99). Although they are not formal members of the E-Lon-schka society, women do assume important offices on the named committees. A designated group of Women Singers has long been associated with the dance and continues to receive great respect in the modern E-Lon-schka. The Head Cook and the other "committee cooks" are central to the spiritual intent and practical function of the E-Lon-schka committee. The ability to host meals and amass an ample supply of rations for the visiting camps and guests is a major tenet of the hospitality associated with the dance.

Although the focus of the E-Lon-schka committee is the sponsorship of the annual dance in their district, the members function as a formal society throughout the year. The committee meets to conduct regular business activity such as fund-raising for the June Dance, organizing sympathy breakfasts when a committee member dies, setting dates for the dances, and holding discussions about passing the drum to a new Keeper. Drum Keepers and their committees also participate in local social dances, funerals, naming ceremonies, hand games, and other traditional events of Osage society.

Today the E-Lon-schka dances are held on three weekends during the month of June, beginning in the Gray Horse District, followed by Hominy, and concluding with the dance in Pawhuska. In the early twentieth century, the dance was held as often as four times a year, which corresponded to the quarterly per-capita payments of revenue from the tribal mineral estate and other sources of communal income. It is generally

conceded that the E-Lon-schka can be held whenever the Drum Keeper chooses to sponsor a dance, but the economic and geographic realities of contemporary Osage life would make this a difficult undertaking, as the majority of participants schedule their vacations from work to attend the June Dances. Several Osage elders remember that "when the dance was really going well," the Drum Keeper would extend it for another four days, and sometimes among the three districts they would dance all summer.[18]

Prior to the first E-Lon-schka dance of the season, the community undertakes increased activity in the three Indian villages where the dances are conducted. The original selection of each village tract corresponded to the area immediately surrounding the three dance houses on the reservation. Today each village is largely defined by the rectangular dance arbors constructed from steel pipes and trusses and covered with a metal roof. The dance area, which consists of fine soil that has a slight roll to it, is prepared by raking and sifting to remove rocks and other hard materials. Wooden benches for the dancers ring the dance area, and rows of bleachers are provided on two sides for spectators and visitors. Other structures include cook sheds and dining shelters for guests from the two visiting districts, plus public rest rooms. Several families from each district maintain smaller camps in which they cook and eat, mostly to entertain extended family and guests. Following the evening sessions, the dancers and their families congregate in these camps to share a light supper and engage in conversation and social activities, including Indian dice, a game of chance and skill (see cat. 90).

The E-Lon-schka dance consists of seven dance sessions, one in the afternoon and one in the evening on Thursday, Friday, and Saturday and a single session on Sunday afternoon that concludes the dance. Each session has an individual atmosphere, the combined result of the accompanying music, the size of the participation, and the special elements and activities associated with it. A session is announced when the Camp Crier rings a large brass bell: the first ring is at one hour before the session and another is at one-half hour before. The host committee enters the arbor as a group, with the drum leading the procession. The drum is placed at the center of the dance area, where the singers are already seated.

FIGURE 6.4 E-Lon-schka dance, Gray Horse dance hall. Courtesy Oklahoma Historical Society.

FIGURE 6.5 Modern dance arbor in Gray Horse, Oklahoma. Courtesy Tyrone Stewart, photographer.

Women, who did not dance in the E-Lon-schka until the 1940s, are not seated in the arbor; they sit on family benches, enter from one of the four openings in the arbor, and then dance around the drum at the outer edges of the dance area. Unlike more secularized dance performances, the sessions of the E-Lon-schka are often halted by the Head Committeeman just as they reach their peak. This is done as a mechanism to keep the dancers anxious to return to the arbor at the beginning of the next session.

There are several special events during the dances. The Committee Dinner at noon on Saturday is the event at which the host Drum Keeper provides a lavish feast for the members of all three E-Lon-schka committees and numerous additional guests. Given the size of the contemporary committees, this dinner often serves more than four hundred people. At the beginning of the Saturday afternoon session, committee members bring large boxes and baskets of groceries and other goods to the dance arbor and place them in a circle around the drum and singers. Visitors, guests, and others are called forward by name to receive a gift of these rations. The Sunday session is devoted to the singing of the named "individual songs" that commemorate various officers on the committee and the memory of specific community members. Each group or individual leads the dancing on his or her song and then conducts a giveaway at its conclusion. It is common for multiple giveaways to be conducted after each song so that the entire schedule of individual songs often takes many hours to complete.

Initiation into the Dance

Male members are formally admitted to the E-Lon-schka through the ceremony of being roached, a reference to the headdress worn by the majority of male dancers. Today this ceremony begins with the entrance of the initiate and his extended family into the arbor during one of the water breaks. The procession is led by the Camp Crier, who requests that the members take notice of the initiate entering the arbor. A preselected individual, often the Head Committeeman or sometimes another member of the committee, acts as the spokesperson for the family. The introduction of the initiate often includes mention of his clan, the English meaning of his Osage name, and some presentation of his extended Osage genealogy. After he concludes his speech, the spokesman takes the eagle feather from the initiate and places it in the socket of the spreader that lies inside the roach headdress.

The family then conducts a giveaway in which they recognize the three Drum Keepers, the singers, their spokesman, and any number of additional individuals, particularly anyone who helped the family assemble the dance clothes and accouterments for the new initiate. In the early twentieth century, it was customary for the initiate to be seated on a blanket when the headdress was tied on. However, today the individual stands before the assembled committees and usually enters the arena wearing the roach headdress, with the eagle feather placed in its holder as the mark of entrance into the dance.

Passing the Drum

Drum Keepers traditionally hold the drum for a self-selected period, which often extends for many years. In the midtwentieth century, several Drum Keepers held it for ten years or more. When one family is ready to "pass the drum" to another, the E-Lon-schka committee convenes to discuss the potential choices and arrive at a consensus decision. The event of passing the drum is of great importance and interest, containing an element of intrigue as rumors circulate that the drum will be passed and people speculate on the possible recipients.

The decision to pass the drum is made public at the conclusion of the Sunday session. If the negotiation has been successfully concluded, the current Drum Keeper moves to the drum, which the singers remove from its stand, places it in front of the new Drum Keeper, and returns to his seat. The new Drum Keeper immediately sets to work to assemble a committee, naming officials and members. When the drum passes at either Gray Horse or Hominy, the new Drum Keeper is responsible for hosting the district at the remaining dances of the year.

The Drum Keeper and his extended family work over the course of the year to prepare the necessary goods, gifts, and food that will be distributed when he pays for the drum and sponsors his first set of dances. The event of "paying for the drum" begins when the committee assembles before the start of the dances on Thursday to share a noon meal. After the dancers from the visiting and host districts have been seated in the arbor, the new Drum Keeper and his family file in and arrange themselves before the assembled members. A number of trunks and bundles are brought into the arena and

FIGURE 6.7 Horse given to the past Drum Keeper in the "paying for the drum" ceremony, Hominy, Oklahoma, ca. 1985. Courtesy Tyrone Stewart, photographer.

FIGURE 6.6 "Brides," Osage County, Oklahoma, ca. 1984. Courtesy Tyrone Stewart, photographer.

several of the new Drum Keeper's female relatives are dressed in traditional Osage wedding outfits (Osage "brides").

The first individual to be recognized in the giveaway is the former Drum Keeper, who receives the traditional gift of a horse with a "wearing blanket" draped over its back. Common recipients of a bride are female relatives of the former Drum Keeper, the Head Committeeman, and the advisors. The brides are escorted out of the dance area, where female relatives "undress the bride" down to shorts and a T-shirt while her bride garments and accouterments are carefully folded and put away. In the early twentieth century, it was common for these "brides" to wear two or three layers of Osage clothes under the wedding coat.[19] Each member of the newly formed committee is recognized and receives a gift from the Drum Keeper, often a Pendleton blanket or shawl. The Drum Keeper completes the giveaway with a sizable monetary gift to the drum.

Dance Clothes

Prior to contact with Europeans, Osage people made their garments exclusively from hides and skins and decorated them primarily with painted designs. The Osage exhibited great skill in their transformation of stone, shell, hair, feathers, bone, horn, and other natural materials into beautifully carved pipes, necklaces, headdresses, musical instruments, dance wands and fans, and other ceremonial objects.[20]

Traditional Osage dress and accouterments underwent extensive modification after the incorporation of European trade goods and stylistic influences from both native and nonnative sources. Glass beads, yarn, satin ribbon, cloth, metal, and other manufactured materials were incorporated into the traditional economy of the Osage people beginning in the late seventeenth century. The introduction of new materials and the tools to work them did little to change the basic style and form of traditional Osage clothing, but it did provide the possibility for expanded aesthetic expression in decorative detail and embellishment.

Since the modern E-Lon-schka dances are the central occasion when Osage people wear traditional-style clothing, the dance is largely responsible for keeping alive the traditional arts required to create them. E-Lon-schka clothing conforms with the basic attire of the Osage people in the midnineteenth century, with the understanding that the distinction between daily utility wear and its ceremonial counterpart was gained through decorative embellishment and the level of accessorizing accouterments. A core inventory for males included leather moccasins, cloth or leather leggings, a breechcloth, and fabric shirts (see cats. 76 and 91). Vests, commercial as well as those constructed from wool stroud cloth, were often substituted for a shirt and, when properly decorated with beadwork, sequins, and ribbon work, were worn as formal male E-Lon-schka attire (see cat. 93). For women, this basic set consisted of moccasins, cloth skirts and "half" leggings, and fabric blouses (see cat. 102). A wearing blanket, most often a large piece of wool stroud cloth, was integral to both men's and women's attire.

Unlike many native communities in Oklahoma and the Great Plains region who developed more homogenous styles of "Indian clothes," Osage people have generally conformed to conservative patterns with respect to taste and style.[21] The traditional clothing worn during the E-Lon-schka dances has remained very consistent over the century that the dance has existed among the Osage people. Modifications have been minor and caused little change in the overall appearance of E-Lon-schka attire. Many tribes in Oklahoma have adopted the E-Lon-schka style of dance clothing, where it is referred to as an Oklahoma Straight Dance outfit. The Straight Dance has become an integral component of social powwows and their associated contest dances.

Osage E-Lon-schka clothing is finely tailored. The overlapping layers of garments and accouterments generally lie flat to the body to accentuate the graceful dance steps used by participants. Accessories are minimal and the vertical orientation of decorative elements, including ribbon work, yarn drop, otter dragger (discussed later in this section), and roach headdress, contribute to the sense of height and grace. A discernible "Osage look" is evident in the clothing itself and the manner in which it is worn. This combination of taste and style is predicated on exacting standards with respect to quality and design. Hallmarks of "Osage work" include precise technical execution and an exactness of design that is accentuated by the selection and juxtaposition of colors. Decorative elaboration in Osage traditional arts is found in the detailed embellishment of E-Lon-schka clothing and accessories, such as beading the ends of the braided fringe found on yarn drops (see cat. 79) and the individual shafts of feathers in a fan.

The traditional fabric arts of the Osage people are central to the creation of E-Lon-schka clothes. Skirts, leggings, breechcloths, and blouses all are made from patterns that have been used for more than a century. Shirts and blouses are variations of a T-shape design decorated with tailored details and ribbon trim. The Osage preference for vibrant colors, complex patterns, and diverse fabrics can be seen in their shirts and blouses. Osage people have particularly excelled in the art forms of ribbon work and finger weaving, using new materials and techniques to perpetuate ancient patterns and their associated symbolism and meaning.

Finger weaving is a term that describes a number of techniques used to produce woven strips without the aid

FIGURE 6.8 Loose fan, ca. 1900. Courtesy Gilcrease Museum.

material with sacred, protective powers.[22] Buffalo hair, spun by hand into long strands, created more pliable fibers that could be used to braid ropes, bridles, and other cordage (see cat. 86). Fine strands of buffalo "yarn" were woven into long sashes for some Osage medicine bundles, where designs were created by working a lighter-colored hair from buffalo calves onto a darker field of adult hair. An expanded set of designs was achieved later when European glass beads were strung on the strands and woven into the belts at the appropriate point.

The fur trade of the seventeenth century introduced two important developments in Native American finger-weaving traditions. The first was the availability of commercial yarn in a broad range of colors, and the second was the adoption of new techniques that greatly expanded the number of possible design elements. At the height of the fur trade, finished sashes were an important trade item, manufactured by a cottage industry that included both European and Native weavers.[23]

Finger-woven sashes have long been important elements in traditional Osage dress. They have been used as belts and garters in both male and female outfits. In woman's attire, a broad finger-woven sash secures the skirt, while smaller woven strips hold the half-leggings in place. A blouse covers the broad woven portion of the sash so that only the long fringe is visible hanging in the back. This fringe provides a kinetic element to the outfit: the dance step used by Osage women incorporates a dip in the knees that causes the fringe to sway in unison from side to side. In the earlier days of the E-Lon-schka dance, men, too, wore fringed sashes to secure their leggings and dance breechcloths, and the fringe would hang from the waist at one or both sides of the dancer. At a later time, the sash was replaced by

of any mechanical devices or tools. Modern finger weaving, which is the product of indigenous and European influences, is an important example of an ancient artistic technique that has been energized through the introduction of new materials and an expanded color palette. In earlier times, Osage women employed a variety of weaving and twining techniques to convert vegetal fibers into mats, bags, ropes, and other utilitarian objects. Rush and nettle fibers were used to construct the storage bags used in medicine bundles. The process of their making was carried out under ceremonial conditions to imbue the

FIGURE 6.9 Buffalo-hair belt. Courtesy Department of Anthropology, Smithsonian Institution.

finger-woven side-drops that simulated the exposed fringe. Male E-Lon-schka dancers wear finger-woven garters to close up the leggings and to provide padding for the long strands of bells that are wound around the legs. When leggings were a part of daily attire in Osage society, men often wore beautifully designed beaded garters below the knee (see cats. 85, 94, 95).

The introduction of satin fabrics, thread, and steel needles greatly affected the artistic endeavors of Native American communities and fostered the development of a diverse set of fabric arts that are collectively referred to as ribbon work. Osage ribbon work came to exemplify a type of ribbon work that developed among the native communities of the Prairie region. While many tribal communities continue to produce ribbon work for decorative detail on traditional clothing, the Osage have earned a position of great stature based on their distinctive patterns, high standards of quality, and the sheer volume of ribbon work they have produced.

Osage ribbon work is made from rayon taffeta that is torn into strips, or "ribbons," that are then basted together into layers. A series of strategic cuts and folds is used to create a wide range of patterns in a technique referred to as "reverse appliqué." Older Osage work is often constructed from three ribbons, but today the Osage are best known for the intricate diamond patterns that use from seven to fifteen ribbons to create works of geometric perfection (see cat. 91). Color selection is an important aspect of Osage ribbon work. It often incorporates a bold juxtaposition of two dark colors with a white or light pastel-colored ribbon that is used as an outline or "piping" for the major design elements.

Ribbon work is a major decorative element for E-Lon-schka clothing. Usually there are matching strips for the leggings, breechcloth, and trailer of the male outfit, and separate patterns are used for the skirts and half-leggings of the women's outfit. The outer edge of the ribbon work for the male Straight Dance outfit is edged in beadwork that is primarily white. Not only does the beadwork offer a higher level of decorative detail, but it also functions to protect the ribbon work from excessive wear. Ribbon work appears as decorative embellishment on wearing blankets, otter drops, vests, and dance shawls.

Roaches are a striking component of male E-Lon-schka attire (see cat. 9). The headdress is constructed from rows of either turkey beard or the long guard hair from porcupines, attached to a flexible base. A row of shorter hair from a deer tail, which has been dyed red or another color, is attached to the outer edge. An ingenious device called a "spreader" sits inside the roach to push the hair into a vertical stance and to provide a means of attaching the headdress to the wearer. The base of the spreader holds a socket for a single golden-eagle tail feather. Older styles of roach spreaders constructed from horn and bone were decorated with carved, incised, and cutout elements (see cat. 92), but by the late nineteenth century German silver was the preferred material for spreaders. German silver, also known as nickel silver, is an alloy of nickel, tin, and copper that is much harder than silver but capable of maintaining a high sheen when buffed and polished. The final element of the headdress is the "scalp feather" ornament that is attached at the outer base of the roach.

The earliest interpretation of the roach headdress has to do with warfare: it provides the physical insignia for a ceremonial official in a tribal war party. The roach is symbolic of the sacred fire, which is revered for its both beneficial and destructive powers. The red of the deer tail along the outer side represents the fire, the black turkey beard depicts the smoke, and the single eagle feather symbolizes the warrior, standing in the flames. The entire headdress is symbolic of a warrior's desire to display the fierce determination of and his identification with the awesome power of fire to destroy and consume his enemy in his defense of the village and its members.[24]

The otter-tail dragger, or "otter drop," which is unique to the traditional regalia of the Grass Dance on the southern plains, may well have been an Osage innovation. The dragger is a narrow strip of fur that hangs from the neck down the back of the dancer. The otter hide is attached to a wool base that is trimmed with ribbon work and then edged with beading. Otter drops are decorated in a tasteful manner that often incorporates a strip of loom beadwork with beaded medallions at each end. Trimmed and decorated feathers, often with the shafts beaded in the gourd stitch technique, commonly hang from the medallions.

E-Lon-schka outfits include accessories decorated with beadwork made in a variety of techniques. This includes the wide, loom-beaded strips that are attached to the leather belts of men and various sizes of appliqué rosettes that decorate the otter drops and beaded handles for fans and tail sticks. The Osage have also used either loomed or appliqué beadwork techniques to create strips that echo the ribbon-work designs used on male dance clothing. Appliqué beadwork in geometric and floral designs also decorates women's blankets.

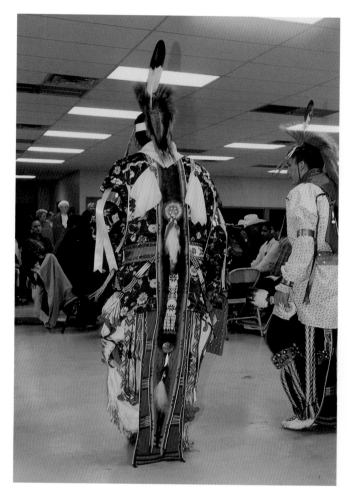

FIGURE 6.10 Otter hide and trailer. © David Ulmer, photographer.

Osage men and women wear a wide range of jewelry in the traditional dress. The majority of the jewelry accessories used in E-Lon-schka clothing are made from German silver. Many dancers wear earrings, with the classic "ball and cone" design a favorite with both sexes. Male E-Lon-schka dancers wear German silver armbands, a neckerchief slide, and wrist bracelets with stamped and engraved designs (see cats. 81, 82, 83, 84). Women wear a matched set of three brooches, or "pins," that are arranged vertically at the center of the bodice of their blouses. These pins are decorated with stamped designs and "pierced" work that displays the influences of the traditional styles of metalwork from the Great Lakes and Prairie regions.

FIGURE 6.11 Little boy's beaded E-Lon-schka suit, Gray Horse, Oklahoma, ca. 1950. Courtesy Gilcrease Museum.

Beads of larger sizes are used for chokers and bando-liers that commonly combine bone "hair pipes" with metal and glass necklace beads. Traditional neckwear for Osage women is a bunch-style necklace made with dozens of strands of faceted, dark "iris" beads that create iridescent reflections of light. Dancers of both sexes typically carry a feather fan, most commonly of golden- or bald-eagle tail feathers. The fan is set in a "flat" or rigid configuration, and its handle is fully beaded with small cut-glass beads (see cat. 87). Male dancers might carry other accouterments such as beaded bags, mirror boards, and whistles (see cats. 12, 23, 88, 89).

Men and women include a variety of wearing blankets in association with their E-Lon-schka attire. For men, this is often a red or blue wool broadcloth blanket with ribbon-work strips and edging that may be further deco-rated with a beaded blanket strip. Blankets made from red wool stroud cloth are traditionally reserved for the firstborn son. Women's wearing blankets have panels of ribbon work running along the two vertical edges, with a wider panel that joins them along the lower horizontal edge. A row of German silver brooches above the hori-zontal row of ribbon work and silk appliqué figures in the shape of horses, hands, and hearts outlined by one or two rows of white beadwork are additional decorative elements for women's blankets (see cat. 1).

Osage Soldier Dance

In traditional Osage society, the return of a victorious war party was met with considerable ceremony and celebration. As the party neared the village, it would be met by a ceremonial official who would sing the Victory Songs and dance at the head of the procession of war-riors and villagers. Religious ceremonies would be conducted to pay homage to the sacred hawks and the charcoal paint used in the ritual preparation of the war party. As intertribal warfare waned in the midnineteenth century, however, the Osage ceased to observe the cere-monies performed to invoke supernatural sanction for defensive action and to celebrate its victorious result.

It was not until World War I that the Osage commu-nity once again found the need to pray for the safe return of its warriors from armed conflict. More than one hun-dred twenty Osage served in the military during that war,

and those at home participated in bond drives and sup-ported the American Red Cross. President Coolidge rec-ognized the patriotism of the Osage people in 1924 when he issued a certificate of appreciation to the members of the tribe for their overwhelming support for the war effort. The following year, the tribe inaugurated the Osage Soldier Peace Dance, using a special $25,000 payment to sponsor a celebration that featured dancing and feasting for both Osage people and their non-Indian neighbors.[25]

The Soldier Dance was an intertribal movement that spread among Native American communities as an outgrowth of their participation in World War I and an expression of their preference for traditional methods to honor servicemen. Singers and composers from the Oto, Ponca, and Omaha tribes influenced the musical repertoire of the Osage Soldier Dance. Male and female participants in the dance form a circle around the drum and dance with a distinctive sideways step. As in the E-Lon-schka dance, individual songs are "placed in the drum" by families to honor a member who had served in the armed forces. Giveaways conducted at the end of individual songs allow the host organizations, singers, and committee people to recognize individuals for their service to the community.

In association with the Soldier Dance, women began to create beautiful wearing blankets that were embel-lished with battle scenes, military insignia, American

FIGURE 6.12 Postcard of Osage Soldier Dance, Pawhuska, Oklahoma, ca. 1926–1939. Photograph by Vince Dillon; cour-tesy Oklahoma Historical Society, Virgil Robbins Collection.

FIGURE 6.13 Veterans Day dance, Pawhuska, Oklahoma, 2002. © David Ulmer, photographer.

flags, and other patriotic motifs rendered in appliqué beadwork. Scenes from blankets include tanks and troops in the trenches, aerial combat between American and German planes, and the names of Osage servicemen. These blankets have been passed down from generation to generation and are used only during the Soldier Dance (see cats. 103 and 104).

As the number of founding members and surviving veterans declined in the 1930s, participation in the Soldier Dance weakened. The entrance of the United States into World War II brought hundreds of Osage into military service and to work in the aircraft factories in nearby Tulsa. As they had before, the entire Osage community participated in bond drives and other activities to support the troops and the general war effort.

In the early 1940s, the Osage Soldier Dance became associated with two national organizations, the American War Mothers and the American Legion. In Pawhuska, the Harold Bigheart Smally Post 198 of the American Legion, and its associated women's auxiliary, assumed maintenance of the Soldier Dance. The female relatives of servicemen in Hominy and Gray Horse affiliated with the American War Mothers and received charters as Chapters 6 and 15, respectively. Soldier Dance celebrations are held in each of the three districts, with the Gray Horse War Mothers sponsoring their dance on the Satur-

day prior to Mothers Day, and Veterans Day observances alternating on a biannual basis between the American Legion Post in Pawhuska and the Hominy War Mothers.

Innovations

Dancing societies and the performance events associated with them have long been important aspects of Osage ceremonial and social life. In the older Osage Tribal Religion, dances with their musical traditions were often associated with the more public events found near the end of the ritual movements and prayers of major tribal ceremonies. The dances have always been associated with the celebratory aspects of life within and among Osage communities.

While most of the basic forms, designs, and techniques used to make and decorate Osage E-Lon-schka clothing and accessories can be traced to the nineteenth century, Osage art and material culture continue to evolve. Osage artists have constantly adopted innovations, new technologies, and materials. While some ribbon work still requires hand stitching, the sewing machine is used when possible. New hues of brightly colored beads are readily incorporated into an expanded design repertoire. Utilitarian advances such as Velcro to replace the hook and eye closures on ribbon shirts only make good sense.

Not all recent innovations have been adopted, however. Ribbon work is difficult to master, and it is time consuming and exacting in its execution. In the late 1970s, an Osage artist experimented with the idea of silk-screening ribbon-work designs on cloth ribbon. Using a sewing machine, an individual could sew the silk-screened strip onto broadcloth and then outline each change in color and pattern with additional machine stitching. From a few feet away, it was not easily distinguished from a handmade strip of ribbon work. However, although it cost a fraction of the price of a handmade piece of ribbon work, few individuals actually used it. Also dismissed was the idea of using zigzag machine stitching to execute ribbon work in the classic four-ribbon patterns.

Today, numerous Osages are actively engaged in producing ribbon work, beadwork, silver work, and other forms of traditional Osage artistry. The intended consumers of their work are either members of the extended family of the artist or other members of the local Osage

community. Osage artists have rarely attempted to com-
mercialize their traditional art forms and market their
works to larger Indian and non-Indian audiences, keeping their works relatively free from the influences of
Western, market-driven forces. The Osage have long
recognized the uniqueness of their artistic traditions
and have been extremely sensitive to possible influences
from other tribes. The development of what some have
termed Pan-Indianism and the more generic Native
American fine arts movement of the early twentieth
century have had little impact on Osage traditional arts.

The E-Lon-schka provides the motivation and impetus
for the perpetuation of traditional Osage arts. The attire
and accessories of Osage E-Lon-schka dancers provide
visible illustration of the general principles that guide
the dance and its organization. Little has changed within
the structure and form of the dance over its history
among the Osage people, yet at the same time important
changes have been instituted with respect to the size of
the committee, the participation of women in the dance
arbor, the use of fund-raisers and raffles to assist in the
financial sponsorship of the dance, and numerous other
adjustments that have been made to adapt the dance to
changing economic and social forces. This has been a
critical aspect of the survival and growth of the E-Lon-
schka and a major force in perpetuating Osage culture
and traditional practices. Ancient forms of structure and
procedures to maintain order provide an arena in which
community circumstances and individual motivation
combine to create contemporary Osage society and its
associated aesthetic expressions.

CAT. 81

BRACELET

late 19th century
German silver
3 × 2 × ½ inches
Department of Anthropology, Smithsonian Institution

German silver armbands and bracelets were originally used as a form of armor to deflect the blows of the enemy. This bracelet from the late nineteenth century shows an eagle bearing a Christian cross on its chest. The eight-pointed elliptical stars bordering the eagle may represent the morning and evening stars—heralds of the sun and the moon. The Osages' first exposure to Christian symbolism, particularly the cross, would have occurred in 1673 at the time Father Jacques Marquette explored the Mississippi River and its tributaries.

CAT. 82
NECKERCHIEF SLIDE

late 19th century
German silver
diameter: 3 inches
Department of Anthropology, Smithsonian Institution

When worn before noon, this German silver neckerchief slide represents the morning star to some clans of the Osage. When worn following noon prayers, the slide is turned upside down, which transforms the overall image inscribed on it into the evening star. The heart with a piercing arrow is a Western concept adopted for personal reasons by the Osage maker of this tie slide.

CAT. 83
TIE SLIDE

ca. 1918
German silver with ruby
diameter: 5 inches
Private collection

This elegantly hand-cut and hand-stamped tie slide is made of German silver, gold, and a ruby imported from Ceylon. The setting was made at Tiffany's in New York in the mid-1920s. This slide was intended for wear at Native American Church services and was made to hold a silk scarf around the neck. Scarves imported from Scotland and Czechoslovakia were preferred. The slide features thirty-two tines that appear to radiate energy from the center ruby, which reflects a deep red glow when it catches the light from the sacred fire in the church service. Symbolizing the morning star, the slide refers to the Osage cosmological order and the rebirth of the sun.

CAT. 84
NECKERCHIEF SLIDE

late 19th century
German silver
diameter: 2 inches
Department of Anthropology, Smithsonian Institution

This slide features symbols of war, including a pipe tomahawk, a bow, a quiver with arrows, a stone pipe, a war ball club with metal spike, and a hawk or eagle's head. A roped border frames these images. The Osage man who commissioned this slide wanted those war symbols to demonstrate his interest in warfare. As a part of treaty agreements, the Osage would stipulate the inclusion of a blacksmith to repair firearms, horse gear, and farming implements. These smiths were also requested to make personalized items such as this slide.

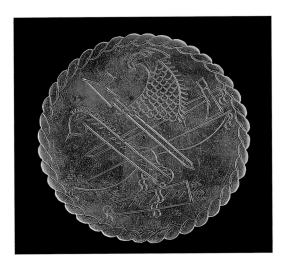

MAN'S GARTERS

cellulose fibers, protein combination, and glass beads
38 × 2¾ inches each
Department of Anthropology, Smithsonian Institution

These appliquéd garters, beaded on hide,
belonged to Chief Bacon Rind. The garters
were tied around the leg below the knees
with hide thongs that are visible behind
the tassels. The tassels hung on the outside
of the leg, moving with the motion of the
wearer. The lightning bolt images under-
neath the pinto horse heads symbolize
speed, and the hands (not to be confused
with the severed hand seen elsewhere in
Osage art) suggest the palm prints of the
owner. The six-pointed stars represent the
morning and evening stars, while the hourglass shapes at the stars' centers are sometimes seen as overhead views of a tornado.
These garters are an exellent example of
the finest imagery illustrating Osage cosmic
forces in beadwork.

CAT. 86

Bison Hair Lead

ca. 1860
glass beads and protein fibers
length: 34 feet
Department of Anthropology, Smithsonian Institution

This type of lead was used to give away horses in ceremonial settings. The plaiting technique, which gives it the maximum strength possible, is so time-consuming that it takes an hour to complete just two inches. Giveaway horses were young and skittish ponies that were not used to being handled, so the lead had to be strong enough to prevent the animals from breaking loose. The ends of the lead are wrapped in red broadcloth with glass beads in the center. The acceptance of the gift would be official when the recipient merely touched the lead with his hand.

CAT. 87

BALD EAGLE FAN

bald eagle feathers, hide, and glass beads
8 × 20 inches
Department of Anthropology, Smithsonian Institution

Chief Bacon Rind commissioned this fan for his personal use. He was especially interested in having an association with the American flag, which is depicted on the handle. The zigzag lines at the base of the handle suggest lightning bolts. The red plumes were meant to inspire courage, and the single green band signifies enduring life.

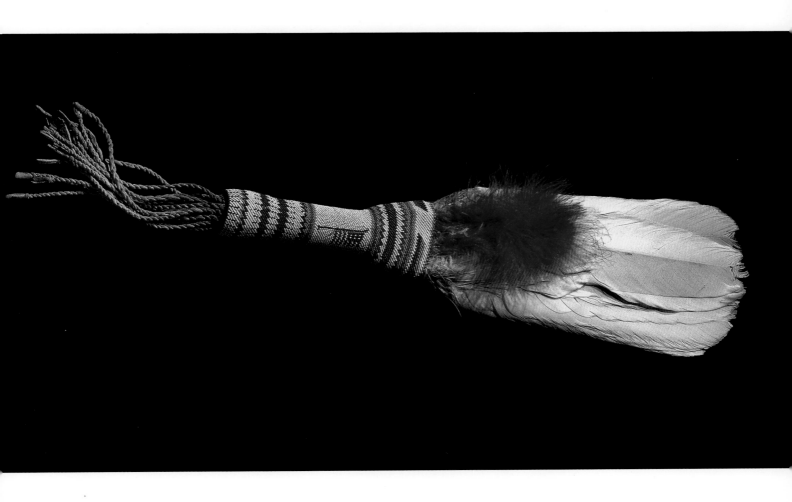

WHISTLE

wood and leather with feather
length: 26 inches
The Field Museum of Natural History, Chicago

This cane whistle was used when attacking an enemy. As long as the attackers were within earshot, the sound emitted would imbue them with a feeling of invincibility, but the sound of these whistles evoked terror in their victims as it signaled their imminent destruction. The incised wavy lines call upon the devastating effects of lightning.

CAT. 89

WHISTLE

wood, leather, yarn, glass beads, feathers, and fur
length: 29¹⁵⁄₁₆ inches
The Field Museum of Natural History, Chicago

This cane whistle is similar to those used in the E-Lon-schka dances of today. The sounding chambers are divided by growth rings, which are bored out near the rim to create a concentrated stream of air that is split by an adjustable reed. The resulting sound imitates a screaming hawk. Historically, in the military order, eight commanders wore hawks stuffed with human hair on their backs. The sound of these whistles inspired courage in all Osage warriors. The blowing of the whistle, with its loud and jolting sounds, instilled fear, panic, and despair in the enemy. The otter fur attached at the tip of this instrument reinforces the power of the hawk by giving it additional speed.

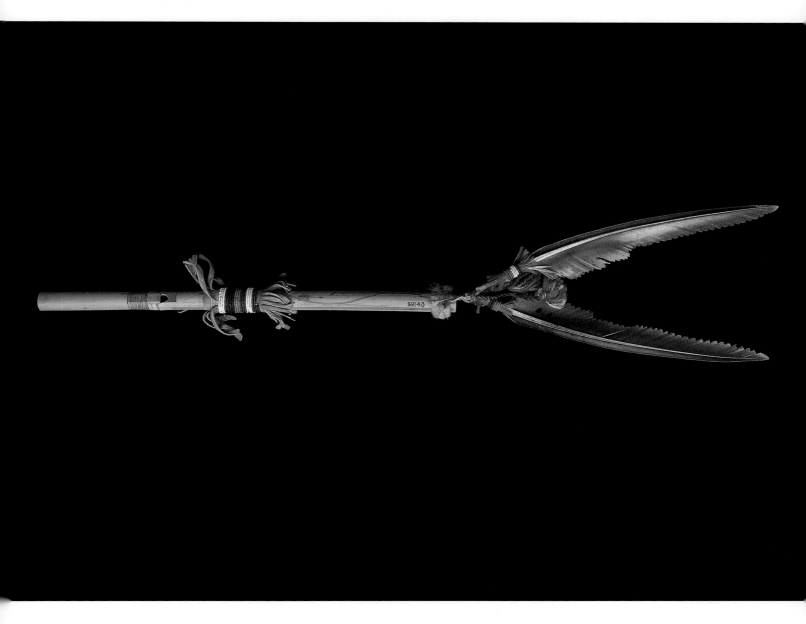

CAT. 90

Dice with Bowl

bone, pigment, and wood
dice average: ¾ inches
Brooklyn Museum of Art, Museum Expedition 1911,
Museum Collection Fund

Games are an important part of Osage festivities. Horse racing and a ballgame known as Shinny were high-stakes games that often involved dangerous physical contact. Dice games, on the other hand, depended more on luck than physical prowess. The game of dice proceeds this way: a given number of players sit across from one another, and a bowl containing the dice is placed between them on a long pile of blankets. One of the players lifts the bowl and then quickly slams it down on the blankets, causing the dice to fall in different scoring patterns, until the player with the highest score wins. Dice games bring together young and old and connect the community in a friendly recreational activity. Of the dice shown here, one is a turtle die, two are falcon dice, and the others are round.

CAT. 91

Dance Trailer and Leggings

trailer: wool, ribbon, and yarn
leggings: wool, yarn, and hide
trailer: 42 15/16 × 9 13/16 × 3/16 inches
leggings: 33 7/8 × 13 3/4 × 3/16 inches
National Museum of the American Indian, Smithsonian Institution

The trailer is one of the four broadcloth pieces worn by all Osage men during dances. The cloth hangs from the waist and falls down the back of the legs, ending just above the ground. Each of the three ribbon sections contains arrows and splayed anthropomorphic figures. The trailer is edged with a border having a lightning pattern.

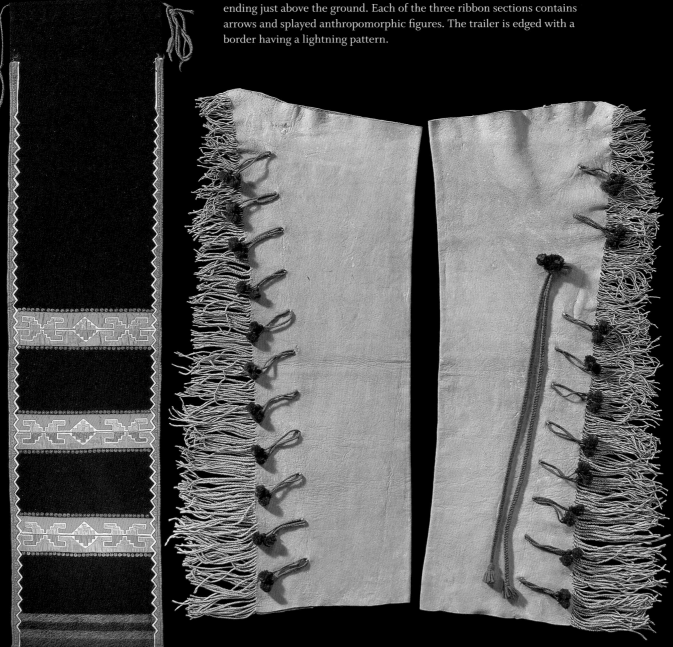

ROACH SPREADER

bone
7⅞ × 2⅜ × 1¾ inches
National Museum of the American Indian, Smithsonian Institution

The elegant shape of this roach platform begins with tight, curving lines
at the front edge by the cylinder. As they expand slightly outward, the lines
become elongated and slightly curved, building momentum as they approach
the forked tines that form the shape of the Osage idea of the *hó-e-ga*, the snare
of life. The stacked hearts are similar to those found in the fireplaces of individual buildings of the Native American Church. Incised dots and decorative
perforations add to the spreader's aesthetic appeal.

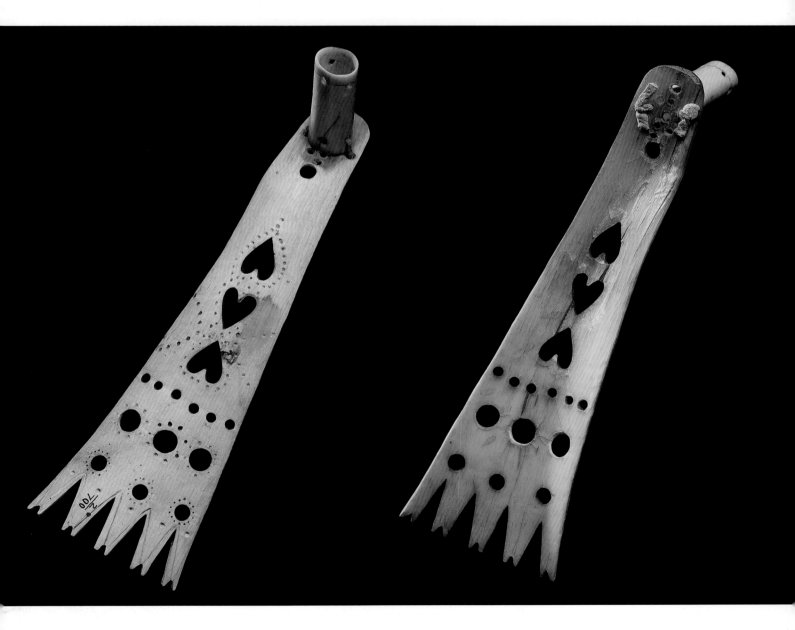

CAT. 93

MAN'S VEST

ca. 1900
wool, cotton, and silk ribbon with glass beads and metal
22½ × 22 × 1½ inches
Courtesy of Beloit College, Logan Museum of Anthropology, 30403

This vest made in the early part of the twentieth century was worn at the E-Lon-schka dances held in the Osage villages each June. The narrow armholes suggest that the garment was worn without a shirt, allowing the dancer to stay relatively cool during the heat of the summer. The hearts on the front are bisected by Christian crosses whose vertical lines extend above and below each heart. On the back of the vest, intricately woven bands of arrows represent the coming together of both the traditional Osage path of life and the Christian road in times of transition.

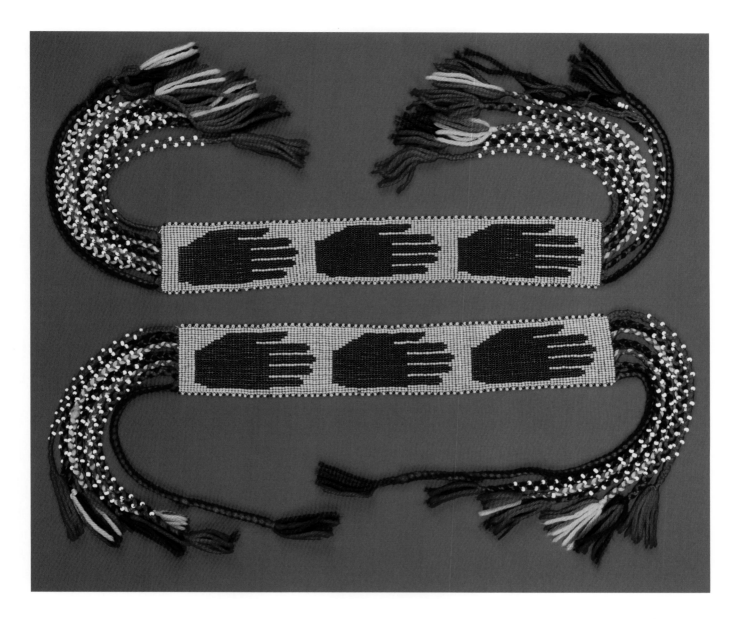

CAT. 94
GARTERS

wool and beads
3 × 30 inches each
Milwaukee Public Museum, James Howard Collection

Garters are worn just below the knee with the fringes running down the outside of the
calf muscles. The bells attached on top of the garters actually cover up the hand motifs,
leaving only the fringe exposed. The flat, open hands may represent the severed hands of
an enemy. Images of hands such as these are reminiscent of war-trophy necklaces made
of human knuckle bones. The owner of this pair of garters may have derived personal
spiritual power from the hidden hands.

CAT. 95
Garters

wool and beads
42 × 2½ inches each
Nancy Pillsbury Shirley, O-TAH-ZHA NAᴺ-ZHE
Collection

These loom-beaded garters feature heart and star motifs at both ends of the beaded field. Stem-like projections connect to the large eight-pointed stars above and below the heart shapes. At the center of each band are pairs of smaller stars whose eight-pointed designs are probably references to four arrow feathers that converge from the four cardinal points of Osage cosmology. The six white lines established by these intersections may represent spiders, which are associated with the invention of weaving. Four beaded strips and two woven strips, all ending in tassels, complete the composition of each garter.

Hair Ornament

feathers, glass beads, wool, and shell
27 × 5 inches
Nancy Pillsbury Shirley, O-TAH-ZHA NA^N-ZHE
Collection

This feather ornament was attached to the
front of a headdress and can be worn on
either the left or right side. Similar feathers
are attached to the Peyote staff. Also known
as scalp feathers, they denote the winning
of war honors. The brown-tinged feathers
are the tail feathers of an adult male bird
from the pheasant family. The black and
white feather is a trimmed golden-eagle
tail feather from a mature bird, which has
been cut to represent lightning. The red
feather medallion is adorned with a freshwater mussel shell that symbolizes the sun
and its life-giving rays. The elongated tri-
angular tip designs and the diamonds on
the bead strips represent ear perforators
and lightning, respectively.

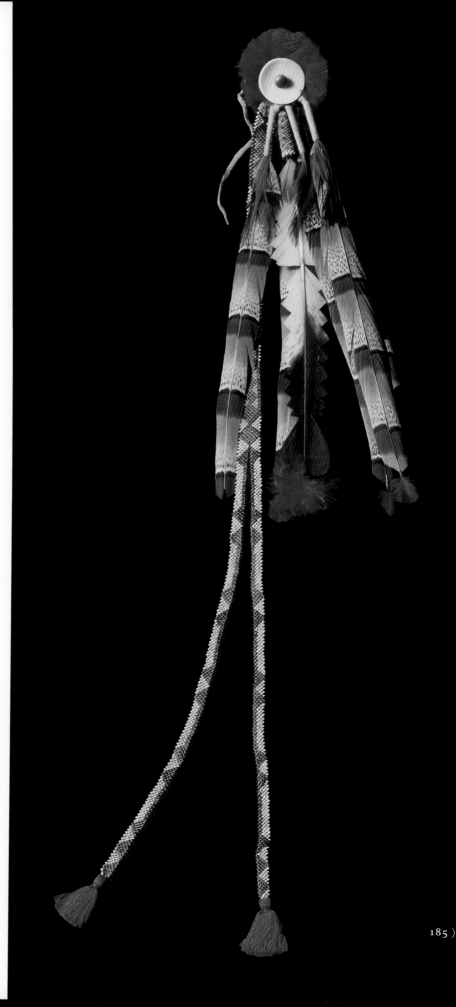

TAIL DANCER'S STICK

wood, glass beads, feather, hide, fur, and metal
17 × 1½ inches
Nancy Pillsbury Shirley, O-TAH-ZHA NA`-ZHE Collection

These sticks are an exclusive symbol of the officer of the E-Lon-schka Tail Dancers, who finish each song within the dance. The Tail Dancers raise their sticks over their heads to be recognized by the Head Singer, who directs the other singers to repeat the song, at which time all the dancers are invited to dance the tail. This stick is adorned with sections of otter fur, and a primary eagle plume is suspended from the end of the shaft. Lightning motifs are executed in the beadwork designs. The Osage adopted the E-Lon-schka dance in the 1880s, and since then it has evolved into an important Osage ritual.

CAT. 98
MOCCASINS

ca. 1915
hide and glass beads
4 × 10 × 10 inches each
Private collection

These moccasins were made by Julia Pryor Mongrain Lookout, one of the most prominent
Osage artists of the twentieth century. She wore them during the special ceremonies that
recognized the Osage participation in World War I and specifically at the presentation of a
certificate of appreciation signed by President Calvin Coolidge and issued by his representatives in Pawhuska in 1924. The flags beaded on each moccasin symbolize the contemporary
Osage expression of patriotism, while the shields located on the flaps and the rims recall
the ancient art of warfare, which so distinguishes Osage history. The lightning motifs on
the sides of the moccasins show power and primal forces, which figure in Osage cosmology.

TAIL DANCER'S BATON

pigment, wood, feathers, and glass beads
Private collection

This early twentieth-century carved and
beaded baton is used by Tail Dancers who
conclude each dance in the E-Lon-schka
celebrations. The heart motif in the beading at the top and bottom decoration refers
to the mating of trumpeter swans, which
in turn are associated with the union of
sky and earth that makes all things possible.
The lightning motifs in the beadwork, along
with the incised sun and relief-carved water
bird at the center of the baton, are important elements in Osage cosmology.

CAT. 100

GARTERS WITH STREAMERS

yarn and glass
Private collection

These blue and red garters of fine woven wool and beadwork are a beautiful display of arrowhead motifs stacked in a tiered arrangement. The pointed edge of each arrowhead is boldly outlined in white beads, which adds to the dramatic presentation of the garters at rest and, especially, in motion.

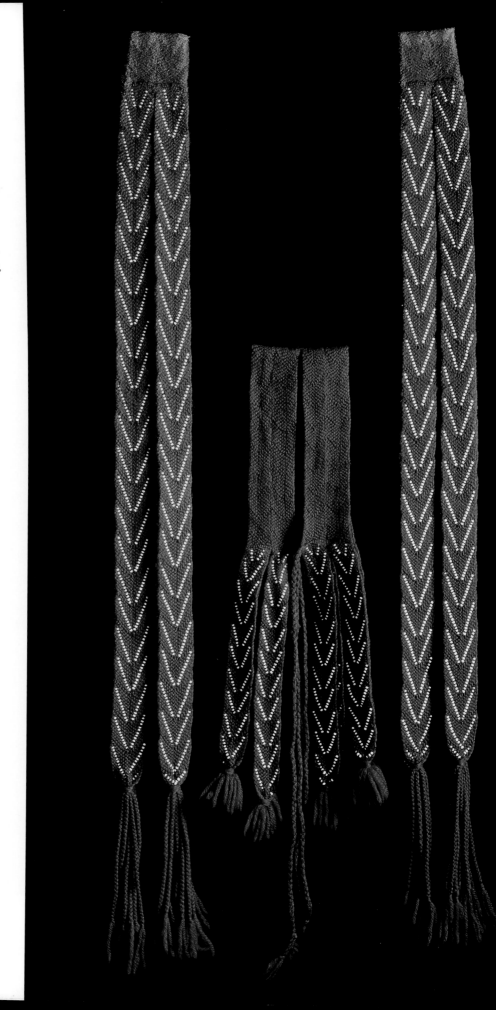

BELT WITH STREAMERS

yarn and glass beads
length: 107 inches
Private collection

This belt of finger-woven wool and bead-work alludes to the Osage Sky clans, expressed in the zigzag lightning patterned fields, which are the belt's primary motifs. The concentric lozenge shapes at the front of the belt also represent lightning bolts, which can cause powerful and destructive prairie fires when they strike the ground.

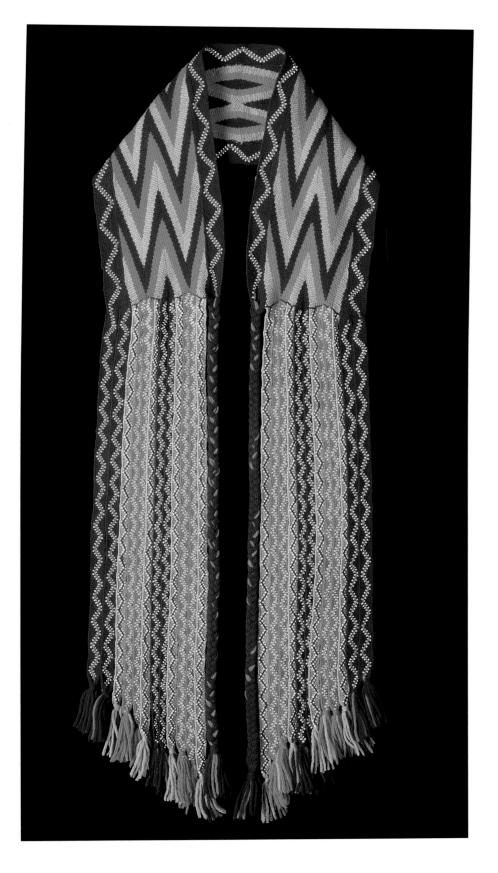

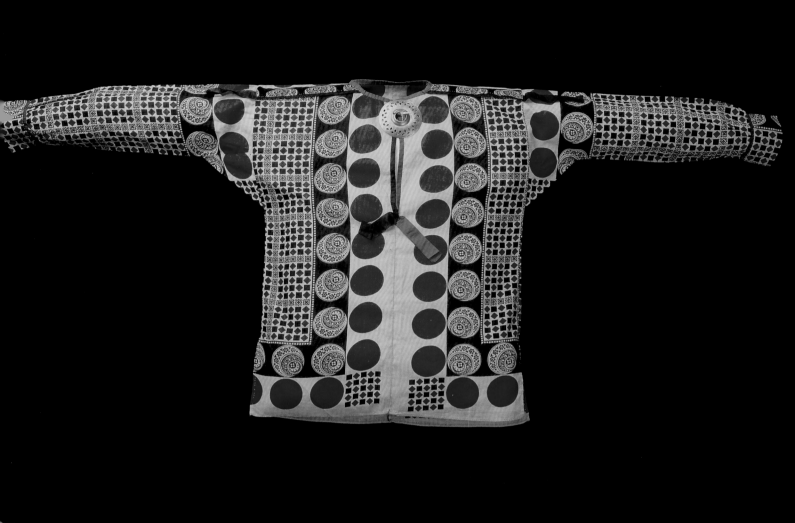

CAT. 102

GIRL'S SCARF SHIRT

ca. 1885
cotton with silver ornament
46 × 22 inches
Department of Anthropology, Smithsonian Institution

This stunning girl's shirt is made from several scarves imported from China. Osage women cut and sewed together different parts of the scarves to achieve an Osage aesthetic. The bold use of red, white, and black indicates a personal preference for war colors. The German silver pin attached to the top complements the circular shapes throughout the shirt. The level of high fashion and the sensuality of the shirt's design were intended to attract suitors and impress others with the well-being and high standing of the young woman's family.

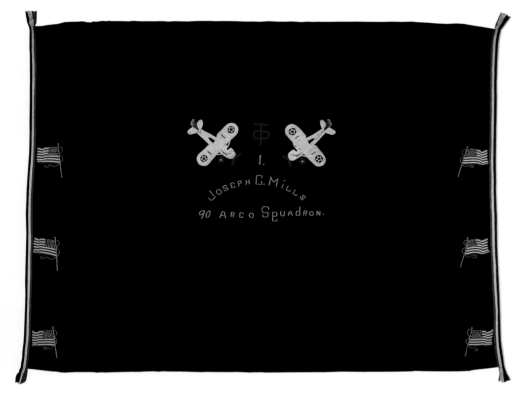

CAT. 103
WAR MOTHERS BLANKET
cloth and glass beads
59¼ × 74½ inches
Osage Tribal Museum

CAT. 104
WAR MOTHERS BLANKET
cloth and glass beads
77¾ × 59 inches
Osage Tribal Museum

CAT. 105
WAR MOTHERS BLANKET
cloth and glass beads
59 × 79½ inches
Osage Tribal Museum

CAT. 106
WAR MOTHERS BLANKET
cloth and glass beads
68½ × 61 inches
Osage Tribal Museum

The War Mothers Society was established after World War I to honor the Osage veterans and their families. These blankets are worn during a dance usually held on Veterans Day. Made from wool broadcloth, these blankets are embellished primarily with beads and silk ribbon. The predominant motifs are the American flag, eagles, airplanes, squadron insignia, and medals of honor. The three different perspectives of the airplane warrant special consideration: the side view of the fuselage; the top view of the wing; and the hawk's-eye view of the tilted tail section. This allows the viewer to see all the important parts of the aircraft. The powerful depiction of the eagle is created by intermingling opaque and metal faceted beads that cause the image to shimmer as if it were alive. Religious devotion is apparent in the placement of the Christian cross above the eagle. Other blankets of this kind depict tanks, pinto horses, and American flags from various points of views. Each blanket identifies the soldier for whom it was made and his or her branch of service.

Oct. 13, 1918
Charles Donovan
115th Inf., 29th Div.
U S A

CHARLES LOOKOUT

"INFANTRY" U.S.A.

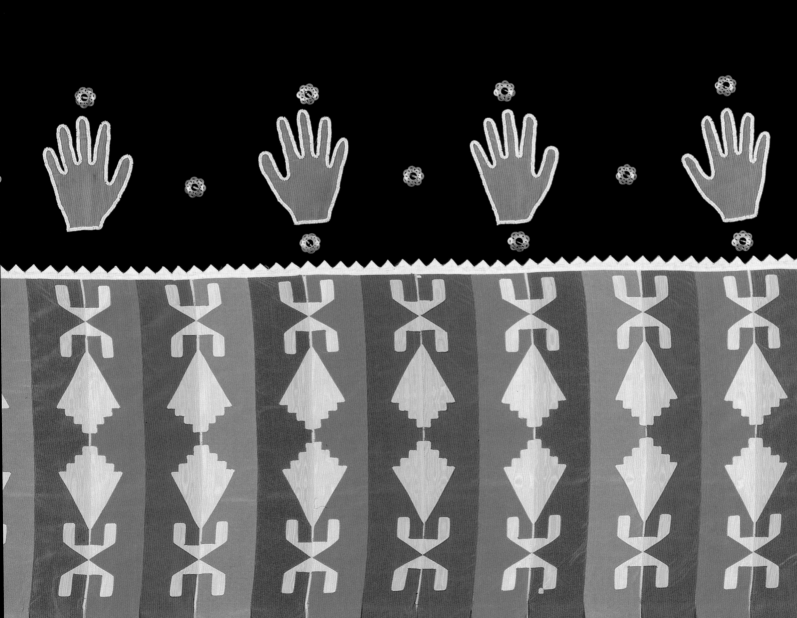

I would say, in layman's terms, that we were a war society and used the elements of the animals,
the other environments, and even the actual wind, the days, the time, the heat, the cold.
We looked through our own eyes and saw the beauty which God had created.
—*Everett Waller, Tulsa, Oklahoma, April 8, 2002*

Today the communities of Hominy, Pawhuska, and Gray Horse, Oklahoma, are a contemporary reflection of the ancient divisions of the Osage people. Members of the three districts are geographically separate yet inextricably united through tribal government. Beyond the present political and economic affairs of the Osage Nation, the past and the present of Osage peoples are celebrated in the spiritually charged environment of the E-Lon-schka dances. At the annual dance in each community, the host village functions as organizer and the other two assume the role of invited guests. Each dance unites the larger Osage community while allowing each district to express its own individuality. Individuality and community are mediated to create the larger Osage society.

This balance of the individual and the community finds inspiration in the ancient philosophy of the Osage people that follows from their conception of the universe and each person's place within it. *Wakonta*, the prevailing force of the universe, created the Osage, then left them to construct their universe in their own way. Unlike many Western stories of creation that set forth the rules to live by, Osage creation stories describe a people entrusted to carry out a worldview of purpose and meaning. That construction of the universe depended on the talents and perseverance of the Osage to divine both the visible and invisible aspects of the universe and charged them to establish order while at the same time drawing from, and even exploiting, chaotic energy. Each person must

also create his or her way within the Osage social realm with its own carefully constructed rules and regulations. So while the clothes of each dancer must adhere to a set standard of elements and components, contemporary outfits at the E-Lon-schka dances display an astonishing range of originality and diversity.

The materials from which Osage arts traditionally are made include otter, hawk, eagle, bison, owl, elk, stone, and wood—materials considered so rich in life force that when used in a work of art, they further imbue the object with aesthetic power. The feeling and weight of an otter turban, the resonance of the struck drum, the sound of knee bells, the fluttering of eagle feathers, the flash of a mirror, and the smells of fry bread and wood fire are all meant to center the Osage in the universe and to establish place and time in the ongoing maneuvers against chaos. The term *aesthetic* in the original Greek sense of the word means "that which is perceived by all the senses," and it is in just such a multidimensional realm that Osage arts are experienced.

Osage art is, first of all, an art of motion. The pipe to be smoked is passed from east to west and back to the east. Dancers in full ritual dress move in the way of the sun as the earth spins on its axis. The motion of art follows the cosmic path, and as the arts move in ritual motion, a microcosm of the universe is created. Drawing energy from the cosmic realm through the motion of art and ritual, chaos is replaced by order in the everyday visible work of the Osage.

Osage arts are based on a highly organized philosophy and a worldview that embraces a keen sense of duality expressed through sets of paired oppositions. The Osage penchant for bilateral symmetry, i.e., expressions of paired oppositions, can be seen in their beadwork, finger weaving, and ribbon work. Just a cursory examination of a ribbon appliqué design in a woman's blanket reveals arrowlike lines with bilateral feather forms, lozenges, and other patterns that all include bisecting lines (see cat. 108). The bisected forms often occur in contrasting light and dark colors, such as red and blue, which are symbolic of the duality of the cosmos.

The orderly presentation of oppositional forms paired in overall designs is further enriched by the paradox that often results from the unpredictability of natural forces—things are not always what they first appear to be. The sky is peace and order, yet its storms and lightning can deal destruction and death. Similarly, at night the earth may be the dark harbor of death and chaos, yet with the reemergence of the sun it gives birth to the sweet new grass of spring on which the buffalo nourish.

The paradoxical nature of oppositions becomes even clearer when one looks more carefully at Osage design. Suddenly the eyes and mind start to work and move in an unfamiliar way, and it becomes clear that there is no background-foreground relationship: what at first appears to be foreground becomes background, and what was background becomes foreground. Each of what was thought to be in opposing grounds surrenders to what was perceived as the opposing element. This perception of reality is brilliantly represented in Osage arts and is an element of what distinguishes their works from other American Indian artistic traditions.

An example of a woman's blanket from the Denver Art Museum Collection illustrates the background-foreground phenomenon as the eye continually makes adjustments to ground rotations (cat. 1). The use of contrasting colors reinforces the effect as the eyes cannot focus on both elements of the pairs at once. The blanket's serrated-edge ribbon work exemplifies the aesthetic paradox. The white lightning serrations give way to the dominance of the black ones and the black to the white ones; the blue and white serrations achieve the same visual effect. When the blankets are draped across the shoulders, the ribbon panels join in two vertical patterns

in the front of the dancers (see cat. 14). Thus the line formed by the joining of the edges separates the panels and results in bilateral symmetrical design. In the Osage community, women dance in a motion to the east, with the left-side ribbon panels on the sky side and the right panel on the earth side. In so doing, the women embody the two cosmic regions and, by extension, the male and female principles, thus alluding to the potential for regeneration and rebirth. But as the women turn to the west, the sky side becomes the earth and the earth side the sky. Again, the rule of paradox.

In the E-Lon-schka dances, the women form an outer circle and the men form an inner ring that, in turn, circles the singers. At the center is the drum. Through the pounding rhythm and booming sound, the drum re-creates the thunder coming from the sky, while the bells of the male dancers make the sound of rain as it falls on the earth, representing fertility in the dance. All the ritual objects and dress associated with the dance help to place the people in actual as well as ritual motion.

Prominent among Osage artistic symbols are heart shapes, which can be seen on blankets, war axes, riding quirts, men's vests, feather drops, roach spreaders, and instruments of the Peyote Church. The heart motif has strong cosmological associations with life-death issues. The heart shape itself probably derives from the profiles of trumpeter swans, which, in preparation for mating, place their beaks tip to tip while bringing their chests together. In this way, the crook-shaped necks of the birds form a heart design, so that one half of the heart is male and the other female. The heart represents a fertility symbol, reminding all that the first task of the Osage, after securing peace and order, is to give birth to the next generation. The white feathers of these birds refer to the sky, masculinity, and peace, while the black feet and beaks recall death, war, and the feminine. Representing both bravery and determination, these birds are known to protect their nests to the death in order to ensure the survival of the next generation.

The stacked heart shapes on the riding quirt from the Linden Museum in Stuttgart also illustrate the paradoxical nature of the heart motif (cat. 6). On one side, the hearts are filled with blood, symbolizing the vitality of the Osage warrior who stands armed for war. On the

FIGURE 7.1 Moundville rattlesnake disc. Courtesy University of Alabama Museums.

reverse, the hearts are emptied, as a reference to death. This symbolism is reinforced by the image of a warrior who now holds a trophy head. Interestingly, the stacked hearts may also represent snake tail rattles. The similarity of this design to Mississippian snake rattles in depictions of these animals on stone discs is remarkable. In keeping with Osage symbolism, the rattlesnake represents quickness and the ability to strike a deadly blow.

In earlier times, a pair of crooked standards covered with swan feathers and down skin would have been carried into battle, and when they were placed together to form a heart shape, it signified that the Osage were completely united in the war effort. The early twentieth-century vest with one heart shape on each side of the front probably also refers to a singleness of purpose and tenacity under duress (cat. 93).

During the Mourning Dances, last held around 1911, the Sky and Earth peoples, arranged in two parallel lines, mourned facing west, with the crook bearers at the front of each group. It may well be that the two standards were positioned to strike up the heart shape, once again referring to the mating swans and their defense of their nest until death. As the standard bearers faced the setting sun in the west, the heart symbolized the realization that new life would come about through death. And in accordance with traditional Osage theology, the deceased spirit, which the mourning party honored, would travel to the invisible world, only to be snared by the *hó-e-ga*,

or mirror board, and placed again on the life path as a newly born Osage (see cats. 12 and 23).

The heart shape is also found in the leaves of the red-bud tree. As one of the first trees to flower in the spring and the last to shed its leaves, redbud trees are associated with long life. The red color of its spring buds is associated with the regenerative powers of the sun. Yet the deep black ashes of the redbud were made into a paint that was applied to the faces of warriors before an attack was launched; the black symbolized the ashes left by wild prairie fires and, by extension, death and the destruction of the enemy. Again, in one entity life and death are paradoxically related.

In dance, in war, and in Osage games of foot racing and dice, there are notions of speed and quickness. Says one Osage expression, "Life is short, be quick about it," and its counterpart says, "Be quick about it, but don't hurry." Thus paradox reaches into the realms of Osage notions of time and velocity, not to mention acceleration. The otter, which is well known for its speed and quickness, provides both material and motif in Osage art. Otter turban headdresses, with the tails extending down the backs of earlier warriors and today's dancers, inspired Osage males to be quick in attack yet do a thorough job (see cat. 107). Zigzag lightning patterns and lightning bolts symbolized by the lozenge shapes found on many Osage works of art symbolize speed as well as lightning's source of power, the sun. The circular shapes of shields and circular designs found on many Osage objects refer to cosmic elements, constellations, individual stars, and the moon, as well as the powers of the sun and fire and their ability to create and destroy.

The duality of speed and careful thoroughness, which can often be seen to be in opposition to each other, are embodied in the traditional Osage art form of finger weaving. The repetitive nature of the process leads an artist to develop a technique whereby speed of motion and dexterity are positive virtues in the lengthy process required to produce large works, such as the belts worn in traditional female attire (see cat. 79). The penchant for speed must be tempered by the considerable care that must be taken to ensure that the tension of the individual threads is consistent throughout the thousands of twining movements needed to create a finished piece. Failure to maintain this consistency produces finger-woven pieces with wavy edges, an unfortunate departure from the exacting standards that the Osage apply to their traditional arts. The maneuvers required to create patterns and designs in finger weaving, coupled with the common insertion of small white beads into the work, amplify the virtues of care and exactness required to make something that will satisfy the discerning eye of an Osage client.

Roach spreaders and roaches themselves further explore Osage notions of speed and warfare (see cats. 4, 9, 92). A spreader is actually a small platform inserted at the base of the roach, causing it to flare in its characteristic manner. The spreader is attached to a cord that loops under the dancer's chin, thus securing the roach. Many of the spreaders made out of bone are empowered with heart motifs. The material spreaders and roaches were made from is also empowering: the spreader was made of elk antler for the platform, and the cylinder above the platform was made of the upper wing bone of an eagle. Elk are associated with strength, speed, and stamina, while the eagle-wing bone stands for the power of flight, speed, and the association of flight with the sky and the sun. The eagle feather anchored in the cylindrical eagle-wing bone provided the warrior with a direct link to *Wakonta*, inspiring the warriors to strike like lightning and move with the velocity of a prairie fire in pursuit of victory. Be quick! But don't hurry. In other words, be swift, but be thorough. The roach itself is made of deer-tail hair and the chest hairs of a wild turkey. The deer hair that is dyed red refers to the power of the prairie fire as well as the fire that Osage warriors sometimes used to destroy enemy villages; the black is mindful of the ashes left behind. One can envision an Osage war party in ritual dress—clan priests carrying sacred bundles and others holding standards with the feathers fluttering in the breeze (see cats. 13 and 51), the roaches and spreaders, black face paint, the blue-painted stuffed hawks attached to the backs of the eight commanding officers—and one can imagine that a heightened confidence arose to ensure the unity of purpose that would result in a strikingly fast and successful mission.

Although intertribal warfare no longer exists, the Osage have applied their military talents to the international realm (see cats. 103 and 104). The flags that decorate moccasins, belts, blankets, and gourd rattles allude to the patriotism that the Osage have displayed in most wars in which the United States has engaged. It may also be that the white and red colors of the American flag represent the sky and forces of peace, and the deep blue suggests the earth and the forces of destruction. The blankets of the War Mothers Society, whose motifs of flags, armored vehicles, and airplanes are rendered in beadwork and sequins, honor those who have fought and those who have died.

War Mothers blankets are good examples of the continuation of the division of domestic and artistic labor along gender lines in Osage society. In the traditional economy of the Osage people, men and women were organized along clear lines of activity and production. In general, men were responsible for the semiannual buffalo hunts that provided the villages with meat, hides, and other materials critical for their survival. Women were in charge of planting and tending the gardens of corn and squash and for finding and harvesting wild plants for food, medicines, and fibers. In the twentieth century, women have created and worn magnificently beaded blankets during the dances that are held to honor the military service and sacrifice of their male relatives. Although Osage women have also served in the military with increasing frequency, this has yet to be recognized through the traditional arts and cultural activities associated with their male counterparts.

A wonderful pipe and pipe stem from the National Museum of Natural History illustrates another element in the lexicon of Osage color symbolism and aesthetic range (see cat. 11). The black stone pipe features a carved human face with a strong vertical nose and close-set eyes rimmed in a narrow red paint line. The black alludes to death, war, and the earth. The eyes represent the vision of *Wakonta*. Paradoxically, the beautiful skull beads on the thong symbolize earth qualities. This object, which could be lit only when it was time for battle, was certainly owned by a strong Earth clan, perhaps the Black Bear people. Yet it was Sky, not Earth, people who were the only ones who could light it, indicating the unity of the people needed in a moment of war and the belief that military action was part and parcel of the cosmic order. The red lines around the eyes represent the eyes of the sun and the sky as they look for war to restore the peace. The bowl of the pipe is another reference to communal unity. Given that the stem represents the body of the pipe, the two parts form the complete being of this primordial man. When lit, the pipe would exude a sacred smoke that moved into the sky to appeal for divine assistance as it was passed to the smokers along the path of the sun.

In the arts of hunting, split-horn headdresses were worn to prepare for the bison hunts. The dances were intended to appease the spirits of the bison so that they could be taken to feed the people, with the understanding that their spirits would one day return from the invisible world. The split-horn headdress from the Brooklyn Art Museum (see cat. 3) has a kingfisher bird attached to the nape of the neck. The kingfisher comes from the sky, but it lives in holes on the banks of rivers. Diving from the sky like a lightning bolt, it strikes the water to catch its prey. In the dances at which men wore such headdresses, the unity of the cosmos was the context in which the quick strike of lightning symbolized the importance of preparations for the hunt.

Osage art is about meaning and purpose. Although the paradoxical forces of life, death, and regeneration are universal human concerns, the Osage obsession with these forces is brilliantly represented in their aesthetic and ritual acts. Their preoccupations with speed, with being one with the universe, and with a strong sense of order have evolved over time as the Osage people have increased their understanding of the world *Wakonta* created. Through close observation of flora, fauna, and the celestial realm, the Osage have determined the qualities, virtues, and principles that they could apply to the challenges of the day, the season, and the life cycle. These concepts are made manifest in the artistic expressions of the Osage people. The symbols associated with their arts and, indeed, the materials they use to make them have been combined to create powerful objects that assisted the elders in their efforts to establish order out of chaos and to ensure the survival of the Osage as a people.

As contemporary Osage people face new challenges with respect to their governance, economy, and society, the arts and the events associated with them provide a sense of continuity and connection to the responses formulated by their ancestors. The elements of traditional thought and practice will continue to evolve in the efforts of Osage people to create order and meaning in their individual and communal lives.

OTTER TURBAN HEADDRESS

hide, otter fur, feathers, beads, metal, shell,
bird beak, and pigment
48 × 8 inches
Osage Tribal Museum

This headdress of a clan priest indicates
that he had achieved all of the thirteen
war honors designated by the military
order. The impressive variety of life symbols demonstrates the different perspectives and functions of each of the original
twenty-four Osage clans. Placed on the
forehead would be the sun emblem, represented by the freshwater mussel shells;
they would be framed by skin sections
from the male trumpeter swan, which is
revered for its ability to fight and protect
its home. Projecting outward from the swan
skin are the upper and lower mandibles
of the ivory-billed woodpecker, a bird that
inspires great courage through its strength,
endurance, tenacity, and speed. The birds'
bills, their insides consecrated with blue
paint, rest on the scalp of the pileated woodpecker. Surrounding the head is a commercially made German silver band attached
to blue-painted otter fur. From the band
hangs a broadcloth trailer that terminates
in a tuft of horsehair. Every object on the
trailer commemorates specific war honors,
which the owner would recite at various
ceremonies when called upon to do so. This
act would demonstrate to all present the
individual's qualifications and his sanction
by the *non-hón-zhin-ga* priests.

CAT. 108

BLANKET

20th century
wool, satin ribbon, and nickel silver thread
59½ × 68 inches
Gilcrease Museum, Tulsa, Oklahoma

When this blanket was worn by a dancer, the two pairs of hands on the dancer's back would give the impression of two people touching the dancer. The use of the complimentary colors green and purple in the silk appliqué heightens the optical impact. The color bars on which the feather motifs and connecting U shapes are sewn are arranged in perfect symmetry, starting with purple-purple at the center and ending with blue. The background of changing color bars, together with the all-white U and feather shapes, sustains an overall optical tension.

1 / EARLY OSAGE ART AND HISTORY

Opening quotation from George Catlin 1844, *Letters and notes on the manners, customs, and conditions of the North American Indians written during eight years' travel (1832–1839) amongst the wildest tribes in North America*, vol. 2 (London: D. Bogue), p. 40.

1. The following discussion of Osage culture history is drawn from Garrick Bailey 1973, *Changes in Osage Social Organization, 1673–1906* (University of Oregon Anthropology Papers, no. 5), and Garrick Bailey 2001, "Osage," in *Handbook of North American Indians* 13 (1) (Washington, D.C.: Smithsonian Institution); see these studies for citations of particular data presented. For a more in-depth discussion of Osage history covering the period up to 1840, see Willard H. Rollings 1992, *The Osage: An Ethnohistorical Study of Hegemony on the Prairie-Plains* (Columbia: University of Missouri Press). John Joseph Mathews 1982, *The Osages: Children of the Middle Waters* (Norman: University of Oklahoma Press), has an excellent discussion of Osage history from an Osage perspective, while Louis Burns 1989, *A History of the Osage People* (Fallbrook, Calif.: CIGA Press), presents a detailed account of Osage history up to the present.

2. See Carl Chapman and Eleanor Chapman 1964, *Indians and Archaeology of Missouri* (Columbia: Missouri Archaeological Society), pp. 96–100, for a brief discussion of Osage archaeological finds, and Carl Chapman 1975, *Archaeology of Missouri* (Columbia: University of Missouri Press) for a more detailed discussion.

3. See George Hyde 1951, *The Pawnee Indians* (Denver: University of Denver Press), p. 15.

4. Hyde 1951, pp. 54–55, 60.

5. For a more detailed discussion of Indian removal and the conflict with the Osage, see three classic studies by Grant Foreman 1933, 1936, 1946, *Advancing the Frontier, Indians and Pioneers*, and *The Last Trek of the Indians* (Norman: University of Oklahoma Press).

6. The material presented in this section is drawn from Garrick Bailey 1964–2003, Osage field notes, except when indicated otherwise.

7. See Chapman and Chapman 1964, *Indians and Archaeology of Missouri*, pp. 96–99.

8. Chapman and Chapman 1964, *Indians and Archaeology of Missouri*, p. 100.

9. See Andrew Hunter Whiteford 1977b, "Fiber Bags of the Great Lakes Indians" (*American Indian Art Magazine* 3), p. 40, and Victor Tixier 1940, *Tixier's Travels on the Osage Prairies* (Norman: University of Oklahoma Press), p. 137.

10. See Tixier 1940, *Travels on Osage Prairies*, pp. 137–39, and Alice Marriot 1974, *Osage Indians*, vol. 2 (New York: Garland), pp. 72–73.

11. See Marriott 1974, *Osage Indians*, pp. 77–81.

12. See Milford Chandler 1973, "Art and Culture," in *Art of the Great Lakes Indians* (Flint, Mich.: Flint Institute of Arts), p. xxv.

13. Chandler 1973, "Art and Culture," p. xxiv.

14. See Barbara Hail 1983, *Hau, Kóla!* (Haffenreffer Museum, Brown University), pp. 51–53.

15. Hail 1983, *Hau, Kóla!* pp. 53–54.

16. Hail 1983, *Hau, Kóla!* pp. 58–60.

17. Hail 1983, *Hau, Kóla!* pp. 61–63, 182.

18. See Chandler 1973, "Art and Culture," pp. xxiv–xxv; Whiteford 1977b, "Fiber Bags," p. 40; and Tixier 1940, *Travels on Osage Prairies*, pp. 137–39.

19. See Richard Conn 1980, "Native American Cloth Appliqué and Ribbonwork," and Alice Marriott and Carol Rachlin 1980, "Southern Plains Ribbonwork Development and Diffusion," both in George Horse Capture, ed., *Native American Ribbonwork* (Cody, Wyo.: Buffalo Bill Historic Center).

2 / OSAGE COSMOLOGY

Opening quotation from Edgar McCarthy 1923, *Peyote: As Used in Religious Worship by the Indians* (Hominy, Okla.: Private printing), p. 10.

1. This term has several different meanings; here it refers to a generic religious man. For another meaning, see Francis La Flesche 1932, *A Dictionary of the Osage Language* (Washington, D.C.: Bureau of American Ethnology, Bulletin 109), p. 194.

2. Francis La Flesche 1928, "The Osage Tribe: Two Versions of the Child-naming Rite," in *Forty-third Annual Report of the Bureau of American Ethnology (1925–26)* (Washington, D.C.: Bureau of American Ethnology), pp. 29–30.

3. La Flesche 1932, *Dictionary of Osage Language*, pp. 193–94.

4. La Flesche 1932, *Dictionary of Osage Language*, p. 193.

5. The ancient Osage priests appear to have defined the atmosphere earlier than Western scientists.

6. Francis La Flesche 1921, "The Osage Tribe: Rite of the Chiefs: Sayings of the Ancient Men," in *Thirty-sixth Annual Report of the Bureau of American Ethnology (1914–15)* (Washington, D.C.: Bureau of American Ethnology), pp. 277.

7. See Garrick Bailey 1995, *The Osage and the Invisible World* (Norman: University of Oklahoma Press), p. 31, for further discussion.

8. Francis La Flesche 1925, "The Osage Tribe: The Rite of Vigil," in *Thirty-ninth Annual Report of the Bureau of American Ethnology (1917–18)* (Washington, D.C.: Bureau of American Ethnology), p. 139.

9. See Bailey 1995, *Osage and Invisible World*, pp. 30–31.

10. See Bailey 1995, *Osage and Invisible World*, pp. 32–33, for a discussion of the Osage concept of the cosmos.

11. Francis La Flesche 1930, "The Osage Tribe: Rite of the Wa-xó-be," in *Forty-fifth Annual Report of the Bureau of American Ethnology (1927–28)* (Washington, D.C.: Bureau of American Ethnology), p. 584.

12. La Flesche 1925, "Rite of Vigil," p. 364.

13. See La Flesche 1930, "Rite of Wa-xó-be," p. 629; La Flesche 1932, *Dictionary of Osage Language*, p. 201.

14. La Flesche 1932, *Dictionary of Osage Language*, p. 194; see also La Flesche 1921, "Rite of Chiefs," p. 302.

15. La Flesche 1925, "Rite of Vigil," p. 83.

16. See La Flesche 1921, "Rite of Chiefs," p. 49, and La Flesche 1925, "Rite of Vigil," pp. 83, 103–6, 316, 364.

17. John Dunn Hunter 1973, *Memoirs of a Captivity among the Indians of North America* (New York: Schocken Press), pp. 191, 193, 197.

18. A special tribal medicine bundle, the *Mon-kon ton-ga wa-xó-be*, was created for this plant. See Bailey 1995, *Osage and Invisible World*, pp. 47–48, 72–73.

19. For lists of plants and animals used for food by the Osages, see Garrick Bailey 1973, "Changes in Osage Social Organization" (*University of Oregon Anthropology Papers*, no. 5), pp. 25–26, and Garrick Bailey 2001, "Osage," in *Handbook of North American Indians* 13 (1) (Washington, D.C.: Smithsonian Institution), p. 479.

20. See Bailey 1995, *Osage and Invisible World*, p. 192.

21. See Bailey 1995, *Osage and Invisible World*, p. 32.

22. See Bailey 1995, *Osage and Invisible World*, p. 34.

23. Francis La Flesche 1939, *War Ceremony and Peace Ceremony of the Osage Indians* (Washington, D.C.: Bureau of American Ethnology, Bulletin 101), p. 228.

24. La Flesche 1930, "Rite of Wa-xó-be," p. 570.

25. See La Flesche 1928, "Two Versions of Child-naming Rite," p. 29, and La Flesche 1932, *War Ceremony and Peace Ceremony*, p. 46.

26. La Flesche 1932, *Dictionary of Osage Language*, pp. 224 and 84, respectively.

27. See La Flesche 1930, "Rite of Wa-xó-be," p. 647.

28. See La Flesche 1921, "Rite of Chiefs," pp. 84–90.

29. See La Flesche 1921, "Rite of Chiefs," plate 6, and La Flesche 1925, "Rite of Vigil," p. 74.

30. See La Flesche 1921, "Rite of Chiefs," p. 102.

31. La Flesche 1921, "Rite of Chiefs," plate 7; La Flesche 1932, *Dictionary of Osage Language*, p. 99; and Garrick Bailey 1964–2003, field notes.

32. See La Flesche 1921, "Rite of Chiefs," pp. 135–37.

33. See Bailey 1995, *Osage and Invisible World*, pp. 36–40, for a list of life symbols by clan.

34. La Flesche 1932, *Dictionary of Osage Language*, pp. 54, 79, 96, and 93, respectively.

35. See La Flesche 1930, "Rite of Wa-xó-be," p. 654.

36. See Francis La Flesche 1920, "Symbolic Man of the Osage Tribe," *Art and Archaeology* 9, pp. 68–72, for a discussion of the symbolism of the pipe.

37. La Flesche 1932, *Dictionary of Osage Language*, p. 185.

38. See La Flesche 1921, "Rite of Chiefs," plate 10.

39. La Flesche 1932, *Dictionary of Osage Language*, pp. 156, 167.

40. See Bailey 1995, *Osage and Invisible World*, pp. 35–42, for a discussion of the clan system.

41. James Owen Dorsey 1888, "Osage Traditions," in *Sixth Annual Report of the Bureau of American Ethnology (1884–85)* (Washington, D.C.: Bureau of American Ethnology), p. 396; also see La Flesche 1930, "Rite of Wa-xó-be," p. 629.

42. See Bailey 1995, *Osage and Invisible World*, pp. 55–60, for a discussion of the types of rituals.

43. See Bailey 1995, *Osage and Invisible World*, pp. 49–50.

44. The clan priests in a west ritual are reported to have painted their faces red and placed "a downy feather from the under cover of the tail of an eagle" on their crown (La Flesche 1939, *War Ceremony and Peace Ceremony*, p. 13).

45. La Flesche 1925, "Rite of Vigil," pp. 67, 70; La Flesche 1930, "Rite of Wa-xó-be," pp. 549–50, 557; see also La Flesche 1920, "Symbolic Man," for a discussion of the "symbolic man."

46. This description applies to a *Xó-ka* in a clan ritual belonging to the Earth division. One would suspect that the figure would be on the opposite, or left, side of a *Xó-ka* in a clan ritual from the Sky division.

47. This description of a *Xó-ka* was for a Puma clan priesthood initiation ritual; see La Flesche 1925, "Rite of Vigil," pp. 73–74.

48. The buffalo robe was worn in rituals relating to hunting and in the child-naming rite of at least some of the clans. See La Flesche 1930, "Rite of Wa-xó-be," p. 707, and La Flesche 1928, "Two Versions of Child-naming Rite," p. 36.

49. La Flesche 1921, "Rite of Chiefs," p. 65.

50. La Flesche 1930, "Rite of Wa-xó-be," pp. 682–83.

51. La Flesche 1925, "Rite of Vigil," p. 93.

52. See La Flesche 1925, "Rite of Vigil," p. 93, and La Flesche 1930, "Rite of Wa-xó-be," p. 647.

53. La Flesche 1920, "Symbolic Man," p. 71.

54. La Flesche 1921, "Rite of Chiefs," p. 92.

55. La Flesche 1930, "Rite of Wa-xó-be," p. 563; see also La Flesche 1925, "Rite of Vigil," pp. 164–70, for the story of the tally sticks.

56. See La Flesche 1925, "Rite of Vigil," pp. 114–15; La Flesche 1930, "Rite of Wa-xó-be," pp. 577–78.

57. La Flesche 1925, "Rite of Vigil," pp. 335–36.

58. La Flesche 1939, *War Ceremony and Peace Ceremony*, pp. 18–19.

59. See La Flesche 1921, "Rite of Chiefs," p. 261, and La Flesche 1939, *War Ceremony and Peace Ceremony*, p. 15.

60. La Flesche 1939, *War Ceremony and Peace Ceremony*, p. 14.

61. See La Flesche 1925, "Rite of Vigil," pp. 234, 364, and La Flesche 1930, "Rite of Wa-xó-be," p. 675.

62. La Flesche 1930, "Rite of Wa-xó-be," pp. 578–79.

63. See Bailey 1995, *Osage and Invisible World*, pp. 220–21.

64. La Flesche 1930, "Rite of Wa-xó-be," p. 577.

65. This was the *ní-ki wí-gi-e* of the Puma clan; see La Flesche 1921, "Rite of Chiefs," pp. 157–211.

66. See La Flesche 1930, "Rite of Wa-xó-be," p. 535.

67. La Flesche 1930, "Rite of Wa-xó-be," p. 675.

68. La Flesche 1925, "Rite of Vigil," p. 91.

3 / OSAGE DAILY LIFE: LIVING LIFE AS A PRAYER

Opening quotation from Francis La Flesche 1921, "The Osage Tribe: Rite of the Chiefs: Sayings of the Ancient Men," in *Thirty-sixth Annual Report of the Bureau of American Ethnology (1914–15)* (Washington, D.C.: Bureau of American Ethnology), p. 50.

1. The following description of village organization applies best to the eighteenth century, while the Osage were still in present-day Missouri. As they were forced westward into what is today Kansas and Oklahoma, the villages began to fragment. However, these new resident villages appear to have retained their identity with one or another of the five original village/bands, and the traditional political organization continued to function to some degree. See Louis F. Burns 1984, *Osage Indian Bands and Clans* (Fallbrook, Calif.: CIGA Press), pp. 1–17.

2. La Flesche 1921, "Rite of Chiefs," p. 45.

3. Francis La Flesche 1932, *A Dictionary of the Osage Language* (Washington, D.C.: Bureau of American Ethnology, Bulletin 109), p. 114.

4. La Flesche 1921, "Rite of Chiefs," p. 68.

5. La Flesche 1921, "Rite of Chiefs," pp. 69–71.

6. La Flesche 1921, "Rite of Chiefs," pp. 67–69. La Flesche is not clear concerning the chief's house. In his text he speaks of it in the singular, as if there was only one chief's house. We assume that what he stated applied to both, with the Sky division families taking coals from the fire of the Sky chief's fireplace and the Earth division families taking theirs from that of the Earth chief.

7. See La Flesche 1930, "The Osage Tribe: Rite of the Wa-xó-be," in *Forty-fifth Annual Report of the Bureau of American Ethnology (1927–28)* (Washington, D.C.: Bureau of American Ethnology), p. 67.

8. See Father Paul M. Ponziglione 1883, letter from Kansas on July 2, 1883, in *Woodstock Letters* 12, p. 297; Father Paul M. Ponziglione 1889, "Indian Traditions Among the Osage," in *Woodstock Letters* 18, pp. 75–76; and Father Paul M. Ponziglione n.d., "Father Schoenmaker and

the Osage," manuscript (St. Louis, Mo.: St. Louis University Library), pp. 24–25.

9. La Flesche 1921, "Rite of Chiefs," p. 68.

10. La Flesche 1921, "Rite of Chiefs," p. 68.

11. See Ponziglione 1889, "Indian Traditions Among Osage," pp. 75–76, and Ponziglione n.d., "Father Schoenmaker and Osage," pp. 24–25.

12. See the stories of the Whistle and Hair bundles in La Flesche 1932, *Dictionary of Osage Language*, pp. 403–6.

13. La Flesche 1939, *War Ceremony and Peace Ceremony of the Osage Indians* (Washington, D.C.: Bureau of American Ethnology, Bulletin 101), p. 4.

14. For child-naming rites, see La Flesche 1928, "The Osage Tribe: Two Versions of the Child-naming Rite," in *Forty-third Annual Report of the Bureau of American Ethnology (1925–26)* (Washington, D.C.: Bureau of American Ethnology).

15. See La Flesche 1939, *War Ceremony and Peace Ceremony*, pp. 140–41.

16. Alice Fletcher and Francis La Flesche n.d., La Flesche Papers 4558, National Anthropological Archives (Washington, D.C.: Smithsonian Institution, Museum of Natural History).

17. La Flesche 1921, "Rite of Chiefs," p. 72.

18. La Flesche 1921, "Rite of Chiefs," p. 72.

19. See Garrick Bailey 1995, *The Osage and the Invisible World* (Norman: University of Oklahoma Press), pp. 54, 291.

20. See La Flesche 1921, "Rite of Chiefs," p. 78.

21. La Flesche 1921, "Rite of Chiefs," p. 70.

22. La Flesche 1939, *War Ceremony and Peace Ceremony*, p. 204.

23. La Flesche 1921, "Rite of Chiefs," p. 69.

24. See La Flesche 1921, "Rite of Chiefs," p. 69; Alice Fletcher and Francis La Flesche 1911, "The Omaha Tribe," in *Twenty-seventh Annual Report of the Bureau of American Ethnology (1905–6)* (Washington, D.C.: Bureau of American Ethnology), p. 58; Ponziglione 1889, "Indian Traditions Among Osage," p. 75; and James Owen Dorsey 1897, "Siouan Sociology: A Posthumous Paper," in *Fifteenth Annual Report of the Bureau of American Ethnology (1893–94)* (Washington, D.C.: Bureau of American Ethnology), p. 233.

25. This term actually translates as "Osage house."

26. For descriptions of Osage villages, dwellings, and furnishings, see Dorsey 1897, "Siouan Sociology," p. 233; Fletcher and La Flesche 1911, "Omaha Tribe," p. 58; Father Paul M. Ponziglione 1878, letter of December 31, 1877, in *Woodstock Letters* 8, p. 101; Ponziglione 1889, "Indian Traditions Among Osage," p. 75; Ponziglione n.d., "Father Schoenmaker and Osage," p. 164; John Bradbury 1817, *Travels in the Interior of America, 1809, 1810 and 1811* (London: Sherwood, Neely and Jones), p. 37; Isaac McCoy 1835, *Annual Report of Indian Affairs within Indian Territory* (Shawanoe Baptist Mission House, Indian Territory [Okla.]: J. Meeker), pp. 17–18; Victor Tixier 1940, *Tixier's Travels on the Osage Prairies* (Norman: University of Oklahoma Press), pp. 117–

18, 134–35; W. W. Graves 1916, *Life and Letters of Father Ponziglione, Schoenmaker and Other Early Jesuits at Osage Mission* (St. Paul, Kans.: W. W. Graves), p. 129; and Thomas J. Farnham 1906, *Travels in the Great Western Prairies, the Anahuac and Rocky Mountains and the Oregon Territory (1843)*, in Reuben G. Thwaites, ed., *Early Western Travels* (Cleveland, Ohio: Arthur A. Clark), p. 132.

27. Carl Chapman and Eleanor Chapman 1964, *Indians and Archaeology of Missouri* (Columbia: Missouri Archaeological Society), p. 100.

28. For a discussion of these bags, see Andrew Hunter Whiteford 1977a, "Fiber Bags of the Great Lakes Indians, Part 1," *American Indian Art Magazine* 2 (3), pp. 52–64; Andrew Hunter Whiteford 1977b, "Fiber Bags of the Great Lakes Indians, Part 2," *American Indian Art Magazine* 3 (1), pp. 40–47, 90; and Andrew Hunter Whiteford 1978, "Tapestry-Twined Bags, Osage Bags and Others," *American Indian Art Magazine* 3 (2), pp. 32–39, 92.

29. Gaylord Torrence 1994, *The American Indian Parfleche* (Seattle: University of Washington Press), pp. 85–91.

30. La Flesche 1921, "Rite of Chiefs," pp. 146–51.

31. See Jedidiah Morse 1822, *A Report of the Secretary of War of the United States, on Indian Affairs Comprising a Narrative of a Tour* (New Haven, Conn.: S. Converse), p. 205; Tixier 1940, *Travels on Osage Prairies*, p. 120; and Graves 1916, *Life and Letters of Father Ponziglione*, p. 148.

32. Francis La Flesche 1925, "The Osage Tribe: The Rite of Vigil," in *Thirty-ninth Annual Report of the Bureau of American Ethnology (1917–18)* (Washington, D.C.: Bureau of American Ethnology), pp. 194–95.

33. See Tixier 1940, *Travels on Osage Prairies*, p. 140, and W. W. Graves 1949, *The First Protestant Osage Missions 1820–1837* (Oswego, Kans.: The Carpenter Press), p. 12.

34. See Tixier 1940, *Travels on Osage Prairies*, pp. 140, 154–55.

35. La Flesche (Fletcher and La Flesche n.d., La Flesche Papers, letter of June 1, 1911) makes the statement "their [the Osages'] hunting ceremony is meager practically nothing." He further suggests that when the Osages and the Omahas separated, the Omaha took most of the hunting rituals while the Osages took most of the war rituals.

36. McCoy 1835, *Annual Report of Indian Affairs*, pp. 203–5; Graves 1949, *First Protestant Osage Missions*, p. 12; and Tixier 1940, *Travels on Osage Prairies*, p. 140.

37. In 1817 the Cherokee attacked the village of the Arkansas Osages while most of the men were away on the summer hunt (Grant Foreman 1936, *Indians and Pioneers* [Norman: University of Oklahoma Press], pp. 47–52).

38. La Flesche 1921, "Rite of Chiefs," p. 67; Graves 1949, *First Protestant Osage Missions*, p. 13; and see Tixier 1940, *Travels on Osage Prairies*, pp. 155, 176–78, 186, 198, 210, 221–25, 238, 258–60.

39. Thomas Marshall 1928, "The Journals of Jules DeMun," *Missouri Historical Society Collections* 5, pp. 192–93.

40. Tixier 1940, *Travels on Osage Prairies*, pp. 140–44, 149–50, 155; Ponziglione n.d., "Father Schoenmaker and Osage," p. 219; and Sister Mary Paul Fitzgerald 1939, *Beacon on the Plains* (Leavenworth, Kans.: Saint Mary College), p. 23.

41. See Fletcher and La Flesche 1911, "Omaha Tribe," p. 58.

42. See Tixier 1940, *Travels on Osage Prairies*, pp. 209–32, for a description of such a war party.

43. See Tixier 1940, *Travels on Osage Prairies*, pp. 186–91.

44. James Edwin Finney 1955, "Reminiscences of a Trader in Osage Country," *The Chronicles of Oklahoma* 33, pp. 147–48.

45. See La Flesche 1939, *War Ceremony and Peace Ceremony*, pp. 201–55, for a description of the ceremony. It was published seven years after his death, and it appears to have been only in draft form. As a result, there many gaps in the materials presented and many unanswered questions about the ceremony.

46. Frank Speck 1907, "Notes on the Ethnology of the Osage Indians," *Transactions of the University* [of Pennsylvania] *Museum* 2 (2), p. 171.

47. See Tixier 1940, *Travels on Osage Prairies*, p. 196.

48. Marshall 1928, "Journals of Jules DeMun," pp. 191–93, 195.

49. See Ponziglione n.d., "Father Schoenmaker and Osage," p. 292; Graves 1949, *First Protestant Osage Missions*, p. 12; and Morse 1822, *Report of Secretary of War*, pp. 203–5.

50. See La Flesche 1928, "Two Versions of Child-naming Rite."

51. La Flesche 1928, "Two Versions of Child-naming Rite," pp. 87–95.

52. Max Moorhead 1954, *Commerce of the Prairies by Josiah Gregg* (Norman: University of Oklahoma Press), p. 429; see also Paul Vissier 1827, *Histoire de la Tribu des Osages* (Paris: Chez Charles Bechet Libraire), p. 57, and Tixier 1940, *Travels on Osage Prairies*, p. 143.

53. Tixier 1940, *Travels on Osage Prairies*, p. 143.

54. Ponziglione n.d., "Father Schoenmaker and Osage," pp. 277–79; see also Fletcher and La Flesche n.d., La Flesche Papers 4558.

55. Ponziglione n.d., "Father Schoenmaker and Osage," pp. 277–79.

56. Tixier 1940, *Travels on Osage Prairies*, p. 183.

57. La Flesche 1911, "Osage Marriage Customs," in *American Anthropologist* 14, pp. 127–30; and La Flesche 1932, *Dictionary of Osage Language*, pp. 94–95.

58. La Flesche 1932, *Dictionary of Osage Language*, pp. 38–39.

59. Quoted in Graves 1949, *First Protestant Osage Missions*, p. 15.

60. Except where noted, the following description of organizing this type of war party is taken from La Flesche 1939, *War Ceremony and Peace Ceremony*, pp. 3–85.

61. Tixier 1940, *Travels on Osage Prairies*, p. 213.

62. La Flesche 1939, *War Ceremony and Peace Ceremony*, pp. 78–79.

63. La Flesche 1939, *War Ceremony and Peace Ceremony*, pp. 85–86.

64. For a list of war honors, see La Flesche 1925, "Rite of Vigil," pp. 179–80.

65. See Francis La Flesche 1917b, "Tribal Rites of the Osage Indians," *Smithsonian Miscellaneous Collections;* and Francis La Flesche 1918, "Researches Among the Osages," *Smithsonian Miscellaneous Collections* 70, pp. 110–13, 118–19.

66. See La Flesche 1928, "Two Versions of Child-naming Rite," pp. 54–55; and La Flesche 1925, "Rite of Vigil," p. 194.

67. La Flesche 1925, "Rite of Vigil," p. 195.

68. La Flesche 1932, *Dictionary of Osage Language*, p. 167.

69. See Fletcher and La Flesche, La Flesche Papers 4558, p. 78.

70. See Burns 1984, *Osage Indian Bands*, pp. 133–35.

71. Tixier 1940, *Travels on Osage Prairies*, p. 138.

72. See La Flesche 1918, "Researches Among the Osages," pp. 110–13.

73. See Fletcher and La Flesche, La Flesche Papers 4558, p. 85.

74. See La Flesche 1925, "Rite of Vigil," pp. 193–94.

75. La Flesche 1925, "Rite of Vigil," p. 238.

76. La Flesche 1925, "Rite of Vigil," p. 54.

77. La Flesche 1930, "Rite of Wa-xó-be," p. 614.

78. Fletcher and La Flesche, La Flesche Papers 4558, p. 78.

79. Fletcher and La Flesche, La Flesche Papers 4558, p. 78.

80. Garrick Bailey 1964–2003, field notes.

81. See La Flesche 1939, *War Ceremony and Peace Ceremony*, pp. 86–143, for a detailed description of the Mourning Dance.

82. Garrick Bailey 1973, "Changes in Osage Social Organization, 1673–1906" (University of Oregon Anthropology Papers, no. 5), pp. 73, 76, 81; and Terry Wilson 1985, *The Underground Reservation: Osage Oil* (Lincoln: University of Nebraska Press), pp. 14, 43.

83. Bailey 1973, "Changes in Osage Social Organization," p. 80.

84. Bailey 1973, "Changes in Osage Social Organization," p. 82.

85. Bailey 1973, "Changes in Osage Social Organization," pp. 110–11.

86. Bailey 1973, "Changes in Osage Social Organization," pp. 86–87; and Bailey 1964–2003, field notes.

87. Bailey 1964–2003, field notes.

88. Bailey 1964–2003, field notes.

4 / THE OSAGE PEYOTE RELIGION

Opening quote from Humpahtoka, ca. 1949; tape-recorded copy provided by Preston Morrell; translation by Lottie Pratt.

1. For bibliographic reference to the voluminous literature on peyote and its religious use by Native Americans, see Edwin F. Anderson 1996, *Peyote: The Divine Cactus*, 2d ed. (Tucson: University of Arizona Press); Weston La Barre 1989, *The Peyote Cult*, 5th ed., enlarged (Norman: University of Oklahoma Press); and Omer C. Stewart 1987, *Peyote Religion, A History* (Norman: University of Oklahoma Press).

2. For a comprehensive history of the Peyote Religion, see J. S. Slotkin 1956, *The Peyote Religion: A Study in Indian-White Relations* (Glencoe, Ill.: Free Press). The definitive source for the history of Peyotism in

specific tribal communities is Stewart 1987, *Peyote Religion, a History*. For the history of Osage Peyotism, see Daniel C. Swan 1990, "West Moon—East Moon: An Ethnohistory of Osage Peyotism" (Ann Arbor, Mich.: University Microfilms International).

3. La Barre 1989, *Peyote Cult*, pp. 36–37; Slotkin 1956, *Peyote Religion: A Study*, pp. 214–16; John R. Swanton 1942, "Source Material on the History of Ethnology of the Caddo Indians," in *Bureau of American Ethnology Bulletin 132* (Smithsonian Institution, Washington, D.C.: U.S. Government Printing Office), pp. 220–24.

4. For information regarding John Wilson and his participation in Peyotism, see La Barre 1989, *Peyote Cult;* James Mooney 1896, "The Ghost Dance Religion and the Sioux Outbreak of 1890" *Annual Report of the Bureau of American Ethnology (1892–1893)* 14: 653–1136 (Smithsonian Institution, Washington, D.C.: U.S. Government Printing Office); Frank Speck 1933, "Notes on the Life of John Wilson, the Revealor of Peyote, as recalled by his nephew George Anderson" *General Magazine and Historical Chronicle* 35, pp. 539–56 (Philadelphia); Melburn D. Thurman 1973, "Supplementary Material on the Life of John Wilson," in *Ethnohistory* 20, pp. 279–87.

5. For information on the development, content, and diffusion of Big Moon Peyotism, see La Barre 1989, *Peyote Cult;* Vincenzo Petrullo 1975, *The Diabolic Root: A Study of Peyotism, the New Indian Religion among the Delawares* (reprint, New York: Octagon Books); and Speck 1933, "Life of John Wilson."

6. Francis La Flesche 1921, "The Osage Tribe: Rite of the Chiefs: Sayings of the Ancient Men," in *Thirty-sixth Annual Report of the Bureau of American Ethnology (1914–15)* (Washington, D.C.: Bureau of American Ethnology), p. 46; Francis La Flesche 1925, "The Osage Tribe: The Rite of Vigil," in *Thirty-ninth Annual Report of the Bureau of American Ethnology (1917–18)* (Washington, D.C.: Bureau of American Ethnology), p. 177.

7. John Joseph Mathews 1982, *The Osages, Children of the Middle Waters*, 4th ed. (Norman: University of Oklahoma Press), p. 740.

8. See Daniel C. Swan 1998, "Early Osage Peyotism," *Plains Anthropologist* 43 (163), pp. 51–71, for a detailed examination of the initial conversion of the Osage to Big Moon Peyotism. Community sources on the history of Osage Peyotism include Henry Haskell, Leroy Logan, Randolph Lookout, Walter Matin, Preston Morrell, Ed Red Eagle Sr., Mary Standingbear, and Josephine Walker.

9. Leroy Logan 1986, oral history interview (Hominy Indian Village, Hominy, Oklahoma; ms. notes courtesy Dan Swan), p. 1A; Kate Lester Jones 1986, "Osage Indians," *Oklahoma Today* 36 (3), p. 33.

10. Logan 1986, interview; Preston Morrell 1986, personal communication with the author; Josephine Walker 1968, oral history interview conducted by Leonard Maker Sr. (Doris Duke Oral History Collection, T-364; transcribed by Debbie Darrow; Norman: University of Oklahoma, Western History Collections).

11. James Owen Dorsey 1884, "An Account of the War Customs of the Osage," *American Naturalist* 18, pp. 115, 117, 121, 123, 125; La Flesche

1921, "Rite of Chiefs," p. 119; La Flesche 1925, "Rite of Vigil," p. 53; Francis La Flesche 1939, *War Ceremony and Peace Ceremony of the Osage Indians* (Washington, D.C.: Bureau of American Ethnology, Bulletin 101), pp. 104, 139–40, 203.

12. See W. David Baird 1980, *The Quapaw Indians: A History of the Downstream People* (Norman: University of Oklahoma Press), p. 180; Mathews 1982, *Children of the Middle Waters*, 4th ed., p. 744; and Petrullo 1975, *Diabolic Root*, p. 103, for additional information regarding Victor Griffin and his activity as a Peyote missionary.

13. Sources on changes in the Osage Peyote Religion since World War II include Leonard Maker Sr., Walter Matin, Preston Morrell, Henry Haskell, Randolph "Smokey" Lookout, and Lottie Pratt.

14. For an early description, see John Francis McDermott, ed., 1940, *Tixier's Travels on the Osage Prairies*, translated from French by Albert J. Salvan (Norman: University of Oklahoma Press), p. 164.

15. Richard E. Schultes 1937, "Peyote, and Plants Used in the Peyote Ceremony," *Harvard University, Botanical Museum Leaflets* 4 (8), pp. 138–39.

16. Logan 1986, interview, p. 1A.

17. Logan 1986, interview, p. 1B; Morrell 1986, personal communication, p. 1B.

18. James H. Howard n.d., manuscript notes (Milwaukee Public Museum, Wis.).

19. Logan 1986, interview, p. 2A; Morrell 1986, personal communication, p. 1B; Lottie Pratt 1995, interview notes (Hominy, Oklahoma; ms. notes courtesy Dan Swan), p. 2A.

20. Morrell 1986, personal communication.

5 / THE RICHEST PEOPLE IN THE WORLD

Opening quotation from Charles Red Corn 2002, *A Pipe for February* (Norman: University of Oklahoma Press), p. 5.

1. Evander Sweet 1903, "Richest People in the World," *The World Today* 5, pp. 1454–58.

2. See Frank Speck 1907, "Notes on the Ethnology of the Osage Indians," *Transactions of the Museum of Science and Art* 2 (2), pp. 159–71.

3. Eugene E. White 1965, *Experiences of a Special Indian Agent* (reprint, Norman: University of Oklahoma Press), p. 202.

4. Sweet 1903, "Richest People in the World."

5. See H. Craig Miner 1989, *The Corporation and the Indian* (Norman: University of Oklahoma Press).

6. For a discussion of the background and provisions of the General Allotment Act of 1887, see Rennard Strickland 1982, *Felix S. Cohen's Handbook of Federal Indian Law* (Charlottesville, Va.: Michie Bobbs-Merrill), pp. 127–41.

7. Terry Wilson 1985, *The Underground Reservation: Osage Oil* (Lincoln: University of Nebraska Press), pp. 101–7.

8. Jessie Bloodworth 1953, *The Osage People and Their Trust Property* (Pawhuska, Okla.: A Field Report of the Bureau of Indian Affairs, Anadarko Area Office, Osage Agency), pp. 166–67.

9. Bloodworth 1953, *Osage People and Trust Property*, pp. 165–66.

10. Bloodworth 1953, *Osage People and Trust Property*, pp. 190–91.

11. In 1901 the Indian Territory Illuminating Oil Company was created out of Foster's Phoenix Oil Company, which held the blanket lease on the Osage Reservation. Kenny A. Franks 1980, *The Oklahoma Petroleum Industry* (Norman: University of Oklahoma Press), p. 36.

12. Carl Coke Rister 1949, *OIL! Titan of the Southwest* (Norman: University of Oklahoma Press), p. 182.

13. James Edwin Finney 1959, "The Indian Territory Illuminating Oil Company," *The Chronicles of Oklahoma* 37, p. 158.

14. Osage Indian Agency 1911, *Superintendents' Annual Narrative and Statistical Reports from Field Jurisdictions of the Bureau of Indian Affairs* (Washington, D.C.: National Archives Microfilm Publications, M1011 roll 95), pp. 40, 42.

15. Lee Slater 1975, *1975 Directory of Oklahoma* (Oklahoma City: State Election Board), p. 333.

16. This figure is based on agency records tabulated by the Osage Tribal Museum. There may have been some additional individuals whose service was unknown to the agency.

17. Wilson 1985, *Underground Reservation*, p. 131.

18. Garrick Bailey 1978, "John Joseph Mathews," in *American Indian Intellectuals*, proceedings of the American Ethnological Society (St. Paul, Minn.: West Publishing), p. 208.

19. James Crowder 1987, *Osage General: Major General Clarence L. Tinker* (Oklahoma City: Office of History, Tinker Air Force Base, U.S. Air Force), p. 77.

20. Garrick Bailey 1964–2003, field notes.

21. Osage Tribal Council 1957, *1907–1957 Osage Indians Semi-Centennial Celebration* (Pawhuska, Okla.: Osage Tribal Council), p. 45.

22. Osage Indian Agency 1919, *Superintendents' Annual Narrative and Statistical Report from Field Jurisdictions of the Bureau of Indian Affairs* (Washington, D.C.: National Archives Microfilm Publications, M1011 roll 95), pp. 8–9.

23. Bailey 1964–2003, field notes.

24. Wilson 1985, *Underground Reservation*, p. 124.

25. Rister 1949, *OIL!* p. 182.

26. Wilson 1985, *Underground Reservation*, p. 123.

27. Kenny A. Franks, Paul F. Lambert, and Carl N. Tyson 1981, *Early Oklahoma Oil: A Photographic History, 1859–1936* (College Station: Texas A&M University Press), p. 4.

28. Franks 1980, *Oklahoma Petroleum Industry*, pp. 101–5.

29. See Slater 1975, *Directory of Oklahoma*, p. 333.

30. Bloodworth 1953, *Osage People and Trust Property*, chart 1.

31. Wilson 1985, *Underground Reservation*, pp. 143–45.

32. Bloodworth 1953, *Osage People and Trust Property*, p. viii.

33. Osage Indian Agency 1929, *Superintendents' Narrative and Annual Statistical Report from Field Jurisdictions of the Bureau of Indian Affairs* (Washington, D.C.: National Archives Microfilm Publications, M1011 roll 96), p. 25.

34. Bailey 1964–2003, field notes.

35. Sister Mary Paul Fitzgerald 1939, *Beacon on the Plains* (Leavenworth, Kans.: Saint Mary College).

36. Wilson 1985, *Underground Reservation*, pp. 77–80.

37. Bailey 1964–2003, field notes.

38. There are several versions of this story; this quote is from James Edwin Finney 1958, "The Osages and Their Agency During the Term of Isaac T. Gibson, Quaker Agent," *The Chronicles of Oklahoma* 36, p. 424.

39. Bailey 1964–2003, field notes.

40. Bailey 1964–2003, field notes.

41. Bailey 1964–2003, field notes.

42. Osage Indian Agency 1924, *Superintendents' Annual Narrative and Statistical Report from Field Jurisdictions of the Bureau of Indian Affairs* (Washington, D.C.: National Archives Microfilm Publications, M1011 roll 96), p. 9.

43. Bailey 1964–2003, field notes.

44. Bailey 1964–2003, field notes.

45. Bailey 1964–2003, field notes.

46. Bailey 1964–2003, field notes.

47. Bailey 1964–2003, field notes.

48. Charles Eastman 1977, "Report on the Economic Condition of the Osage Indians in Oklahoma," *The Chronicles of Oklahoma* 60, pp. 343–45; and Bailey 1964–2003, field notes.

49. Bailey 1964–2003, field notes.

50. Eastman 1977, "Report on Economic Condition," pp. 343–45.

51. Bailey 1964–2003, field notes.

52. Bailey 1964–2003, field notes.

53. Bailey 1964–2003, field notes.

54. Bailey 1964–2003, field notes.

55. Bailey 1964–2003, field notes.

56. Bailey 1964–2003, field notes.

57. Bailey 1964–2003, field notes.

58. Anonymous 1930, "Beautiful Cups Awarded in Indian Golf Tournament," *The American Indian* 4 (12), p. 11.

59. Osage Indian Agency 1929, *Annual Report*, p. 22.

60. Gerda Sebbelov 1911, "The Osage War Dance," *The Museum Journal of the University of Pennsylvania* 2, pp. 71–74; and Bailey 1964–2003, field notes.

61. Bloodworth 1953, *Osage People and Trust Property*, pp. 167–69.

62. Wilson 1985, *Underground Reservation*, p. 79.

63. Bailey 1964–2003, field notes.

64. Wilson 1985, *Underground Reservation*, p. 188.

6 / Osage Dancing Societies and Organizations

Opening quotation from Frederick M. Lookout 1998, notes on the Osage E-Lon-schka ceremony (manuscript copy courtesy Dan Swan).

1. See works of Garrick Bailey and Francis La Flesche for examples and interpretation of these traditions.

2. Francis La Flesche 1914, "Ceremonies and Rituals of the Osage," in *Explorations and Fieldwork of the Smithsonian Institution* (Washington, D.C.: U.S. Government Printing Office), *Smithsonian Miscellaneous Collections* 63 (8), pp. 66–67; Francis La Flesche 1917a, p. 121; Francis La Flesche 1921, "The Osage Tribe: Rite of the Chiefs: Sayings of the Ancient Men," in *Thirty-sixth Annual Report of the Bureau of American Ethnology (1914–15)* (Washington, D.C.: Bureau of American Ethnology), p. 84; Francis La Flesche 1928, "The Osage Tribe: Two Versions of the Child-naming Rite," in *Forty-third Annual Report of the Bureau of American Ethnology (1925–26)* (Washington, D.C.: Bureau of American Ethnology), p. 73; Frank Speck 1907, "Notes on the Ethnology of the Osage Indians," in *Transactions of the Museum of Science and Art* 2 (2), p. 165.

3. Garrick Bailey 1995, *The Osage and the Invisible World: From the Works of Francis La Flesche* (Norman: University of Oklahoma Press), p. 18; Leonard Maker Sr. 1968b, p. 4.

4. Allison Lee Granberry 1987, "The Expression of Osage Identity: Ethnic Unity and the In-Lon-Schka" (Master's thesis, Department of Anthropology, Tulsa: University of Oklahoma), p. 65.

5. Clark Wissler 1916, "General Discussion of Shamanistic and Dancing Societies" *Anthropological Papers of the American Museum of Natural History* 11 (12), pp. 853–76.

6. Edward Red Eagle Sr. 1984, public presentation (Pawhuska Ilonschka Centennial Program, transcribed by James Cooley); Newman Little Walker 1984, public presentation (Pawhuska Ilonschka Centennial Program, transcribed by James Cooley); Alice Anne Callahan 1977, "The ÍN-Lon-Schka (Playground-of-the-Eldest-Son), The June Ceremonial Dance of the Osages: A Study in American Indian Arts" (Ann Arbor, Mich.: University Microfilms International), p. 57.

7. U. S. Bureau of Indian Affairs 1894, "Report of the Osage Agent" (Washington, D.C.: U.S. Government Printing Office), p. 242.

8. Mary Nora Standingbear 1985, notes and comments on Osage Peyotism (manuscript notes courtesy Dan Swan).

9. Walter Matin Sr. 1976, oral history interview conducted by Abraham Conklin (Hominy Indian Village, Hominy, Oklahoma; manuscript notes courtesy Dan Swan), p. 1A; Leroy Logan 1986,

oral history interview (Hominy Indian Village, Hominy, Oklahoma; manuscript notes courtesy Dan Swan), p. 1A; Maker 1968b, p. 6.

10. Matin 1976, interview, p. 1A.

11. Granberry 1987, "Expression of Osage Identity," p. 40; Rose Albert Hill 1967, oral history interview conducted by Robert L. Miller (Doris Duke Oral History Collection, T-107; transcribed by Nora Kerr; Norman: University of Oklahoma, Western History Collections), p. 8.

12. Norman Feder 1980, "Some Notes on the Osage War Dance," *Moccasin Tracks* (November), pp. 4–5.

13. U.S. Bureau of Indian Affairs 1873, "Report of the Osage Agent" (Washington, D.C.: U.S. Government Printing Office), p. 216.

14. Feder 1980, "Osage War Dance," p. 5; Speck 1907, "Ethnology of Osage Indians," pp. 170–71; Kate Pearson Burrell 1903, "As Osage Indians Live Today," *Sturm's Oklahoma Magazine* 2, p. 89; U.S. Bureau of Indian Affairs 1894, "Report of the Osage Agent," p. 242.

15. Feder 1980, "Osage War Dance," p. 5.

16. Frederick M. Lookout 1996, personal communication with author.

17. Feder 1980, "Osage War Dance," p. 6.

18. Rose Kirk Pipestem 1978, personal communication; Mary Standingbear n.d., personal communication.

19. Lenora Morrell Shannon n.d., personal communication with author.

20. See the works of Francis La Flesche and Garrick Bailey for descriptions and drawings of these objects.

21. Howard 1965, *The Ponca Tribe*, p. 219.

22. Garrick Bailey 1995, *Osage and Invisible World*, p. 52.

23. Robert J. Austin 2000, *A Manual of Fingerweaving* (Pottsboro, Tex.: Crazy Crow Trading Post), pp. 5–6.

24. Murie 1914, "Pawnee Indian Societies," p. 616. Francis La Flesche 1939, *War Ceremony and Peace Ceremony of the Osage Indians* (Washington, D.C.: Bureau of American Ethnology, Bulletin 101), p. 97.

25. Terry Wilson 1985, *The Underground Reservation: Osage Oil* (Lincoln: University of Nebraska Press), pp. 131–32.

) References (

Anderson, Edward F.
1996   *Peyote: The Divine Cactus.* 2d ed. Tucson: University of Arizona Press.

Anonymous
1930   "Beautiful Cups Awarded in Indian Golf Tournament." *The American Indian* 4 (12): 11.

Austin, Robert J.
2000   *A Manual of Fingerweaving.* Pottsboro, Tex.: Crazy Crow Trading Post.

Bailey, Garrick
1964–2003   Field notes.
1973   "Changes in Osage Social Organization 1673–1906." *University of Oregon Anthropology Papers,* no. 5.
1978   "John Joseph Mathews." In *American Indian Intellectuals.* Proceedings of the American Ethnological Society. St. Paul, Minn.: West Publishing.
1995   *The Osage and the Invisible World: From the Works of Francis La Flesche.* Norman: University of Oklahoma Press.
2001   "Osage." In *Handbook of North American Indians* 13 (1): 476–97. Washington, D.C.: Smithsonian Institution.

Baird, W. David
1980   *The Quapaw Indians: A History of the Downstream People.* Norman: University of Oklahoma Press.

Bloodworth, Jessie
1953   *The Osage People and Their Trust Property.* Pawhuska, Okla.: A Field Report of the Bureau of Indian Affairs, Anadarko Area Office, Osage Agency.

Bradbury, John
1817   *Travels in the Interior of America, 1809, 1810 and 1811.* London: Sherwood, Neely and Jones.

Burns, Louis F.
1984   *Osage Indian Bands and Clans.* Fallbrook, Calif.: CIGA Press.
1989   *A History of the Osage People.* Fallbrook, Calif.: CIGA Press.

Burrell, Kate Pearson
1903   "As Osage Indians Live Today." *Sturm's Oklahoma Magazine* 2: 84–89.

Callahan, Alice Anne
1977   "The ÍN-Lon-Schka (Playground-of-the-Eldest-Son), The June Ceremonial Dance of the Osages: A Study in American Indian Arts." Ann Arbor, Mich.: University Microfilms International.

Catlin, George
1844   *Letters and notes on the manners, customs, and conditions of the North American Indians written during eight years' travel (1832–1839) amongst the wildest tribes in North America.* 2 vols. London: D. Bogue.

Chandler, Milford
1973   "Art and Culture." In *Art of the Great Lakes Indians.* Flint, Mich.: Flint Institute of Arts.

Chapman, Carl
1975   *Archaeology of Missouri.* Columbia: University of Missouri Press.

Chapman, Carl, and Eleanor Chapman
1964   *Indians and Archaeology of Missouri.* Columbia: Missouri Archaeological Society.

Conn, Richard G.
1980   "Native American Cloth Appliqué and Ribbonwork: Their Origin and Diffusion in the Plains." In *Native American Ribbonwork: A Rainbow Tradition,* edited by George Horse Capture. Cody, Wyo.: Buffalo Bill Historic Center.

Crowder, James
1987   *Osage General: Major General Clarence L. Tinker.* Oklahoma City: Office of History, Tinker Air Force Base, U.S. Air Force.

Din, Gilbert C., and Abraham P. Nasatir
1983   *The Imperial Osages: Spanish-Indian Diplomacy in the Mississippi Valley.* Norman: University of Oklahoma Press.

Dorsey, James Owen
1884   "An Account of the War Customs of the Osage." *American Naturalist* 18: 113–33.
1888   "Osage Traditions." *Sixth Annual Report of the Bureau of American Ethnology (1884–85),* pp. 373–96. Washington, D.C.
1897   "Siouan Sociology: A Posthumous Paper." *Fifteenth Annual Report of the Bureau of American Ethnology (1893–94),* pp. 205–44. Washington, D.C.

Eastman, Charles
1977   "Report on the Economic Condition of the Osage Indians in Oklahoma, 1924." *The Chronicles of Oklahoma* 60: 343–45.

Farnham, Thomas J.
1906   *Travels in the Great Western Prairies, the Anahauc and Rocky Mountains and the Oregon Territory (1843).* 2 vols. *Early Western Travels,* edited by Reuben G. Thwaites. Cleveland, Ohio: Arthur A. Clark.

Feder, Norman
1980   "Some Notes on the Osage War Dance." *Moccasin Tracks* (November): 4–7.

Finney, James Edwin
1955   "Reminiscences of a Trader in Osage Country." *The Chronicles of Oklahoma* 33: 145–58.
1958   "The Osages and Their Agency During the Term of Isaac T. Gibson, Quaker Agent." *The Chronicles of Oklahoma* 36: 416–28.

1959   "The Indian Territory Illuminating Oil Company." *The Chronicles of Oklahoma* 37: 149–61.

Fitzgerald, Sister Mary Paul
1939   *Beacon on the Plains.* Leavenworth, Kans.: Saint Mary College.

Fletcher, Alice, and Francis La Flesche
n.d.   La Flesche Papers. National Anthropological Archives, Museum of Natural History, Smithsonian Institution, Washington, D.C.
1911   "The Omaha Tribe." *Twenty-seventh Annual Report of the Bureau of American Ethnology (1905–6).* Washington, D.C.

Foreman, Grant
1933   *Advancing the Frontier.* Norman: University of Oklahoma Press.
1936   *Indians and Pioneers.* Norman: University of Oklahoma Press.
1946   *The Last Trek of the Indians.* Norman: University of Oklahoma Press.

Franks, Kenny A.
1980   *The Oklahoma Petroleum Industry.* Norman: University of Oklahoma Press.

Franks, Kenny A., Paul F. Lambert, and Carl N. Tyson
1981   *Early Oklahoma Oil: A Photographic History, 1859–1936.* College Station: Texas A&M University Press.

Granberry, Allison Lee
1987   "The Expression of Osage Identity: Ethnic Unity and the In-Lon-Schka." Master's thesis, Department of Anthropology. Tulsa: University of Oklahoma.

Graves, W. W.
1916   *Life and Letters of Father Ponziglione, Schoenmaker and Other Early Jesuits at Osage Mission.* St. Paul, Kans: W. W. Graves.
1949   *The First Protestant Osage Missions 1820–1837.* Oswego, Kans: The Carpenter Press.

Hail, Barbara A.
1983   *Hau, Kóla!* Mount Hope Grant, R.I.: Haffenreffer Museum, Brown University.

Haskell, Henry
1985–1987   Comments on the Osage Peyote Religion. Manuscript notes courtesy of Dan Swan.

Hill, Rose Albert
1967   Oral history interview. Conducted by Robert L. Miller, Doris Duke Oral History Collection, T-107. Transcribed by Nora Kerr. Norman: University of Oklahoma, Western History Collections.

Howard, James H.
n.d.   Manuscript notes. Milwaukee Public Museum, Wis.
1965   *The Ponca Tribe.* Bureau of American Ethnology, Bulletin 195, Washington, D.C.

Humpahtoka
ca. 1949   Tape-recorded interview. Translated by Lottie Pratt. Copy courtesy Preston Morrell.

Hunter, John Dunn
1973   *Memoirs of a Captivity among the Indians of North America.* New York: Schocken Press.

Hyde, George
1951   *The Pawnee Indians.* Denver: University of Denver Press.

Irving, Washington
1854   *A Tour of the Prairies.* New York: G. P. Putnam.

Jackson, Donald, ed.
1966   *The Journals of Zebulon Montgomery Pike.* 2 vols. Norman: University of Oklahoma Press.

Jones, Kate Lester
1986   "Osage Indians." *Oklahoma Today* 36 (3): 32–36.

La Barre, Weston
1989   *The Peyote Cult.* 5th ed., enlarged. Norman: University of Oklahoma Press.

La Flesche, Francis
1911   "Osage Marriage Customs." *American Anthropologist,* n.s., 14: 127–30.
1914   "Ceremonies and Rituals of the Osage." *Explorations and Fieldwork of the Smithsonian Institution. Smithsonian Miscellaneous Collections* 63 (8): 66–69. Washington, D.C.: U.S. Government Printing Office.
1915   "Omaha and Osage Traditions of Separation." *Proceedings of the International Congress of Americanists* 19: 459–62.
1917a   "Work Among the Osage Indians." *Smithsonian Miscellaneous Collections* 66: 118–21. Washington, D.C.: U.S. Government Printing Office.
1917b   "Tribal Rites of the Osage Indians." *Smithsonian Miscellaneous Collections* 68: 84–90. Washington, D.C.: U.S. Government Printing Office.
1918   "Researches Among the Osages." *Smithsonian Miscellaneous Collections* 70: 110–13, 118–19. Washington, D.C.: U.S. Government Printing Office.
1920   "Symbolic Man of the Osage Tribe." *Art and Archaeology* 9: 68–72.
1921   "The Osage Tribe: Rite of the Chiefs: Sayings of the Ancient Men." *Thirty-sixth Annual Report of the Bureau of American Ethnology (1914–15),* pp. 35–604. Washington, D.C.
1925   "The Osage Tribe: The Rite of Vigil." *Thirty-ninth Annual Report of the Bureau of American Ethnology (1917–18),* pp. 31–630. Washington, D.C.
1928   "The Osage Tribe: Two Versions of the Child-naming Rite." *Forty-third Annual Report of the Bureau of American Ethnology (1925–26),* pp. 29–164. Washington, D.C.
1930   "The Osage Tribe: Rite of the Wa-xó-be." *Forty-fifth Annual Report of the Bureau of American Ethnology (1927–28),* pp. 523–833. Washington, D.C.

1932 *A Dictionary of the Osage Language.* Bureau of American Ethnology, Bulletin 109. Washington, D.C.

1939 *War Ceremony and Peace Ceremony of the Osage Indians.* Bureau of American Ethnology, Bulletin 101, Washington, D.C.

Little Walker, Newman

1984 Public presentation. Pawhuska Ilonschka Centennial Program. Transcribed by James Cooley.

Logan, Leroy

1985 Comments to the Osage language class. Community Center, Hominy, Oklahoma. Manuscript notes courtesy Dan Swan.

1986 Oral history interview. Hominy Indian Village, Hominy, Oklahoma. Manuscript notes courtesy Dan Swan.

Lookout, Frederick Morris

1996 Personal communication with the author.

1998 Notes on the Osage E-Lon-schka ceremony. Manuscript copy courtesy Dan Swan.

Lookout, Randolph "Smokey"

1985 Comments on the Lookout family church. Manuscript notes courtesy Dan Swan.

Maker Sr., Leonard

1968a Oral history interview. Conducted by Katherine Maker. Doris Duke Oral History Collection, T-344-1. Transcribed by Monte Coombes. Norman: University of Oklahoma, Western History Collections.

1968b Oral history interview. Conducted by Katherine Maker. Doris Duke Oral History Collection, T-356. Transcribed by Flora Quinata. Norman: University of Oklahoma, Western History Collections.

Marriott, Alice

1974 *Osage Indians.* Vol. 2. New York: Garland Publishing.

Marriott, Alice, and Carol Rachin

1980 "Southern Plains Ribbonwork Development and Diffusion." In *Native American Ribbonwork: A Rainbow Tradition,* edited by George Horse Capture. Cody, Wyo.: Buffalo Bill Historical Center.

Marshall, Thomas, ed.

1928 "The Journals of Jules DeMun." Translated by Nettie Beauregard. *Missouri Historical Society Collections* 5: 167–208.

Mathews, John Joseph

1982 *The Osages, Children of the Middle Waters.* 4th ed. Norman: University of Oklahoma Press. (Originally published in 1961.)

Matin Sr., Walter

1976 Oral history interview. Conducted by Abraham Conklin. Hominy Indian Village, Hominy, Oklahoma. Manuscript notes courtesy Dan Swan.

McCarthy, Edgar

1923 *Peyote: As Used in Religious Worship by the Indians.* Hominy, Okla.: Private printing.

McCoy, Isaac

1835 *Annual Report of Indian Affairs within Indian Territory.* Shawanoe Baptist Mission House, Indian Territory (Okla.): J. Meeker.

McDermott, John Francis, ed.

1940 *Tixier's Travels on the Osage Prairies.* Translated from French by Albert J. Salvan. Norman: University of Oklahoma Press.

Miner, H. Craig

1989 *The Corporation and the Indian.* Norman: University of Oklahoma Press.

Mooney, James

1896 "The Ghost Dance Religion and the Sioux Outbreak of 1890." *Annual Report of the Bureau of American Ethnology (1892–1893)* 14: 653–1136. Smithsonian Institution. Washington, D.C.: U.S. Government Printing Office.

Moorhead, Max, ed.

1954 *Commerce of the Prairies by Josiah Gregg.* Norman: University of Oklahoma Press.

Morrell, Preston

1984–2000 Notes and comments on Black Dog Peyotism. Hominy, Oklahoma. Manuscript notes courtesy Dan Swan.

1986 Personal communication with the author.

Morse, Jedidiah

1822 *A Report of the Secretary of War of the United States, on Indian Affairs Comprising a Narrative of a Tour.* New Haven, Conn.: S. Converse.

Murie, James R.

1914 "Pawnee Indian Societies." *Anthropological Papers of the American Museum of Natural History* 11 (7): 545–645.

Nasatir, A. P., ed.

1930 "An Account of Spanish Louisiana, 1785." *The Missouri Historical Review* 24: 521–36.

Osage Indian Agency

1911 *Superintendents' Annual Narrative and Statistical Report from Field Jurisdictions of the Bureau of Indian Affairs.* Washington, D.C.: National Archives Microfilm Publications, M1011 roll 95.

1919 *Superintendents' Annual Narrative and Statistical Report from Field Jurisdictions of the Bureau of Indian Affairs.* Washington, D.C.: National Archives Microfilm Publications, M1011 roll 95.

1924 *Superintendents' Annual Narrative and Statistical Report from Field Jurisdictions of the Bureau of Indian Affairs.* Washington, D.C.: National Archives Microfilm Publications, M1011 roll 96.

1929 *Superintendents' Annual Narrative and Statistical Report from Field Jurisdictions of the Bureau of Indian Affairs.* Washington D.C.: National Archives Microfilm Publications, M1011 roll 96.

Osage Tribal Council
1957 *1907–1957 Osage Indians Semi-Centennial Celebration.* Pawhuska, Okla.: Osage Tribal Council.

Petrullo, Vincenzo
1975 *The Diabolic Root: A Study of Peyotism, the New Indian Religion among the Delawares.* Reprint, New York: Octagon Books.

Pipestem, Rose Kirk
1978 Comments on the Osage Ilonschka. Manuscript notes courtesy Dan Swan.

Ponziglione, Father Paul M., S.J.
n.d. "Father Schoenmaker and the Osage." Manuscript. St. Louis University Library, St. Louis, Mo.
1878 Letter of Father Ponziglione, December 31, 1877. *Woodstock Letters* 8: 99–105.
1883 Kansas, Letter from Father Ponziglione, July 2, 1883. *Woodstock Letters* 12: 292–98.
1889 "Indian Traditions among the Osage." *Woodstock Letters* 18: 68–76.

Pratt, Lottie
1995 Interview notes. Hominy, Oklahoma. Manuscript notes courtesy Dan Swan.

Red Corn, Charles
2002 *A Pipe for February.* Norman: University of Oklahoma Press.

Red Eagle Sr., Edward
1967 Oral history interview. Doris Duke Oral History Collection, T-108. Norman: University of Oklahoma, Western History Collections.
1984 Public presentation. Pawhuska Ilonschka Centennial Program. Transcribed by James Cooley.
1985 Notes and comments on Osage Peyotism. Manuscript notes courtesy Dan Swan.

Rister, Carl Coke
1949 *OIL! Titan of the Southwest.* Norman: University of Oklahoma Press.

Rollings, Willard H.
1992 *The Osage: An Ethnohistorical Study of Hegemony on the Prairie-Plains.* Columbia: University of Missouri Press.

Schultes, Richard E.
1937 "Peyote, and Plants Used in the Peyote Ceremony." *Harvard University, Botanical Museum Leaflets* 4 (8): 129–51.

Sebbelov, Gerda
1911 "The Osage War Dance." *The Museum Journal of the University of Pennsylvania* 2: 71–74.

Shannon, Lenora Morrell
n.d. Personal communication with the author.
1984–1988 Notes and comments on Osage Peyotism. Manuscript notes courtesy Dan Swan.

Slater, Lee
1975 *1975 Directory of Oklahoma.* Oklahoma City: State Election Board.

Slotkin, J. S.
1955 "Peyotism, 1521–1891." *American Anthropologist* 57: 202–30.
1956 *The Peyote Religion: A Study in Indian-White Relations.* Glencoe, Ill.: Free Press.

Speck, Frank
1907 "Notes on the Ethnology of the Osage Indians." *Transactions of the Museum of Science and Art* 2 (2): 159–71.
1933 "Notes on the Life of John Wilson, the Revealor of Peyote, as recalled by his nephew George Anderson." *General Magazine and Historical Chronicle* 35: 539–56. Philadelphia.

Standing Bear, Mary Nora Lookout
1985 Comments on the history of Osage Peyotism. Manuscript notes courtesy Daniel C. Swan.

Stewart, Omer C.
1987 *Peyote Religion, A History.* Norman: University of Oklahoma Press.

Strickland, Rennard, ed.
1982 *Felix S. Cohen's Handbook of Federal Indian Law, 1982 Edition.* Charlottesville, Va.: Michie Bobbs-Merrill.

Swan, Daniel C.
1990 "West Moon—East Moon: An Ethnohistory of Osage Peyotism." Ann Arbor, Mich.: University Microfilms International.
1998 "Early Osage Peyotism." *Plains Anthropologist* 43 (163): 51–71.

Swanton, John R.
1942 "Source Material on the History of Ethnology of the Caddo Indians." Bureau of American Ethnology Bulletin 132. Smithsonian Institution. Washington, D.C.: U.S. Government Printing Office.

Sweet, Evander
1903 "Richest People in the World." *The World Today* 5: 1454–58.

Thurman, Melburn D.
1973 "Supplementary Material on the Life of John Wilson." *Ethnohistory* 20: 279–87.

Tixier, Victor
1940 *Tixier's Travels on the Osage Prairies.* Edited by John F. McDermott. Norman: University of Oklahoma Press.

Torrence, Gaylord
1994 *The American Indian Parfleche: A Tradition of Abstract Painting.* Seattle: University of Washington Press and Des Moines Art Center.

U.S. Bureau of Indian Affairs
1873 "Report of the Osage Agent," Commissioners Report, pp. 215–18. Washington, D.C.: U.S. Government Printing Office.

1894   "Report of the Osage Agent," Commissioners Report,
        pp. 241–45. Washington, D.C.: U.S. Government Printing
        Office.

Vissier, Paul

1827   *Histoire de la Tribu des Osages.* Paris: Chez Charles Bechet
        Libraire.

Voget, Fred W.

1974   *Osage Indian.* Vol. 1. New York: Garland Publishing.

Walker, Josephine

1968   Oral history interview. Conducted by Leonard Maker Sr.
        Doris Duke Oral History Collection, T-364. Transcribed by
        Debbie Darrow. Norman: University of Oklahoma, Western
        History Collections.

White, Eugene E.

[1893] 1965   *Experiences of a Special Indian Agent.* Reprint, Norman:
        University of Oklahoma Press.

Whiteford, Andrew Hunter

1977a   "Fiber Bags of the Great Lakes Indians." Part 1. *American Indian
        Art Magazine* 2 (3): 52–64, 85.

1977b   "Fiber Bags of the Great Lakes Indians." Part 2. *American Indian
        Art Magazine* 3 (1): 40–47, 90.

1978   "Tapestry-Twined Bags, Osage Bags and Others." *American
        Indian Art Magazine* 3 (2): 32–39, 92.

Wilson, Terry

1985   *The Underground Reservation: Osage Oil.* Lincoln: University
        of Nebraska Press.

Wissler, Clark

1916   "General Discussion of Shamanistic and Dancing Societies."
        *Anthropological Papers of the American Museum of Natural
        History* 11 (12): 853–76.

Figures and color plates are indicated with
bold type.

agriculture, 6, 53–54, 56, 66
airplane motif, **151, 192–93**
Á-ki-da, 50, 52, **94c**
alligator motif, **97**
allotment process, 138–39, 149
altars, Peyote, **110, 111, 112–13, 116**
American Legion, 169
American War Mothers, 169, **192c**
antlers: club, **76**; European tools, 8–9; quirts, **16,
76**; roach spreaders, **14,** 198
appliqué work. *See* ribbon work
Arapahoe people, 7
armor, **17, 105, 171**
arrow/arrowhead motifs: cradleboards, **68–69, 106;**
garters, **189;** leggings, **180;** mirror boards, **22;**
neckerchief slides, **172;** Peyote staff, **117, 117;**
vest, **182**
arrows for rituals, 37

baby boards. *See* cradleboards
background-foreground relationships, **82,** 196, **202**
Bacon Rind, Chief (Star That Travels), **62;** belongings
of, **12, 39, 150, 173, 175;** E-Lon-schka dance, **159**
bags, 36, **52–53, 85–86, 92–93, 134–35,** 148, **165**
basketry, 52
beadwork: overview, 9–10; bags, **85–86, 134–35,
165;** belts/sashes, **153, 190;** blankets, **192–93;**
boxes, **127;** children's clothing, **103;** cradleboards,
68–69, 106; fans, **119, 128, 131–32, 152, 175;**
garters, **173, 183–84, 189;** hair ornament, **185;**
headdresses, **79, 82, 84, 154–55,** 166, **167–68,
200–201;** horse regalia, **174;** jacket, **151;** leggings,
150; moccasins, **124, 187;** necklaces, **20, 40;**
rattles, **12, 121, 129, 130;** shield, **77;** Tail Dancer
batons, **186, 188;** vest, **182**
Bear clan, 36, 37, 61
bear claws, **17, 42**
bears in Osage cosmology, 32–33
beaver, 32
bells: belts, 61; blankets, **24–25;** cradleboards,
68–69, 106; garters, **183;** headdresses, **79, 100;**
rattles, **12;** weapons, **17, 78, 89, 101**
belts/sashes, 36, 59, 61, **153, 165, 190**
Big Hills people, 49, 67, 145
Big Moon altars, **110, 111.** *See also* Peyote Religion
bilingualism, 137, 138, 144
bird beaks, 61
birds: generally, 119–20; heron motif, **97;** kingfishers, **13c,** 199; in Osage cosmology, 29;

pelicans, 32, 50, 53; woodpeckers, 23, 55, **84,
200–201.** *See also* feathers
birth-death pairing, 28–29
birth rankings, 56–57
bison: as design motif, **87, 92–93;** hunting, 54–55,
56, 66; in Osage cosmology, 30, 32
bison materials: bags, 10, 36, 52; belts/sashes, **153,
165;** headdress, **84;** horse regalia, **83, 174;** Peace
Ceremony, 55; quirt, **81;** robes, 8, 35, 36, 57, 63,
204 *n*48; sacred bundles, 36; spoon, **99**
Black Bear clan: fans, **150, 152;** headdresses, **13, 19;**
leggings, **150**
Black Dog, Chief, **91, 112, 113**
black symbolism: bow and arrows, 37; face painting,
35, 197; hatchet pipe, **43;** shields, **88, 96;** swan
materials, 196
blankets: children's, **102;** decoration styles, 8,
10, 196; E-Lon-schka, **163, 164;** foliage motif,
24–25; hand motif, **202;** horse motif, **11;** Peyote
ceremonies, 122, **122;** Soldier Dance, **168–69;**
as trade goods, 8; warfare motifs, **192–93,** 198;
as wedding gifts, 58; for yarn, 10, 53
blue symbolism, 36, 64, **76**
bone, **178–79, 181.** *See also* antlers
bonnets. *See* headdresses
bow and arrows, 37, **71, 80**
Bow clan, 37, 61
bowls, 8, **70, 178–79**
boxes, Peyote, **121, 126–27**
bracelets, **167, 171**
breastplates, **17, 105**
broadcloth: hatchet, **78;** headdresses, **79, 82, 100;**
horse regalia, **83;** shield, **91**
brooches/pins, **114, 167, 191**
buffalo. *See* bison
Buffalo Bull clan, 36, 55
Buffalo Face clan, 36
bundles: clan, 36, 61, 64, 148; sacred, 36, 50, 51,
148, 204 *n*18
Burbank field, 141
burial/death rituals, 51, 55, 65–66

Caddo people, 5, 6, 109, 110
Cahokia people, 3
calumet dance, 51–52
calumets, **75, 98c**
Camp Crier, 161, 162
cane whistles, **176–77**
carving. *See* stone carving; woodwork
Catlin, George, 3, 8
catlinite: European tools, 8–9; pipes, **18, 21, 44,
45, 87, 95**
Cattail clan, 36, 55

cedar: bags, **134–35;** boxes, 121, **126–27;** burial
rituals, 65; as design motif, **102;** in Osage
cosmology, 32; Peyote ceremonies, 117
celestial bodies. *See* star motif; sun *entries*
Ceremonial Mourners, 66
Ceremonial War Leaders, 55
charcoal, sacred, 60–61, 62
Charcoal Dance, **61,** 158
Cherokee people, 6–7, 206 *n*37
Cheyenne people, 7
chiefs, 50–51, 52, 56. *See also* Bacon Rind, Chief
(Star That Travels); Black Dog, Chief
children: blankets, **102;** clothing, 57, 63, **103, 151,
167;** haircuts, 57, **57;** importance of, 30, 56, 63;
marriage ages, 57–58; men's status, 66; naming
rituals, 56–57; toys, **104–7;** women's roles, 59, 63
chokers, **40**
Chouteau, René Auguste, 6
Christian symbols: blanket, **192;** bracelet, **171;** Peyote
Religion, 118, 123; rattles, **12, 129;** vest, **182**
churches: Christian, 138, 144; Peyote, **111, 114, 115,**
146. *See also* Native American Church
ci-ge, 56
clan bundles, 36, 51, 61, 64, 148
clans: loss of, 67; marriages, 58, 59; rituals, 34–35,
55, 56–57, 60; structure of, 33; village organization, 52
Claremore's Village, 6, 7, 112, 113
Clermont, 7
cloth as trade goods, 8
clothing: and artistic tradition, 148–49; belts/sashes,
36, 59, 61, **153, 165, 190;** children's, 57, 63, **103,
151, 167;** coats/jackets, 58–59, **72–73, 151;** decoration styles, 8, 10; doll, **104–5;** moccasins, **103,
124, 187;** Peyote generally, 121–22; shirts, **14–15,
103, 191;** transitions, 8, 143; vests, **164, 182, 197;**
wedding, 58–59, **72–73, 163;** women's roles, 63;
Xó-ka's, 35–36. *See also* E-Lon-schka clothing/
accessories
clubs, war, 37, 61, **76, 90, 97–98**
coats/jackets, 58–59, **72–73, 151**
colonial era, 5–6
Colorado Springs, 146
color symbolism: children's buffalo robe, 63; face/
body painting, 35, 49, 64, 197; hawk skin, 36;
headdresses, 166; leggings, **150c;** in Osage cosmology, 29; personal fan, **175;** Peyote clothing,
124c; pipes, **43, 87;** ritual instruments, 37; in
shell gorgets, **40c;** swan materials, 196; trade
goods, 9; weapons, 37, **76, 88, 90, 96**
Comanche people, 7–8, 111
Committee Dinner, 162
Company of the Indies, 5

hatchet, **78**

hatchet pipe, **43**

hawk feathers: headdress, **13**; Peace Ceremony, 55; Peyote staffs, 118; shields, **89, 91**

hawks: in Osage cosmology, 29, 32; symbolism, **19c, 177c**

hawk skins, 36

Head Committeeman, 160, 162

Head Cook, 161

headdresses: E-Lon-schka, 162, 166; for hunting rituals, **13, 79, 82, 84, 100**, 199; otter turban, 122, 197, **200–201**; Peyote staffs, 118, **118**; roach spreaders for, **14, 19**, 166, **181**, 198; Soldier Dance, **154–55**

head effigy pipe, **44**

head-right shares, 138–39, 140, 141–42, 147, 149

Head Singer, 160, **186c**

healing remedies, 30

heart motif: garters, **184**; hatchet, **78**; hatchet pipe, **43**; neckerchief slides, **172**; Peyote altars, 110, 111; quirts, **16**; roach spreaders, **14, 181**; symbolism of, 196–97; Tail Dancer baton, **188**; vest, **182**

Heart-Stays people, 49, 113, 145, 158

heron motif, **97**

hó-e-ga, **14, 16, 22**, 28, **35, 47, 71, 181**

Hominy village/area: allotment process, 139, 145; E-Lon-schka, 67, 158, 159, 161, 163; Peyote Religion, 112, 114; Soldier Dance, 169

Honored Man, 52

horns: headdresses, **13, 79, 82, 84, 100**, 199; spoons, **99**

horsehair: headdresses, **79, 82, 100, 154–55, 200–201**; Peyote fans, **133**; shields, **77**

horses: arrival/impact, 4, 6, 8; as design motif, **11, 81, 95, 102, 173**; as gifts, 58, 159, 163; regalia, **83, 163, 174**

House of Mystery, 34

houses, 50, 52, 137, 145–46, 148

human figures/motif: blankets, **102**; bowl, **70**; club, **98**; Peyote staff, **125c**; pipes, **21, 44**, 198–99; quirt, **81**; ritual symbolism, 35–36. *See also* hand motif

humans in Osage cosmology, 29–31, 195

Humpahtokah, 109

Hunka, 28, 33

hunting: chiefs' responsibilities, 50, 54, 56; as design motif, **16, 71**; impact of relocated Indians, 7; men's roles, 59–60; rituals, **13**, 51, 199; seasonal patterns, 6, 54–55, 56, 66; trade impact, 5; village coordination, 49, 54; weapons, **71, 80**

income levels, oil boom years, 140, 141–42, 147

Indian Removal Act, 7

Indian Territory, 66–67, 138

Indian Territory Illuminating Oil Company, 208 *n*11

infants, 57

in-gthon, 56

Isolated Earth clan, 55

ivory-billed woodpeckers, 55, **200–201**

jackets/coats, 58–59, **72–73**, 151

jewelry: bracelets, 167, **171**; E-Lon-schka dances, 167–68; introduction of European items, 9; neckerchief slides, **172**; necklaces, 9, **20, 42, 46**; Peyote ceremonies, 122; pins/brooches, **114**, 167, **191**

Joliet, Louis, 3

Kansa people, 3, 67, 158

ká-zhin-ga, 56

Keeper of the Little Old Men, 51

kingfishers, **13c**, 199

Kiowa people, 7–8, 11

kshón-ga, 56

Laclède, Pierre, 5

La Flesche, Francis, **13c**, 27–28, 37

lance, **101**

land-water pairing, 28, 33–35. *See also* earth-sky pairing

language, 137, 138, 144

Last to Come clans, 33, 34–35

Law, John, 5

leatherwork: bags, 53, **85–86**; beadwork, 9–10; breastplate, **17**; headdress, **100**; jacket, **151**; leggings, **150**; quirts, **16, 81**; shield, **96**

left-right pairing: belt, **153**; blankets/dances, 196; in Osage cosmology, 28–29; sacred bundles, 36; village organization, 52

leggings: beadwork, 10, **150**; broadcloth, 8; child's, **103**; dance, 166, **180**; dolls, **104–5**; ribbon work, 10

liberty bonds, 140

life-death pairing, 28–29, 31–33, 196–97

life symbols, 31–33

lightning motif: bags/boxes, **127, 134–35**; belts/ sashes, **153, 190**; blankets, **102**; fans, **128, 131, 152, 175**; garters, **173**; hair ornament, **185**; jewelry, **42**; leggings, **180**; moccasins, **124, 187**; musical instruments, **12, 123, 130, 132**; symbolism, 123, 197; Tail Dancer instruments, **186, 188**; weapons, **89, 97–98**; whistles, **176–77**

Lisa, Manuel, 6

Little Moon Peyotism, 111, 112

Little Old Men, 51

Little Osage, 49, 145

longbows, **71**

longhouses, 52, 137

Lookout, Frederick Morris, **130c**, 157

Lookout, Henry, **135c**

Lookout, Julia, **130c, 151c, 152c, 153c, 155c, 187c**

Lookout Church, 114

looms, 10, **93c**

Louisiana, colonization/purchase, 5–6

macaw feathers, **128**

man root (ginseng), 30, 32, 50, 204 *n*18

Marland Oil Company, 141

Marquette, Jacques, 3

marriage, 57–59, 60, **72–73**

masculine-feminine pairing: blankets, **24–25**, 196; dances, 196; in gender roles, 56, 63; in Osage cosmology, 28

Mathews, John Joseph, 140

Matin, Walter, 159

mayapples, 30

McCarthy, Edgar, 27

medicine bundles, 36, 50, 51, 204 *n*18

men's roles, overview, 59–60

metal containers, 8–9, 52, 148

metalwork: blankets, **24–25**, 168; breastplate, **17**; clubs, **90, 97**; dolls, **104–5**; fan, **133**; hand mirrors, **22, 47**; hatchet, **78**; headdresses, **79, 82, 84**, 166, **200–201**; lance, **101**; pipes, **43, 45**; quirt, **16**; shield, **91**. *See also* jewelry

Mexico, 109, 142

Miles, Leo, 160

military service (U.S.): as design motif, **24–25**, 151, **155**, 168–69, 198; World War I and II, 140, 144, 169. *See also* warfare *entries*

milkweed, 30

mí-na, 56

mineral rights, 138–39, 149

mirror boards, **22, 47**

mí-zhin, 58

moccasins, **103, 124, 187**

moiety structure, 33

Mongrain, Steve, **152c**

Mon-kon ton-ga wa-xó-be, 204 *n*18

Moon Head (John Wilson), 67, **110**, 110–11, 112–14, 118

Moon Head pin, **114**

morning prayers, 49

Morrell, Preston, **118**

Mourning Dance, 66, 67, 148, 197

mourning rituals, 51, 55, 65–66

musical instruments. *See* drums/drumming; rattles

Mysterious Hills, 53–54

naming rituals, 51, 56–57

Naval Reserve, 140

neckerchief slides, **172**

necklaces, 9, **20, 40, 42**

New Mexico, 142

New Year ceremony, 53

night-day pairing, 28–29, 36, 37

non-hón-zhin-ga. See priests

Noonagan, "Irish Pat," **130c**

north-south pairing, 52, 60

o-dón ceremony, 62

oil industry/royalties, 137, 138, 139–41, 147

) Photography Credits (

p. 7: courtesy Missouri Historical Society, St. Louis; pp. 11, 72: photos © by the Denver Art Museum; pp. 12, 21, 39, 40, 74, 75, 76, 77, 78, 124, 171, 172, 173, 174, 175, 191: Department of Anthropology, Smithsonian Institution (cat. nos. 364529, E276133, 364513, 364538, 367868, E277833, E200493, 291090, E364512, E364510, 364537-0, 364533, 364534, E364517, 276518, E364531, 367863); pp. 13, 42, 83, 178: Brooklyn Museum of Art, Museum Expedition 1911, Museum Collection Fund (11.694.9050, 11.694.9032, 11.694.9009, 11.694.9006, 11.694.9000); pp. 14, 15: courtesy, National Museum of the American Indian, Smithsonian Institution (02/0738, 10/3014), photos by Ernest Amoroso; pp. 16, 97: Linden-Museum Stuttgart; pp. 17, 22, 23, 91, 102, 103, 104, 105, 106, 107, 134, 192, 193, 200: Osage Tribal Museum, photos by David Ulmer; pp. 18, 43, 44, 45, 46, 70, 84, 85, 86, 87, 88, 89, 90, 92, 93, 94, 99, 100, 180, 181: courtesy National Museum of the American Indian, Smithsonian Institution (02/0885, 10/2890, 19/6283, 02/0887, 02/1003, 16/9090, 02/1127, 02/1113, 02/1031, 00/6609, 21/4463, 02/0699, 02/0753, 02/0861, 02/0985, 02/0987, 02/0986, 02/1085, 16/9576, 02/0670, 24/4156 B, D, 02/0700); pp. 19, 20, 25, 130, 131, 132, 133, 151, 152, 153, 154, 167, 169, 172, 187, 188, 189, 190: photos by David Ulmer; p. 35: Smithsonian Institution, National Anthropological Archives; pp. 41, 79, 176, 177: © The Field Museum,

Chicago (A114219_01d, A114218_03d, A114266_01d, A114267_01d); pp. 47, 183: Milwaukee Public Museum, James Howard Collection; pp. 57, 58, 62, 66, 137, 140, 144: courtesy Osage Tribal Museum; p. 61: © University of Oklahoma Press, 1940, 1968; p. 67: Jackson County Parks and Recreation, Missouri, photo by David Ulmer; pp. 68, 125, 126, 129, 203: Gilcrease Museum, Tulsa, Oklahoma, photos by David Ulmer; p. 71: collection of Nordamerika Native Museum, Zürich, Switzerland; p. 80: The Spurlock Museum, University of Illinois at Urbana-Champaign; p. 81: © 1990 The Detroit Institute of Arts; p. 82: Missouri Historical Society, St. Louis, photo by Melinda Muirhead Smith; pp. 95: Philbrook Museum of Art, Tulsa, Oklahoma, photo by David Ulmer; pp. 96, 182: Beloit College, Logan Museum of Anthropology (LMA 31207.1, 30403); p. 98: collection of Mr. and Mrs. Timothy L. Drone, Saint Louis, Missouri, photo by David Ulmer; p. 101: Missouri Historical Society, St. Louis, photo by Cary Horton; pp. 109, 113, 115: photos by Daniel C. Swan; p. 110: courtesy University of Oklahoma Library, Western History Collections, Phillips Collection; p. 110: courtesy Andrew Gray, photo by Chaz Vandiver; pp. 111, 114: courtesy National Anthropological Archives, Smithsonian Institution (90-7259, 98-8729); pp. 113, 159, 165, 167: courtesy Gilcrease Museum, Tulsa, Oklahoma; p. 114: courtesy E. Sean StandingBear; p. 116: courtesy Daniel C. Swan, illustration

by Bobby C. Martin and Gregory D. Carmack; p. 117: collection of William Fletcher, photo by Shane Culpepper; p. 118: courtesy Daniel C. Swan, photo by Shane Culpepper; p. 119: Preston Morrell Collection, courtesy Daniel C. Swan; pp. 119, 120: courtesy Gilcrease Museum, Tulsa, Oklahoma, Mary Whitesell Collection; p. 120: courtesy Daniel C. Swan; p. 122: courtesy John Nunley, photo by David Ulmer; p. 123: Preston Morrell Collection, photo by Daniel C. Swan; p. 127: University of Pennsylvania Museum of Archaeology and Anthropology; pp. 128, 185, 186: Nancy Pillsbury Shirley, O-TAH-ZHA NA^N-ZHE Collection, photos by David Ulmer; p. 150: U.S. Cavalry Museum, Fort Riley, Kansas, photo by Dan Donnert, Ksu Photographic Services; p. 158: courtesy Oklahoma Historical Society (15637), Ruth Mohler Collection, photo by Vince Dillon; p. 159: courtesy Oklahoma Historical Society, Perry, Cherokee Strip Museum Collection (19413.75.178.914.4); p. 161: courtesy Oklahoma Historical Society (16662); pp. 162, 163: photos by Tyrone Stewart; p. 165: courtesy Department of Anthropology, Smithsonian Institution (E263122); p. 168: courtesy Oklahoma Historical Society, Virgil Robbins Collection (16336), photo by Vince Dillon; p. 184: Nancy Pillsbury Shirley, O-TAH-ZHA NA^N-ZHE Collection, photo by Jean Paul Torno; p. 197: courtesy University of Alabama Museums.